DISCARD

The Philosophy of Leibniz

Fourteen of the most important
books on Leibniz's philosophy
reprinted in fifteen volumes

Edited by
R. C. Sleigh, Jr.

A GARLAND SERIES

Logic and Reality in Leibniz's Metaphysics

G. H. R. Parkinson

Garland Publishing, Inc.
New York & London
1985

Library of Congress Cataloging in Publication Data

Parkinson, G. H. R. (George Henry Radcliffe)
Logic and reality in Leibniz's metaphysics.

(The Philosophy of Leibniz)
Reprint. Originally published: Oxford :
Clarendon Press, 1965.
Includes bibliographical references and index.
1. Leibniz, Gottfried Wilhelm, Freiherr von, 1646–1716.
I. Title. II. Series.
B2598.P37   1985   193   84-48428
ISBN 0-8240-6541-7 (alk. paper)

The volumes in this series are printed on
acid-free, 250-year-life paper.

Printed in the United States of America

LOGIC AND REALITY
IN LEIBNIZ'S
METAPHYSICS

LOGIC AND REALITY
IN LEIBNIZ'S
METAPHYSICS

BY

G. H. R. PARKINSON

SENIOR LECTURER IN PHILOSOPHY
UNIVERSITY OF READING

OXFORD
AT THE CLARENDON PRESS
1965

Oxford University Press, Amen House, London E.C.4

GLASGOW NEW YORK TORONTO MELBOURNE WELLINGTON
BOMBAY CALCUTTA MADRAS KARACHI LAHORE DACCA
CAPE TOWN SALISBURY NAIROBI IBADAN ACCRA
KUALA LUMPUR HONG KONG

PRINTED IN GREAT BRITAIN
AT THE UNIVERSITY PRESS, OXFORD
BY VIVIAN RIDLER
PRINTER TO THE UNIVERSITY

PREFACE

I AM indebted to many who have written about Leibniz, particularly to Bertrand Russell, whose writings I have found stimulating even when I have disagreed with them, and to Louis Couturat, whose *Opuscules et fragments inédits de Leibniz* has, like his book on Leibniz's logic, been an indispensable tool. It is also a pleasure to express my gratitude to Mrs. W. C. Kneale, who read a version of this book in typescript and made many valuable suggestions, and to my wife, for her constant help and encouragement.

G.H.R.P.

Reading 1964

CONTENTS

ABBREVIATIONS

I. LEIBNIZ'S WORKS

(a) COLLECTED EDITIONS

A   *Gottfried Wilhelm Leibniz: Sämtliche Schriften und Briefe*, Academy edition (Darmstadt and Berlin, 1923–   ). References are to series and volume.

Bodemann   *Die Leibniz-Handschriften der Königlichen Öffentlichen Bibliothek zu Hannover*, edited by E. Bodemann (Hanover and Leipzig, 1895).

C   *Opuscules et Fragments inédits de Leibniz*, edited by L. Couturat (Paris, 1903).

Dutens   *G. G. Leibnitii Opera Omnia*, edited by L. Dutens, 6 vols. (Geneva, 1768).

FC   *Nouvelles Lettres et Opuscules inédits de Leibniz*, edited by Foucher de Careil (Paris, 1857).

G   *Die philosophischen Schriften von Gottfried Wilhelm Leibniz*, edited by C. I. Gerhardt, 7 vols. (Berlin, 1875–90).

G. M.   *Leibnizens mathematische Schriften*, edited by C. I. Gerhardt, 7 vols. (Berlin and Halle, 1849–63).

Grua   *G. W. Leibniz: Textes inédits*, edited by G. Grua (Paris, 1948).

L   *Gottfried Wilhelm Leibniz: Philosophical Papers and Letters*, edited and translated by L. E. Loemker (Chicago, 1956).

Schmidt   *Gottfried Wilhelm Leibniz: Fragmente zur Logik*, edited and translated by F. Schmidt (Berlin, 1960).

(b) SEPARATE WORKS

To Clarke   *Correspondance Leibniz-Clarke*, edited by A. Robinet (Paris, 1957). Clarke's translation (1717) is contained in L 1095 ff., and has been published separately by H. G. Alexander (Manchester, 1956). References are to Leibniz's papers, and are given by paper and section.

DM   *Discours de Métaphysique*, edited by H. Lestienne (2nd edition, Paris, 1952). This text has been the basis of a separate translation of the *Discours* by P. G. Lucas and L. Grint (Manchester, 1953); cf. L 465 ff.

Mon.	*Principes de la philosophie ou Monadologie*, edited by A. Robinet (Paris, 1954).
NE	*Nouveaux Essais sur l'entendement humain*. The text is that of A vi. 6, which supersedes that in G v. References are to book, chapter, and section.
PNG	*Principes de la Nature et de la Grace*, edited by A. Robinet (in the same volume as the *Monadologie*).

For the convenience of the English reader, reference has been made where possible to the translations by L. E. Loemker. Although not always accurate, these are by far the widest selections from Leibniz at present available in English. Translations cited in the text are by the author, unless mention is made to the contrary.

II. OTHER WORKS

Bocheński	*Formale Logik*, by I. M. Bocheński (Freiburg, 1956).
C. L.	*La Logique de Leibniz*, by L. Couturat (Paris, 1901).
Fischer–Kabitz	*Gottfried Wilhelm von Leibniz*, by Kuno Fischer, 5th ed., revised by W. Kabitz (Heidelberg, 1920).
Friedmann	*Leibniz et Spinoza*, by G. Friedmann (Paris, 1946).
Gebhardt	*Spinoza: Opera*, edited by C. Gebhardt, 4 vols. (Heidelberg, 1925).
Haldane and Ross	*The Philosophical Works of Descartes*, translated by E. S. Haldane and G. R. T. Ross, 2 vols. (Cambridge, 1911).
Jungius	*Logica Hamburgensis*, by J. Jungius, edited by R. W. Meyer (Hamburg, 1957).
Kauppi	*Über die Leibnizsche Logik*, by R. Kauppi (Helsinki, 1960).
Kneale	*The Development of Logic*, by W. and M. Kneale (Oxford, 1962).
Lewis	*A Survey of Symbolic Logic*, by C. I. Lewis, 2nd ed. (New York, 1960).
Mahnke	*Leibnizens Synthese von Universalmathematik und Individual-metaphysik*, by D. Mahnke (Halle, 1925)
RMM	*Revue de Métaphysique et de Morale*.
Russell	*A Critical Exposition of the Philosophy of Leibniz*, by Bertrand Russell, 2nd ed. (London, 1937).
Stebbing	*A Modern Introduction to Logic*, by L. S. Stebbing, 4th ed. (London, 1945).

INTRODUCTION

THE writings of metaphysicians are notoriously obscure, and those of Leibniz are no exception. It is not that the construction of his sentences is unusually involved, nor that he is a cryptic or allusive writer; nevertheless there must be many readers who, on reaching the end of one of his metaphysical works, have wondered what it meant. Others may have a different sort of difficulty; they may believe themselves to understand much, if not all, of what is said, but are unable to see why they are expected to accept it as true. Either, then, what Leibniz writes is regarded as unintelligible, or it is regarded as intelligible, but as a mere fabrication, a philosophical fairy-tale.[1] There is, however, at least one approach to Leibniz's metaphysics which many readers have found helpful, the approach from his logic. This is particularly associated with the name of Bertrand Russell, whose *Critical Exposition of the Philosophy of Leibniz* was first published in 1900. Similar views were put forward independently by Louis Couturat,[2] but he was concerned more with Leibniz's logic than with his metaphysics.

Russell summed up his ideas about Leibniz in the statement that Leibniz's philosophy was 'almost entirely derived from his logic'.[3] This might seem a strange thesis, in view of the fact that logic is generally regarded as a purely conceptual study which makes no assertions about the external world, whereas metaphysics makes very general statements about the nature of what exists. Russell would no doubt accept this, but would point out that he did not say that Leibniz's philosophy rested wholly on his logic. In Russell's opinion, the proposition that there is an external world is one which Leibniz asserts on the basis, not of logic, but of sense-perception.[4] But although the

---

[1] Cf. Russell, p. xiii.

[2] Besides *La Logique de Leibniz* (Paris, 1901), see 'Sur la métaphysique de Leibniz', *RMM*, 1902.   [3] Russell, p. v.   [4] Russell, p. 9.

senses enable us to assert that there is an external world, it is logic that tells us what such a world must be like, if it exists. The way to understand Leibniz's metaphysical views, then, is to trace them back to their origins in his logic; or, to change the metaphor, they are to be understood as being a description of the way the world looks when seen through a certain kind of logical spectacles.

Such, in rough outline, was the thesis Russell put forward in 1900. Since then, much more of Leibniz's work in the field of logic and metaphysics has been published, the selections published by Couturat in 1903 and by Grua in 1948 being especially important. Russell took account of some of Couturat's material when he wrote a short preface to the second edition of his *Critical Exposition* in 1937,[1] but his discussion of it was only perfunctory. There is another respect in which there have been relevant changes since 1900. Not only have many more of Leibniz's writings become generally available, but views about logic have altered—to a great extent because of Russell's own logical investigations, which still lay ahead of him when he first wrote about Leibniz. There are, then, good reasons for a reconsideration of the relations between Leibniz's logic and his metaphysics, which will be the task of this essay.[2]

---

[1] Russell, pp. v–ix.

[2] Mention may be made here of a recent study of Leibniz's logic and metaphysics, Gottfried Martin's *Leibniz: Logik und Metaphysik* (Cologne, 1960). This is a widely ranging introduction to the subject, covering in a relatively short space not only Leibniz's logic in the generally accepted sense, but his mathematics and science also, as well as paying considerable attention to the historical background of the issues raised. Its value is limited, however, by the fact that it is based almost entirely on those of Leibniz's works which were accessible to Russell in 1900; hardly any reference is made to Couturat's selections, and none whatever to those of Grua. Martin's reason for this seems to be (op. cit., pars. 3, 7, and 16) a wish to restrict himself to works published by Leibniz, or which Martin regards as prepared for publication by him. Yet many of the works which he excludes are far from being rough notes—and even if they were, the rough notes of a Leibniz are surely of interest—but are carefully worked-out essays. To ignore these is to deprive oneself of a valuable aid to the understanding of Leibniz; it is to ignore, indeed, Leibniz's own warning that 'The man who knows me only

A discussion of the relations between Leibniz's logic and his metaphysics must find answers to a number of problems. As already mentioned, Leibniz does not derive metaphysical propositions, in the sense of general propositions about the nature of what exists, from his logic alone. What he derives are necessary, but conditional, propositions about what the world must be like, if there is a world; these may be called consequences which relate to metaphysics, rather than metaphysical without qualification. First, then, it must be seen whether these consequences are validly derived by Leibniz. Second, it must be decided whether Leibniz derived from his logic all the consequences relating to metaphysics that are derivable from it. Russell argued that he did not; that whereas his logic pulled him towards a monism, such as that of Spinoza, his religious prejudices, or at any rate the need to accommodate himself to the religious prejudices of his time, pulled him away from it.

To be concerned with these two tasks is to be concerned simply with the way in which conclusions follow or do not follow from certain premisses—that is, with what may in a sense be called the consistency and completeness of the Leibnizian system. There is, however, another problem, which concerns the soundness of the premisses themselves. According to Russell, they are not sound, and it is probable that most contemporary philosophers would agree with this estimate of Leibniz's logic. It will be argued here, however, that careful attention to what Leibniz wrote will show that some (though not all) of Russell's criticisms are unjustified. Besides considering the worth of Leibniz's logical views, it will also be asked how much of the metaphysics discussed is of value. No one is likely to claim today that Leibniz's metaphysical system is true as a whole; rather, the question is whether it consists merely

by my published works does not know me' (To Placcius, 1696. Dutens, vi, 1, p. 65).

I am grateful to Mr. P. G. Lucas, whose English translation of Martin's book (*Leibniz: Logic and Metaphysics*) had not appeared at the time when this essay was being written, for enabling me to become acquainted with Martin's work.

of a collection of logical fallacies and unsupported assertions, or whether it contains some genuine insights into philosophical problems.

Such, then, are the aims of this essay: to study the consequences relating to metaphysics which Leibniz derived, or should have derived, from his logic, and to evaluate that logic and the metaphysics which is related to it. Something must now be said about the limits of the inquiry. First, it is not claimed that what is about to be discussed is the whole of Leibniz's metaphysics, though it will become clear that it is an important part of it. Second, it is not argued that Leibniz could have given no reasons for his metaphysical views besides the ones to be discussed here. This marks a point of difference from Russell and Couturat, who claimed not only that Leibniz's metaphysics was largely derived from his logic, but that the only reasons Leibniz had for his assertions about what the world must be like were logical reasons. Here, on the other hand, Leibniz's logic is regarded as one source of these assertions, but not necessarily the only source. Finally, the metaphysical views in question are those of the mature Leibniz, and his early works will be cited only in so far as they are in harmony with those of his maturity. The same condition applies to the many works of Leibniz that cannot even be approximately dated. Russell, too, restricted himself to the philosophy of Leibniz's maturity,[1] which he regarded as dating from the year 1686, in which Leibniz reached the age of forty. This agrees with Leibniz's own estimate,[2] and so may safely be accepted.

[1] This is not always remembered by Russell's critics, who sometimes seem to think that he can be refuted by showing that the derivation of metaphysics from logic was not Leibniz's earliest philosophical concern. See, e.g., A. Rivaud, RMM, 1914, p. 119; Friedmann, p. 46; Mahnke, pp. 68 ff.

[2] In a letter to Burnett dated 18 May 1697 (G iii. 205) Leibniz says that he is satisfied only with the philosophical views which he has held for roughly the last twelve years.

I

The Nature of the Proposition

§ 1.1. When Russell said that Leibniz's metaphysics was almost entirely derived from his logic he had in mind, not Leibniz's contributions to symbolic logic, but his views about the structure of the proposition and about truth. Here an important distinction must be drawn. Leibniz would have agreed that his views about truth have consequences which relate to metaphysics; he drew such inferences explicitly, and on many occasions. He would have agreed, too, that what he says about the nature of truth presupposes a certain view about the structure of the proposition. However, he does not state explicitly that the latter view has of itself any consequences which relate to metaphysics; nor, indeed, does Russell say that he does, but only that he should have done.[1] The first task, then, must be to examine Leibniz's account of the structure of the proposition, to see if it has the consequences Russell says that it has.

Before an account of the structure of the proposition can properly be discussed, it must of course be explained what it is whose structure is in question. The term 'proposition' is traditionally taken to refer to what is true or false, as distinct from (for example) a command or a request.[2] Leibniz's use of the terms which are translated here as 'proposition'[3] is in accordance with this; in one passage, indeed, he refers to 'a proposition,

[1] See below, § 2.1.
[2] See, e.g., Jungius, p. 1. The tradition goes back to Aristotle, *De Interpretatione*, 17^a2 ff.
[3] *Propositio, enuntiatio, la proposition.* That the first two terms are equivalent is shown, for example, by C 364 and C 513, where Leibniz uses the two words in what is evidently the same sense. Again, in many other passages he says of an *enuntiatio* what he also says of a *propositio*. Compare, for example, C 238 and C 513 with C 49; C 262 and C 513 with C 67; C 238 and C 513 with C 52; C 519 with C 85; and C 259 with C 49.

i.e. (*sive*) the true or the false'.[1] His views about the structure of 'the true or the false' may be thought to be familiar. There can be few students of Leibniz who will not assert confidently that he believed every proposition to be of the subject-predicate form, that is, that 'every proposition has a subject and a predicate'.[2] In a sense, Leibniz did believe this; certainly, he sometimes says,[3] and often implies,[4] that every proposition has a subject and a predicate. But to discover exactly what he means by this is a large undertaking, which will occupy the remainder of this chapter and much of the next.

Although the subject of discussion has been stated to be Leibniz's views about the structure of the proposition, it will be convenient not to attempt an examination of 'the proposition' simply, but to accept a division which Leibniz makes between various types of propositions, and to consider the structure of each type in turn. One type is the categorical proposition, and Leibniz mentions hypothetical, disjunctive, and modal propositions as being other types.[5] He also says that the categorical proposition is the basis of all the rest,[5] and it is therefore obvious that this type of proposition must be discussed first.

In every categorical proposition, says Leibniz, there is a 'subject' and a 'predicate'.[6] In his usage, these terms are ambiguous. Sometimes he regards the subject of a proposition as what the proposition is about, and the predicate as something which is ascribed to a subject—a quality, say, or something done to or by the subject. He speaks, for example, of 'the subject which is Caesar'; he says that among Adam's predicates is that of having such and such a posterity, or, that he is the first man, placed in the Garden of Eden, and from whose side God extracted Eve.[7] Again, in the proposition that Leibniz will make a journey, the execution of the journey is said to be the

[1] C 512.   [2] Russell, p. 4.   [3] C 397.
[4] C 1, 10, 16–17, 401, 518 (L 412); G vii. 309.
[5] C 49.   [6] C 77, 85; cf. C 49.
[7] Subject: *DM*, par. 13; cf. *DM*, par. 8; G ii. 52 (L 512); Grua, p. 537. Predicate: G ii. 19, 42.

predicate;[1] consequently Leibniz speaks sometimes of a 'predicate or event'.[2] Sometimes, on the other hand, Leibniz speaks of the terms of a proposition—that is, the subject and the predicate—as concepts, and as being used in reasoning.[3] Sometimes he speaks, not of concepts *as* terms, but of the concepts *of* terms.[4] These usages are not sharply distinguished, Leibniz passing easily from talking about the subject or predicate to talking about the concept of the one or the other.[5] Finally, subject and predicate are sometimes counted as a word or words,[6] and a meaningful word, or rather noun (*nomen*), is regarded by Leibniz as the *sign* of a concept.[7]

Leibniz is not to be blamed for these ambiguities; he did not create them but inherited them, since they are to be found in the Scholastics and to some extent in Aristotle.[8] However, it is important to have a consistent terminology, and in the remainder of this essay the word 'subject' will be taken to mean exclusively what a proposition is about. A distinction will be drawn between the 'subject' in this sense and the 'concept of the subject', whilst the words which refer to the subject will be

[1] G ii. 52. Cf. *DM*, par. 13, in which Caesar's future dictatorship is predicated of him.

[2] G ii. 46; *DM*, par. 14. Cf. G vii. 226 (L 378) and C 324, which state that a predicate can be a thing (*res*).

[3] Terms as concepts: C 43, 52 (L 364), 243, 346; G vii. 292. Used in reasoning: C 49 (L 361).

[4] C 49, 50, 388, 402; G ii. 56.   [5] C 388.   [6] C 241.

[7] C 432. Cf. C 286, 351, 497; G vii. 204; A ii. 1, 228.

[8] *Subjectum* renders Aristotle's *hupokeimenon*, *praedicatum* his *kategoroumenon*. In the *Categories* Aristotle clearly regards the former as that of which something is said—a particular man, say, or a body—and the latter as that which is said of something, as when it is said of Socrates that he is a man (1ª21–1ᵇ3). The same usage is to be found in the *Summulae Logicales* of Petrus Hispanus: 'A subject is that of which something is said; a predicate is what is said of another' (1.07: quoted by Meyer, Jungius, p. 67). The Scholastics also said that a 'term'—i.e. a subject or predicate—could be a concept, a *terminus mentalis* (Bocheński, p. 176). This tradition may go back to Aristotle's view that a proposition is a synthesis of concepts (*De Interpretatione*, 16ª9–14; *De Anima*, 430ª27). Finally, the Scholastics sometimes regarded subject and predicate as words (Bocheński, p. 176; Kneale, pp. 50, 178, 205).

called the 'subject expression'. Similarly, the 'predicate' of a proposition will be taken to be what is ascribed to the subject, and a distinction will be drawn between the 'predicate', the 'concept of the predicate', and the 'predicate expression'. It will be necessary later[1] to make further distinctions between the senses of the word 'predicate', but those already drawn are adequate for the immediate task of giving at any rate a rough account of what Leibniz means by saying that in every categorical proposition there is a subject and a predicate.

Before this task can be undertaken, however, there is one more distinction to be drawn, that between a proposition and the sentence or other symbols[2] by which the proposition is expressed. Although Leibniz says that we use symbols whenever we think or reason,[3] he does not believe that a proposition is nothing but symbols; his reason for this being that truths remain the same even when the symbols by which they are expressed are changed.[4] Leibniz would say, therefore, that one may speak of the proposition that man is a rational animal, but that one should not, strictly speaking, call the sentence 'Man is a rational animal' a proposition; rather, one should say that it expresses a proposition. However, it would be tedious to refer constantly to 'the proposition expressed by the sentence . . .', and in what follows phrases such as 'the proposition "S is P"' will be used as a shorthand way of referring to the proposition expressed by the sentence 'S is P'.

It is obvious that a subject, in the sense just given to the term, cannot literally be in a proposition; the flesh and blood Socrates, for example, is not in the proposition that Socrates is mortal. In saying that there is a subject and predicate in every categorical proposition Leibniz seems to mean that to assert a categorical proposition is to affirm or deny a predicate of a subject. He says, for example,[5] 'I call a "categorical proposition"

---

[1] See below, § 2.3.

[2] The word 'symbol' is here used in a wide sense to refer to words as well as, for example, to the signs used in mathematics.

[3] G vii. 191 (L 281), 204.

[4] G iv. 158 (L 199); cf. G vii. 191.   [5] C 49.

A is *B*, or *A* is not *B*, i.e. (*seu*) it is false that *A* is *B*.' The context shows that the signs *A* and *B* can be replaced respectively by any subject expression, such as 'the wise man', and any predicate expression, such as 'a believer'.[1] This gives a sentence which expresses a proposition in which a predicate is ascribed to a subject, and since Leibniz's definition is said to hold for all categorical propositions, he can be said to believe that in any such proposition a predicate is affirmed or denied of a subject. It is also clear that he believes that the concepts of the subject and of the predicate are in a sense 'in' every proposition, since he says that in every categorical proposition[2] 'the predicate is said to be in the subject, i.e. (*seu*) the concept of the predicate is involved in the concept of the subject'. It follows from this[3] that he would say that any sentence which expresses a proposition will contain both a subject expression and a predicate expression.

§ 1.2. Now that the meaning of the terms 'subject' and 'predicate' in Leibniz's writings has been explained, more can be said of what Leibniz thinks about the nature of predication. He discusses this issue in terms both of subject and predicate, and of their concepts; whether this is the same view expressed differently, or whether Leibniz has different theories about the nature of predication, will be seen later. The account which he gives in conceptual terms has already been mentioned in passing;[4] it involves the notion of the 'involvement' (more usually the 'inclusion' or 'containment') of the concept of the predicate in that of the subject. This will now be discussed in greater detail. For the purposes of the discussion, it will be convenient to divide categorical propositions into the four types recognized by traditional logic—universal affirmative, universal negative,

---

[1] Subject to certain conditions, unspecified by Leibniz, which exclude meaningless sentences such as 'The wise man is a square root'.

[2] C 85. He writes 'In every proposition', but the context shows that every categorical proposition is meant. Cf. C 51 (L 362–3) and C 397.

[3] Cf. p. 7, n. 7. See also C 49, cited above.

[4] Cf. the reference to C 85 made in § 1.1 *ad fin.*

particular affirmative, and particular negative—and to examine each in turn.

Leibniz's views on the universal affirmative proposition can be introduced by a passage from *Calculus Consequentiarum*, a logical paper written probably in 1679.[1]

> When, in a universal affirmative proposition, I say 'Every man is an animal', what I mean is (*hoc volo*) that the concept of animal is involved in the concept of man; for the concept of man is to be a rational animal. And when I say 'Every pious man is happy', I mean that the man who understands the nature of piety will also understand that true happiness is contained in it.

Propositions expressed by a sentence in which the predicate expression is a verb or a phrase containing a verb are to be regarded in the same way. For example, to say 'The wise man believes' is to say that the wise man is a believer,[2] i.e. that the concept of a wise man includes the concept of a believer.

This raises several problems. It has to be explained what Leibniz means when he speaks of 'the concept of' such and such, and when he says that one concept is included or contained in another. It must also be explained what he means by stating that when one says 'Every man is an animal' one means something else, and why he should say that what is meant is that the concept of animal is included in that of man,[3] and not, for example, that the class of men is included in that of animals— why, in other words, he should regard the proposition from

---

[1] C. L., p. 326, n. 3. The passage cited is from C 85.

[2] C 49 (L 360). This may explain why Leibniz sometimes says that in every categorical proposition there is a copula (C 77, 85). By 'copula' he usually means the verb 'is' and its equivalents in other languages (C 244, 282, 289. This follows Scholastic tradition: Bocheński, p. 201). Now, it is obviously false that whenever one expresses a proposition in words one uses a sentence which contains the copula, in this sense of the term. On the other hand, it might be argued that such a sentence is to be preferred to an equivalent sentence which does not contain the copula, in that the former makes the concept of the predicate clearer. For example, the sentence 'The wise man is a believer' makes the concept of the predicate—that of a believer—clearer than 'The wise man believes'.

[3] Cf. C 51, 235.

the 'intensional' rather than from the 'extensional' point of view.[1]

The first task is to explain Leibniz's use of the term 'the concept of' such and such. The subject, which is an important one, can perhaps best be introduced by a brief consideration of modern usage. As now used, the term 'concept of' generally relates to what is understood by a word or phrase.[2] For example, someone who speaks of 'my concept of man' is referring to the way in which he understands the word 'man', while to speak of 'the medieval concept of man' is to speak of the way in which medieval men understood the word 'man' and its equivalents in other languages. Finally, to speak simply of 'the concept of man' is to speak of the way in which the word 'man' and its equivalents are generally understood.

Leibniz defines a concept as a 'simple thinkable' (*simplex cogitabile*), opposing it to a 'complex thinkable', which is a proposition.[3] Described in this way, his use of the term 'concept' might seem to be quite different from modern usage. However, it has already been seen that he regards concepts as related to meaningful words,[4] saying that a word has meaning if it is the sign of a concept, and he makes clear that a meaningless word is a word without a concept.[5] A 'simple thinkable', then, is that of which a meaningful word or phrase is a sign. It must be emphasized, however, that Leibniz believes that a concept can exist without a word; that is, he believes that to have a concept is not necessarily to be a word-user. For example, he says that God has concepts,[6] and God does not literally speak or write. But since Leibniz has also argued that

---

[1] Cf. C. L., pp. 15, 361, 387, 438.

[2] 'Generally', in that it is seriously asked whether animals and infants have concepts. However, it can be argued that the question asked is whether animals and infants resemble in certain respects those who understand what words mean, so that the understanding of words is involved even here, although at one remove.   [3] C 512.

[4] To be exact, to some words, such as nouns (cf. § 1.1, p. 7). Particles are regarded by Leibniz as the signs of 'modes of conceiving' (C 432, 434); they constitute the form rather than the matter of discourse (C 288).

[5] C 512.   [6] Cf. § 5.4, p. 141.

human beings cannot think or reason without the use of symbols, such as words,[1] he would agree that to say that a human being has concepts is to say that he understands certain words; that is, that he knows what they mean.

A distinction was drawn earlier between the concept of man and concepts of man such as that which a certain individual might have, or the medieval concept of man. This may be expressed by saying that the individual in question, or medieval men in general, have or had a concept of man, as opposed to the concept of man. Roughly speaking, for someone to have a concept of X it is sufficient that the word X shall mean something to him; but if he is to have *the* concept of X, he must know *the* meaning of the word X. Such a distinction is important for Leibniz. It is obvious that he must maintain that someone who says 'The wise man believes' is saying that *the* concept, rather than *a* concept, of a wise man includes that of a believer. To take the man as saying the latter would be to take him as saying, for example, that some people think of the wise man as a believer, which is not what he does say. Leibniz must argue, then, that to say that the wise man is a believer is to say that anyone who understands the meaning of the words 'wise man' will think of a wise man as a believer; that is, it is to say that the concept of a wise man includes the concept of a believer. That this is what Leibniz would argue is also indicated by his assertion[2] that when one says 'Every pious man is happy' one means that the man who understands the nature of piety will also understand that happiness is contained in it. This seems to mean that the man who understands the meaning of the word 'piety' will know that it contains the meaning of the word 'happiness'.

The distinction between 'the concept of' and 'a concept of' is also presupposed by Leibniz's theory of truth. The theory will be discussed in detail in Chapter III; for the moment it is enough to say that Leibniz argues that in every true proposition the concept of the predicate is included in that of the subject,

[1] § 1.1, p. 8.   [2] C 85, quoted on p. 10.

and in every false proposition it is not.[1] This means that someone who asserts a false proposition about, say, the wise man is
indeed saying that a certain concept is included in that of a wise
man, but the concept of a wise man that he has in mind is not
the concept of a wise man.

The notion of a concept (as opposed to *the* concept) of such
and such is also presupposed by Leibniz's division of concepts
into various grades, to which there correspond various grades
of knowledge. At the bottom of the scale come what Leibniz
calls 'obscure' concepts and 'obscure' knowledge. One has an
'obscure' concept of a flower, say, when one remembers that
one has seen such a flower, but cannot recognize the flower
when one meets it.[2] To be able to recognize the flower is to
have 'clear knowledge' (and, it may be inferred, a clear concept)
of it.[2] 'Clear knowledge' is divided into two types, 'confused'
and 'distinct'. I have 'confused' knowledge when[3] 'I cannot
enumerate separately the marks which are sufficient to distinguish a thing from others, though that thing actually has
such marks and requisites, into which its concept can be
analysed'. To be able to analyse one's concepts, to be able to
state the distinguishing marks by which one recognizes things,
is to have concepts and knowledge that are 'distinct'.[4] An
assayer, for example, has a 'distinct concept' of gold, because
he knows the 'marks and tests'[5] by which gold is distinguished
from other substances. In all these cases, Leibniz is speaking of
the concepts that *we* have, which may or may not be *the* concept of whatever we are talking about. In most of what follows,
however, the subject of discussion will be *the* concept of such
and such.

There is one more point to be added in clarification of Leibniz's use of the term 'the concept of'. It was mentioned above
that, according to modern usage, concepts can change; for

---

[1] G vii. 199–200; C 388.   [2] G iv. 422 (L 449).

[3] Ibid. Cf. G vii. 293 (L 352–3); *DM*, par. 24.

[4] G iv. 423 (L 449); *DM*, par. 24; C 50 (L 361); C 512.

[5] G iv. 423; *DM*, par. 24.

example, we now speak of the medieval concept of man, and it is possible that what we now call simply 'the concept of man' may at some time be referred to as 'the twentieth-century concept of man'. Leibniz, on the other hand, would say that the concept of man does not change. Although he does not consider in this connexion the concept of man as such, he often speaks of the concept of this or that individual man as being one unchanging concept.[1] What he seems to mean is that although, for example, people's concepts of Julius Caesar have changed over the years, and may continue to change, these are various approximations to the one correct way of interpreting the term 'Julius Caesar', which does not change. Such a concept is perhaps best regarded as the way in which an omniscient being thinks of Caesar; it is the concept of Caesar possessed by someone who has a complete knowledge of what is involved in being Caesar.[2]

It might be objected to Leibniz that many words change their meanings in the course of time, so that one cannot properly speak of *the* meaning of any such word. Leibniz does not seem to consider this objection, but he could consistently reply that a change in meaning does not imply that a concept has changed, but rather that a word which once stood for one concept now stands for another. Take, for example, the word 'enthusiasm', which means to a modern reader something different from what it meant to a reader in the seventeenth century. Some might express this change in meaning by saying that the concept of enthusiasm has changed; Leibniz, however, could say that a word which was the sign of one concept is now the sign of another.

§ 1.3. It is now time to consider what Leibniz means by the 'inclusion' of one concept in another. This question can be answered by reference to one of Leibniz's earliest philosophical ideas, the idea that there are a number of primitive concepts, from a combination of which all others are formed, much as

<hr>

[1] e.g. *DM*, par. 8; C 520 (L 414).   [2] Cf. § 2.4, p. 53.

words are formed by combining the letters of the alphabet.[1]
Because of this analogy Leibniz proposed to call a list of such
concepts an 'alphabet of human thoughts'.[2] Concepts which
are formed by a combination of primitive concepts are called
'derivative';[3] for example, if the concepts of animal and
rational[4] are primitive, then the concept of rational animal is
derivative. The analogy between concept-formation and word-
formation is not complete, however, in that whereas there is
a correct order for the letters of a word, the order of primitive
concepts in one which is derivative is immaterial—one may
just as well say 'animal rational' as 'rational animal'.[5]

The fact that a concept is derivative is not always obvious,
in the way that it is obvious that a word is composed of letters.
This is because one concept can be identical with several, which
define it.[6] Such a concept can be analysed into others, which
may be said to compose it.[7] The concept of man, for example,
would be regarded by Leibniz as identical with a group of
concepts—for example, those of rational and animal. These in
turn could be analysed into others, until eventually there are
reached concepts which are unanalysable or primitive.[8] A concept is said to 'contain' another if all the primitive concepts of
that other are in it.[9] This does not mean, however, that a man
who says that one concept includes another need know, or even
claim to know, which primitive concepts compose each. Someone who says, for example, that the concept of man contains

[1] G vii. 185 (L 362), 292 (L 351), 516 (L 756); C 346. For the date of the
idea, see Fischer–Kabitz, p. 712.

[2] G vii. 11, 185, 199, 292; C 220–1, 430, 435.

[3] G vii. 293 (L 353).

[4] In current usage one would speak rather of the concepts of rationality
and animality, but Leibniz does not (cf. C 51, 53, 85). Although he sometimes refers to concepts by abstract nouns, as in C 85, on the whole he
prefers to avoid such words (e.g. C 356, 360, 400).

[5] G vii. 292, 525 (L 767); NE, 3. 3. 10.

[6] Concepts as definable, DM, par. 24. A definition has the form 'a is the
same as de', C 406.   [7] C 50, 258, 513.

[8] Someone who is able to carry out such an analysis has what Leibniz calls
'adequate' knowledge. G iv. 423 (L 450); DM, par. 24; C 220, 512.

[9] A vi. 1, 198 (par. 80).

that of animal is indeed saying that all the primitive concepts of the latter are contained in the former. But all that he need show to prove his point is that the concept of animal, whether primitive or derived, is one of the concepts which make up the concept of man—whatever the full analysis of that concept may be.

In saying that the concept of animal is included in the concept of man, in that the latter is analysable into, say, the concepts of animal and rational, Leibniz is using the word 'include' as it would normally be used. But in one respect his use of the word (and of the equivalent word 'contain') is wider than is normal. In the case of an identical proposition, such as 'Every man is a man', it would not normally be said that the concept of the subject is stated to *include* that of the predicate. Leibniz, however, would say this[1]—as he obviously must, if he is to say that in every categorical proposition the concept of the predicate is stated to be included in that of the subject. Stated more generally, Leibniz's use of the term 'inclusion' is such that for a concept A to include a concept B it is not necessary that there should be discoverable among the primitive concepts of A concepts which are not discoverable in B. All that is necessary is that each primitive concept of B should be a primitive concept of A.

This discussion, it will be remembered, arose out of Leibniz's statement that when one says 'Every man is an animal', what one means is that the concept of animal is included in that of man. It has now been explained what Leibniz means by the term 'concept of', and by the statement that one concept is included in another. Other questions, however, remain. The first of these is what Leibniz means here by stating that when a man says a certain thing, he means something else. Leibniz plainly thinks that something is concealed, but it is not clear what is thought to conceal what. He might mean that the sentence 'Every man is an animal' misleads one about the structure of the proposition that the concept of man contains

[1] *NE*, 4.17.8 (A vi. 6, 486).

that of animal; that is, that the sentence is what has been called[1] 'logically inappropriate' to the proposition it expresses. Again, he might mean that the sentence is logically inappropriate to the proposition whose appropriate linguistic expression is 'The concept of man includes that of animal'. If this were so, he would be saying that one linguistic expression of a proposition is to be preferred to another.[2] Finally, he might mean that to assert one proposition is to be committed to the assertion of another, which is preferable to it—the proposition that the concept of man includes that of animal being preferable to the proposition that every man is an animal.

Elsewhere Leibniz seems to have no objection to speaking of the proposition that every S is P;[3] in such cases he may be taken to mean that in the sentence 'Every S is P' the copula, 'is', expresses the unanalysed (though analysable) notion of predication.[4] Again, he does not in this context draw the distinction between proposition and linguistic expression which the first two interpretations demand, so that it seems most likely that the third is correct. It now has to be seen why he should prefer to the proposition that every man is an animal the proposition that the concept of man includes that of animal, and should also prefer this to the proposition that the class of animals includes that of human beings, to which one is also committed by the assertion that every man is an animal.[5] Couturat has argued[6] that it was an excessive respect for the authority of Aristotle which made Leibniz prefer the intensional to the extensional point of view. But it is by no means certain that Leibniz would accept anything on Aristotle's

---

[1] Stebbing, p. 79.
[2] This point of view is adopted by Stebbing, loc. cit.
[3] e.g. C 193 ff., 323, 384-5, 410 ff.
[4] For a fuller account of such a use, cf. Kneale, p. 64.
[5] This is not to say that Leibniz never treats propositions extensionally. One passage, for example, states 'When I say "Every man is an animal", I mean that men are to be sought among the animals' (C 235: cf. C 193 ff., 292 ff., 323, 384-5, 410 ff.). However, he usually prefers the intensional approach (C. L., pp. 23, 438).   [6] C. L., p. 438.

authority alone. He does not, on the whole, conceal his debts to other philosophers, and he is ready to mention any points on which he agrees with Aristotle,[1] but this is not the same as accepting something as true because he believes that Aristotle had said it. Certainly, if his only reason for adopting the intensional approach was a belief that this was Aristotle's approach also, then this would do him no credit. However, he mentions explicitly another, and much better, reason: that concepts 'do not depend on the existence of individuals'.[2] He does not enlarge on this, but what he says is sufficient to show that he proposes to regard universal affirmative propositions as being without what is now called 'existential import', that is, as not asserting the existence of what is talked about. For example, if someone says 'Every perfectly wise man is happy', this suggests that there are perfectly wise men; so, too, does the proposition 'The class of perfectly wise men is included in the class of beings which are happy'. All this implies that the proposition will only be true if perfectly wise men exist; yet one might wish to say that the proposition is true even if there are no perfectly wise men. According to Leibniz, one would then be saying that the concept of a perfectly wise man includes the concept of being happy, whether or not the first concept has instances. Leibniz is proposing to treat all universal affirmative propositions in this way, so that the truth of any such proposition does not depend upon the existence of its subject. Similarly, in speaking of the universal negative proposition, Leibniz says[3] that this 'is understood of concepts, not of existing things, so that if I say "No man is an animal" I do not understand this of existing men alone'.

It may be replied to Leibniz that it is possible to deny existential import to a universal proposition, not by regarding it intensionally, but by regarding it as a hypothetical proposition. For example, the proposition that everyone who is wise is happy could be taken as saying that for all x, if x is wise then x is happy. Leibniz would not disagree; he himself sometimes regards the universal affirmative proposition in a similar way,[1] though, for reasons which will be seen later,[2] he prefers the intensional approach. In any case, none of this affects the point which is being made here: namely, that it was just the desire to deny existential import to the universal proposition, rather than mere reverence for Aristotle, which made Leibniz adopt the intensional approach to the proposition.

This might seem surprising, since it contradicts the commonly held view that Leibniz ascribed existential import to universal propositions.[3] It will be worth while, then, to examine the reasons for holding this view. There are two such reasons: first, that Leibniz accepted certain logical doctrines which demand that universal propositions should have existential import, and second, that he explicitly ascribed existential import to them. The logical doctrines referred to are that subalternation and *conversio per accidens* are valid;[4] in other words, Leibniz held that from 'Every A is B' one can validly infer 'Some A is B' (subalternation), and also 'Some B is A' (*conversio per accidens*). If, as is usual, a proposition introduced by the word 'some' is assumed to have existential import, whilst a universal proposition is assumed not to have it, these inferences are invalid—'Something which is A is B' and 'Something which is B is A' do not follow from 'If anything is A, it is B'. The usual way of preserving the validity of subalternation and *conversio per accidens* is to say that the universal proposition has existential import.

A paper written by Leibniz in his maturity, and generally known as *Difficultates quaedam Logicae*,[5] deals with just these

---

[1] Cf. C 252, quoted on p. 22.   [2] § 1.6.

[3] e.g. C. L., p. 349; Kneale, p. 323. If an attempt is made to weaken the testimony of C 53 by pointing out that it comes from a work written in 1679, before Leibniz's maturity as a philosopher, it may be replied that C 387, which has also been cited above, comes from *Generales Inquisitiones de Analysi Notionum et Veritatum* (sometimes abbreviated to *Generales Inquisitiones*), an important paper on logic written in 1686.

[4] C. L., pp. 351, 359–61, 386. Of the many passages in which Leibniz asserts their validity, C 43, 46, 80–81, 303, and 306 may be cited.

[5] G vii. 211 ff., written after 1690 (C. L., pp. 358–9). On this paper,

problems.[1] Leibniz points out that 'Every laugher is a man' is true even if no man laughs, whereas its converse, 'Some man is a laugher', is not true unless some man actually laughs. 'The former speaks of possibles, the latter of actuals.'[2] But instead of solving the difficulty by giving the universal affirmative proposition existential import, Leibniz solves it by denying such import to the particular proposition, remarking that

A similar difficulty does not occur if you remain within the limits of possibles (*in terminis possibilium*). . . . It must therefore be said that the conclusion 'Some man is a laugher' is true in the region of ideas, i.e. if you take 'laugher' for a certain species of possible being.[2]

This seems clear confirmation of the view that for Leibniz the universal affirmative proposition does not have existential import. It is unfortunate that he did not leave the matter there, but went on[3] to discuss the difficulty in terms by which he thought to clarify the possible source of error in a *conversio per accidens*, but which turned out to be a source of confusion themselves. *Conversio per accidens*, he writes, can be proved as follows. To say 'Every laugher is a man' is to say 'A laugher and a laughing man are equivalent'. Now, a laugher is an entity (*ex hypothesi*); therefore, by the equivalence just stated, a laughing man is an entity, which is to say that[4] some man is a laugher. Leibniz points out that for the argument to be valid, the term 'entity' (*ens*) in the conclusion must have the same sense as in 'A laugher is an entity'. If it is taken to refer to possibility, i.e. to the 'region of ideas', then to say that some man is a laugher is similarly to talk about what is possible. If, on the other hand, 'entity' is taken to refer to what really exists, it will be true that some man actually laughs.[3] Here Leibniz seems to consider the possibility of giving the universal affirmative proposition existential im-

cf. C. L., pp. 358 ff.; Kauppi, pp. 46 and 211 ff.; Kneale, p. 339; Lewis, pp. 14–15.
    [1] To be exact, it deals explicitly only with *conversio per accidens*, but what Leibniz says is easily applicable to subalternation.
    [2] G vii. 211.
    [3] G vii. 214.   [4] G vii. 212.

port, and to say that if, and only if, it has such import, then the particular affirmative which is inferred from it has existential import also. But at the end of the same paragraph[1] he says that the conclusion that some man is a laugher does not mean that some man actually laughs. What follows, he says, is that some species of man coincides with the term 'laugher', and he has previously[2] taken the phrase 'species of man' to refer to the 'region of ideas'. It seems, then, that after considering the possibility of giving existential import to the universal affirmative proposition, he decides finally in favour of the non-existential (that is, intensional) interpretation, and takes the term 'entity' in this context to refer to possibility[3] and not to actuality.

He then goes on to say[4] that 'in all propositions it is tacitly assumed that the ingredient term is an entity'. Couturat takes this to mean an *existent* entity, and to show that Leibniz ascribed existential import to all propositions.[5] But it is clear from what has just been said that the most that can be inferred from this is that every universal proposition *can* have an existential interpretation, just as it can also have a non-existential interpretation.[6] It has also just been argued that Leibniz prefers the second of these, so that it is probable that the statement that in every proposition the ingredient term is assumed to be an entity means that in every proposition it is assumed that what is talked about is *possible*, which is by no means the same as saying that it is assumed that it exists.[7]

In sum, *Difficultates quaedam Logicae* does not show that Leibniz ascribed existential import to the universal affirmative proposition; rather, it tends to confirm the view that he did not. The other evidence which Couturat brings in support of

---

[1] G vii. 214.   [2] G vii. 211–12.

[3] As he often does: e.g. C 259, 261, 271; G vii. 319 (L 602); Grua, p. 325; Bodemann, Phil. vii. C 77, quoted by Kauppi, p. 46.

[4] G vii. 214.   [5] C. L., p. 360.   [6] Cf. Kauppi, pp. 215 ff.

[7] Couturat himself has to add (C. L., p. 360) that later in the same paper it is said that the universal affirmative proposition is only hypothetical (G vii. 216–17). He therefore has to make the unnecessary supposition that Leibniz has contradicted himself.

his interpretation is inconclusive. He refers, for example, to a paper in which *ens* is used for *terminus*.[1] But this need only mean that Leibniz sometimes postulated that for anything to be called a 'term' it must be possible, which, indeed, he sometimes states explicitly.[2] Finally, Couturat cites a passage which states that 'Granted that *A* is *B*, then *A* can be called "something"'.[3] But this can hardly mean that a universal affirmative proposition has existential import, since it is followed by '"Every *B* is *C*" means "If *A* is *B*, *A* is also *C*"', which denies such import. It can still be said, then, that Leibniz's reason for viewing the proposition intensionally was that this did not commit him to saying that the subject of a universal proposition actually exists.

Much of this section has been concerned with the topic of inclusion, whether of one class in another or of one concept in another. Leibniz has other ways of regarding the universal affirmative proposition, and indeed all categorical propositions; however, these do not seem to affect what has already been said, and a brief mention of three further ways in which he treats the proposition that every *A* is *B* will be sufficient. These are:

(i) '*A* not-*B* is a non-entity',[4] or '*A* not-*B* is not a thing'.[5]

(ii) 'Every *A* is the same as some *B*'—e.g. 'Every man is the same as some animal'.[6]

(iii) '*A* is the same as *AB*.'[7] So, for example, 'Man-animal and man are equivalent; i.e. if anyone says that you are a man, he says that you are an animal'.[8]

Leibniz does not regard these as superseding his account in terms of inclusion; towards the end of the *Generales Inquisitiones*, in which (i) and (iii) are used, he remarks:[9] 'Every

---

[1] C. L., p. 349, referring to C 324–6.

[2] Clearly in C 360, and more obscurely in C 393, to which Couturat also refers.   [3] C. L., p. 349, referring to C 252.

[4] G vii. 212; C 233.   [5] C 392, 394.   [6] C 233.

[7] G vii. 212; C 259, 262–3, 300, 366, 378.   [8] G vii. 212.

[9] C 395. On this paper, cf. p. 19, n. 3.

proposition in common speech comes to this, that it is said what term contains what.' Nor does he ever seem to state that when we say that every *A* is *B*, what we mean is (say) that *A* is the same as *AB*. In the *Generales Inquisitiones* he says that what he is looking for are suitable *signs* (*propria signa*),[1] and it is possible that he would argue that (i), (ii), and (iii) are sentences which express the proposition that the concept of *A* contains that of *B*. Perhaps it is their comparative remoteness from ordinary ways of thinking which makes Leibniz reluctant to say that any of these three is what is meant when someone says 'Every *A* is *B*'.

§ 1.4. There now remain for discussion the other types of categorical proposition mentioned earlier[2]—the universal negative, the particular affirmative, and particular negative. In the course of the inquiry it will also be seen how Leibniz deals with what is traditionally called the 'singular' proposition, of which the subject is not some *X*, in the sense of several *X*, but one *X* only. The universal negative does not cause Leibniz much difficulty. He has argued that to say that every pious man is happy is to say that the concept of happiness is included in that of piety, and he would also argue that if we say that no pious man is miserable, we are saying that the concept of misery is *excluded* from that of piety.[3] It is obvious that if universal negative propositions are regarded in this way, then it cannot be true that in every categorical proposition the concept of the predicate is said to be included in that of the subject, and this may be why Leibniz sometimes implies that it is only in universal affirmative propositions that the concept of the subject is said to include that of the predicate.[4] If his statement is to cover all propositions, and if the universal negative proposition is regarded in terms of exclusion, then he must say that in every categorical proposition the concept of the predicate is said to be included in or excluded from that of the subject.

[1] C 393.   [2] § 1.2.
[3] Cf. G vii. 208.   [4] Cf. C 402.

However, the universal negative proposition can be treated in a way which does not involve the notion of exclusion, by saying that in every such proposition the concept of a negative predicate is stated to be included in that of the subject. For example, the proposition that no pious man is miserable could be regarded as saying that the concept of non-misery is included in that of the pious man.[1] This would make it possible for Leibniz to say that in every universal proposition, affirmative or negative, the concept of the predicate is said to be included in that of the subject. But this is only a matter of terminology, and there is no evidence that Leibniz thought it to be anything else. In the passages which mention or imply the concepts of negative predicates[1] he is simply concerned to find a convenient symbolism for propositions; there is no hint of an assertion that whenever one utters a proposition, *really* one always means that one concept is included in another.

Particular propositions need more elaborate discussion. It has often been pointed out that the word 'some' is ambiguous. It can be used to mean 'some only', as when one says that some Europeans are Englishmen; it can also be used to mean 'not none', as when one answers the question, 'Are all these people Europeans?' by saying 'I don't know, but some are'. In modern logic the word is given the latter sense, and 'some' is taken to mean 'not none; i.e. at least one, and perhaps all'. Leibniz does not show himself to be aware of this distinction, and in his account of the particular proposition he seems to assume first one usage and then the other. Sometimes he argues that to say that some S is P is to deny that no S is P, and that to say that some S is not P is to deny that every S is P.[2] If these are meant as definitions and not simply as statements of what a particular proposition implies—that is, if the phrase 'is to deny that' means 'is the same as denying that' and not 'implies that one must deny that'—then they are only correct if the word 'some' means 'not none'. For one may deny that no S is P on the grounds that only one S is P, or that more than one (but not every) S is P, or that every S is P. Similarly, one may deny that every S is P on the grounds that only one S is not P, or that more than one (but not every) S is not P, or that every S is not P. The defect of these definitions from the point of view of inclusion is that they involve the notion of the denial of a universal proposition, which is not explained in terms of the inclusion or exclusion of concepts. However, Leibniz gives another account of the particular proposition which does not have this defect.

Take, for example, the particular affirmative proposition that some metal is gold.[1] All gold is metal: that is, the concept of gold includes that of metal, or in other terms the concept of gold consists of the concept of metal plus some other concept. Leibniz now turns this round,[1] and argues that to say that some metal is gold is to say that the concept of metal added to some other concept includes the concept of gold. More generally,[2]

If a proposition is a particular affirmative, then the predicate is not contained in the concept of the subject regarded by itself, but in the concept of the subject taken with some addition, i.e. in some species of the subject.

Two features of this view require comment. First, Leibniz is using that wider sense of 'contain' or 'include' which has already been mentioned.[3] For example, if one adds to the concept of metal the concept of being soluble in *aqua regia*, the concept which results would normally be said to be identical with that of gold. Leibniz would agree that the two concepts are identical, but would add that in his usage the first concept can also be said to 'include' the concept of gold. Second, the use of the word 'species' in the passage quoted suggests that Leibniz is thinking of a particular affirmative proposition as being about some S in the sense of 'some only'. For example, if gold is said to be a species of metal, this means that some metal is gold, and some is not. This appears to be confirmed by

[1] C 51.   [2] C 85; cf. C 55.   [3] § 1.3.

another fact, which may also serve to introduce one of Leibniz's accounts of the particular negative proposition. To say 'Only some *S* is *P*' is equivalent to saying 'Only some *S* is not *P*'; the first proposition implies the second, and the second the first. That is, when 'some' means 'some only', a particular affirmative and a particular negative proposition are equivalent. The relevance of this is that Leibniz sometimes defines a particular negative proposition in a way which is in effect the same as his definition of a particular affirmative proposition. It has been seen that he argues that to say that some *S* is *P* is to say that the concept of *S*, with something added, includes that of *P*. Similarly, he argues that to say that some *S* is not *P* is to say that something is lacking from the concept of *S* which is required in that of *P*.[1] For example, to say that some metal is not gold is to say that something is missing from the concept of metal which is required for the concept of gold; that is, it is to say that something can be a metal without its concept containing all the concepts which constitute that of gold. In explanation of this, it may be added that in speaking of something being lacking Leibniz seems to mean 'something, but not everything'. If all the component concepts of gold were said to be lacking from the concept of metal, it would be being said that the concept of metal is excluded from that of gold, and the proposition would not be a particular negative, but the universal negative 'No metal is gold'.

This definition of the particular negative is clearly not in terms of inclusion, since the notion of something *lacking* from the concept of the subject is vital to it. However, Leibniz gives another definition which is in terms of inclusion and which, like the corresponding definition of the universal negative, involves mention of the concept of a negative predicate. According to this, to say that some metal is not gold is to say that some metal is non-gold.[2] This can be expressed in terms of inclusion as 'The concept of metal, with some addition, includes that of non-gold'. The only comment which need be

[1] C 63–64.   [2] C 86.

made on this definition is that, as in the case of the universal negative proposition, there is no indication that Leibniz believes an account of a proposition to be in any way more fundamental by virtue of the fact that it is given in terms of inclusion.[1] It is, however, obviously more convenient for Leibniz to be able to say that in every categorical proposition the concept of the predicate is said to be included in that of the subject, instead of having to say that this applies without qualification to the universal affirmative proposition alone, and giving separate accounts of the other types of categorical proposition.

It remains to say something of Leibniz's account of the singular proposition, which is about one individual only. Some of the logicians whose works were known to Leibniz regarded such a proposition as a form of particular proposition;[2] Leibniz, on the other hand, regards it as a form of universal proposition. He discusses this matter at greatest length in one of his earliest works, the *De Arte Combinatoria*,[3] but the arguments put forward there are consistent with his mature views,[4] and may therefore be cited here. He argues that if one says, for example, that Socrates is the son of Sophroniscus, this is the same as saying 'Whoever is Socrates is the son of Sophroniscus' or 'Every Socrates is the son of Sophroniscus'.[5] Again, supposing Socrates to have no brother, it will be correct to say that every son of Sophroniscus is Socrates; or again, if I say 'I give and bequeath to Titius all the garments I have', no one will doubt that if I have only one garment, this is owed to him.[6] When one asserts a singular proposition, then, one is saying that the concept of the predicate (a negative predicate in the case of a negative proposition) is included in that of the

[1] Cf. p. 24, above.
[2] Leibniz cites Johannes Hospinianus, whose book on the moods of the syllogism he had studied, and says that Hospinianus' equation of singular with particular propositions is widely held (A vi. 1, 182).
[3] Published in 1666. See A vi. 1, 182–3; also A vi. 1, 520 (1669?).
[4] Cf. *NE*, 4. 17. 8 (1703–5) and C 323.
[5] A vi. 1, 182. Cf. *NE*, 4. 17. 8. [6] A vi. 1, 182–3.

subject, just as when one asserts a universal proposition. Leibniz does not deny, however, that there is a logical difference between a proposition such as 'Every man is mortal' and one such as 'Socrates is mortal', even though in each case the concept of mortality is said to be included in that of the subject. The difference lies in the concept of the subject itself, the concept of Socrates being what Leibniz calls 'complete', whereas the concept of man is not.[1] What this means will be discussed later, in connexion with Leibniz's theory of substance.[2]

§ 1.5. Besides giving an account of the categorical proposition in terms of the inclusion of concepts, Leibniz also says that in a categorical proposition the *predicate* is said to be included in the *subject*.[3] Here he could be using the words 'subject' and 'predicate' to stand for what we have called the *concepts* of subject and predicate,[4] which would be a repetition in other words of the view which has already been discussed. There seems to be no conclusive evidence that he is not doing so;[5] however,

[1] C 375.

[2] See below, § 5.1. It may be added that in *Difficultates quaedam Logicae* (cf. p. 19, n. 5) Leibniz suggests a somewhat different account of the singular proposition. He points out (G vii. 211) that singular propositions can be contradictories (he writes, 'can be opposed')—e.g. that if 'The Apostle Peter is a soldier' is true, 'The Apostle Peter is not a soldier' is false, and conversely. But if the first of these propositions is a form of universal affirmative, its contradictory, which is also a singular proposition, must be a form of particular negative. Again, the syllogism 'Every writer is a man, some writer is the Apostle Peter, therefore the Apostle Peter is a man' is a valid syllogism in the third figure; but in this figure the conclusion must be particular. Leibniz's solution to these difficulties is to say that a singular proposition is equivalent to a particular and to a universal proposition; or, that in the singular proposition 'The Apostle Peter is a man', 'Some Apostle Peter' and 'Every Apostle Peter' coincide (ibid.). How this is to be reconciled with what Leibniz says elsewhere about singular propositions is not clear.   [3] C 51, 85.   [4] Cf. § 1.1.

[5] In *DM*, par. 8, and in C 401–2 Leibniz may seem to draw a distinction between subject and predicate and their concepts when he says (*DM*, par. 8) that when the predicate is not contained expressly in the subject of a true proposition it must be in it virtually, *and therefore* the subject term must always contain the predicate term. It will be argued later, however (§ 3.1), that 'subject' and 'predicate' here refer to the concepts of subject and

let us suppose that he is distinguishing here between subject and predicate on the one hand and their concepts on the other. If this is so, it is not clear what sense is to be given to the word 'in' when it is stated that the predicate is said to be in the subject.

Take, for example, the proposition that Alexander the Great is a king. It is clear that the quality of being a king is not in Alexander in the sense that the concept of being a king is in the concept of Alexander. The concept of being a king is one of the concepts which make up the concept of Alexander, but the quality of being a king is not one of the qualities which make up Alexander. Alexander *has* qualities, he is not constituted by his qualities. In other words, a subject is not a sum of predicates; predicates are what are stated of a subject. That Leibniz accepts this view is shown, for example, by the fact that he does not agree with Locke's argument[1] that the concept of a subject stripped of all predicates is empty, as he might be expected to do if he thought that a subject is a sum of predicates. Instead he says that if we do separate its predicates from a subject, it is only to be expected that what is left has no predicates; this does not mean, however, that the separation cannot meaningfully, and indeed usefully, be made.[2]

It might be suggested next that the quality of being a king is predicate, so that what is meant is that in a true proposition the concept of the predicate is never added to that of the subject; it is always present in the concept of the subject, and anyone who has this concept could (cf. C 402) give an *a priori* proof of the truth of the proposition in question.

[1] *Essay concerning Human Understanding*, 2. 23. 2.

[2] *NE*, 2. 23. 2. Against this, it might be pointed out that in *DM*, par. 9, Leibniz writes that what Aquinas had said of the angels or intelligences— namely, that each individual is an *infima species*—may be extended to cover all individuals without exception. (Cf. G ii. 54, 131. The reference to Aquinas is either to *Summa Theologica*, i, Qu. 50, Art. 4, or to *Summa contra Gentiles*, 2. 93.) This, it may be argued, suggests that Leibniz at least toyed with the idea that a subject, or at any rate an individual, is nothing but a sum of predicates. However, what is at issue in this passage is the nature of the difference between individuals; Leibniz is saying that this is a difference between the predicates of individuals—it is, in Aristotelian language, a difference in form and not, as Aristotle had said, a difference in matter alone. This does not seem to imply that Leibniz thinks an individual to be nothing but predicates. (See also § 5.2, below.)

in Alexander in the sense that Alexander is its *substratum*. Leibniz, however, would not accept this. He would reply—surely with justification—that to speak of a *substratum* in this sense is only to use a metaphor to express the fact that several predicates are conceived of the same subject.[1] He would say much the same of the suggestion[2] that a predicate 'inheres' in the subject. To talk about inherence, he says, is (in so far as it is intelligible) to talk about a mode or state of the subject.[3] It seems, then, that to say that a predicate is in the subject is only another way of saying that it is a predicate *of* the subject, or a predicate which *belongs to* the subject.[4] It follows that the statement that in a categorical proposition the predicate is said to be contained in the subject, if taken to refer to something other than the inclusion of concepts, must be taken to mean no more than that in every categorical proposition a predicate is attributed to or conceived of a subject.[5]

Leibniz's assertion that in every categorical proposition the predicate is said to be in the subject has been thought to imply that he believed every such proposition to be about something which exists.[6] It is clear that this contradicts the view stated earlier, that Leibniz preferred to regard propositions from the standpoint of intension because this does not imply the existence of the subject of a proposition. Philosophers are not always consistent, and Leibniz need be no exception; however, the evidence does not seem to show that there is any inconsistency here. For example, Leibniz discusses propositions in which the subject is an abstraction,[7] even though he thinks that what is abstract is not real.[8] Again, he would accept as subject expressions such phrases as 'all, if any, who laugh' or 'all supposed laughers',[9] which again implies that he did not think that the

---

[1] *NE*, 2. 23. 1.

[2] To be found, for example, in Kneale, p. 323.

[3] G ii. 458 (L 987).

[4] *DM*, par. 8. In his use of the phrase 'belong to' Leibniz is perhaps influenced by the Aristotelian term *huparchein*.

[5] *DM*, par. 8; *NE*, 2. 23. 1.   [6] Kneale, p. 324.

[7] e.g. C 389–91; *NE*, 3. 8. 1, 4. 8. 12.   [8] C 8.   [9] G vii. 216.

subject of a proposition always exists. This does not mean that Leibniz's logic is indifferent to questions about what exists; the next chapter will show that it is not.[1] All that is said here is that Leibniz does not use the term 'subject of a proposition' in such a way as to refer only to what exists.

§ 1.6. It has already been mentioned[2] that Leibniz recognizes other types of proposition besides the categorical, and it is now time to discuss his account of these. The categorical proposition, he writes,[3] is presupposed by 'modal, hypothetical, disjunctive, and all other propositions'. Here, then, he has listed three types of proposition other than the categorical, and has hinted that there are others. It is not clear, however, what others he has in mind, as his discussion seems restricted to the three types already mentioned. By 'modal propositions' he means what is usually meant by the term, namely, propositions which assert either possibility or necessity. He has little to say about these propositions as such, what he has to say about necessity and possibility concerning either necessary truths or the way in which possibility is established. These topics can conveniently be discussed later,[4] leaving for discussion here Leibniz's views about disjunctive and hypothetical propositions. Hypothetical propositions will be considered first.

If Leibniz is to maintain strictly the thesis that all propositions are of the subject-predicate form, he will have to argue that when one says, for example, 'If this is salt, then it will dissolve in water', one is not asserting the *proposition* that if this is salt, then it will dissolve in water. For what one says has an antecedent and a consequent, not a subject and a predicate. But it would be paradoxical to dismiss as mere nonsense the sentence uttered; this must therefore be regarded as expressing a proposition, but in such a way that it does not make clear the subject and predicate of the proposition expressed. Such is the position which Leibniz should hold if he is to say both that

---

[1] Cf. § 2.2, pp. 40 ff.   [2] § 1.1, p. 6.   [3] C 49.
[4] See below, §§ 3.4 and 4.2.

'If . . . then' sentences have meaning, and that all propositions
are of the subject-predicate form. It seems, however, that this
is not his position. He does not speak of hypothetical sentences,
but of hypothetical propositions,[1] and the course of his arguments gives no indication that this is a mistake. Broadly, his
view seems to be that although there are hypothetical propositions, these can be regarded as propositions of the subject-
predicate form. That this is so can be seen from the way in
which he discusses the hypothetical proposition 'From the proposition "*A* is *B*" there follows the proposition "*C* is *D*"'.[2]
The proposition '*A* is *B*', Leibniz says, can be regarded as a
term—namely, 'the fact that *A* is *B*', or 'the *B*-ness of *A*'—
and corresponding substitutions can be made for the proposition '*C* is *D*'. 'From this', Leibniz continues,[2] 'there arises a new
proposition: the fact that *A* is *B* is, or contains, the fact that *C*
is *D*: or, the *B*-ness of *A* contains the *D*-ness of *C*: or, the *B*-ness
of *A* is the *D*-ness of *C*.'

Here there is no suggestion that what is generally called a
hypothetical proposition is really a subject-predicate proposition
in a misleading verbal guise. All that is said is that a subject-
predicate proposition 'arises from', that is, follows from, what
is clearly regarded as another proposition. This is confirmed
by other passages, such as 'When we say "From *A* is *B* there
follows *E* is *F*", *it is the same as if* we were to say "*A*'s being *B*
(*A esse B*) is *E*'s being *F*"'; ' "If *A* contains *B*, *C* contains *D*"
can be formed in this way: "*A*'s containing *B* (*A continere B*)
contains *C*'s containing *D*"'; and 'If, as I hope, I can *conceive*
hypothetical propositions *as* categoricals . . .'.[3] Indeed, even
when Leibniz seems to imply that there are only categorical
propositions, by saying that 'A hypothetical proposition is
merely a categorical proposition, the antecedent being changed
into the subject and the consequent into the predicate', he
concludes 'And so categorical propositions *would be enough*'.[4]

[1] e.g. C 262, 377, 407.   [2] C 389.
[3] C 260, 407, and 377 respectively. (Translator's italics.)
[4] C 262. (Translator's italics.)

It appears, then, that Leibniz did not believe all propositions to be of the subject-predicate form, but that he did think it possible to do without hypothetical propositions, since any such proposition can always be replaced by an equivalent subject-predicate proposition. It may also be assumed (though Leibniz does not seem to say this explicitly) that he thought that the converse is not true, in that very many categorical propositions, such as 'Leibniz was born in A.D. 1646', cannot be replaced by hypothetical propositions. It could therefore be said that his view is that although there are hypothetical propositions, it is as if there were only subject-predicate propositions. This seems to be what Leibniz means when he says or implies that all propositions are of the subject-predicate form,[1] a view which he expresses perhaps more precisely by saying that all other propositions presuppose the categorical proposition as their basis (*fundamentum*).[2] In the rest of this essay this view will be called the thesis that all propositions which are not of the subject-predicate form can be 'reduced' to those which are.[3]

One feature of Leibniz's account of the hypothetical proposition remains to be clarified. It has been seen that he argues that any such proposition is reducible to one which is of subject-predicate form; what is not yet clear, however, is how the proposition to which it is reduced is to be regarded in terms of inclusion—whether it is to be said that the subject includes the predicate, or the concept of the subject includes the concept of the predicate. Take, for example, the proposition 'If Caesar is victorious, then Pompey will be angry'. Using Leibniz's formula 'The B-ness of A contains the D-ness of C',[4] this may be rendered as 'The victoriousness of Caesar contains the future angriness of Pompey'.[5] This, however, could mislead, in that it might be thought to mean that Caesar is in fact victorious,

[1] Cf. § 1.1, p. 6.   [2] C 49.   [3] Cf. Russell, p. 9.
[4] Cf. p. 32, above.
[5] For the way in which Leibniz would render the genitive case, see below, § 2.3.
824195   D

which was not stated in the original hypothetical proposition. It seems best, then, to take the formula as meaning 'The concept of the B-ness of A contains the concept of the D-ness of C', and to suppose that Leibniz's translation of a hypothetical proposition is made in terms of the concepts of subject and predicate. The proposition 'The victoriousness of Caesar contains the future angriness of Pompey' may be taken to represent the proposition 'Caesar is victorious, therefore Pompey will be angry'.[1]

It is obvious that there are difficulties in Leibniz's account of the hypothetical proposition, but for the moment our task is one of exposition rather than of criticism. It now remains to discuss what Leibniz says about the disjunctive proposition—that is, about propositions of the form 'p or q', where 'p' and 'q' stand for propositions. It is a commonplace of modern logic that the word 'or' and its equivalents can be used to join propositions in either of two ways, generally described as the 'exclusive' and 'non-exclusive' senses of 'or'. When 'or' has the non-exclusive sense, a proposition of the form 'p or q' is true if at least one of the propositions represented by 'p' and 'q' is true. If 'or' has the exclusive sense, then a proposition of the form 'p or q' is true only if one and one only of the propositions represented by 'p' and 'q' is true. Leibniz does not show himself to be aware of this distinction,[2] but the disjunctive proposition which he defines is clearly of the exclusive sort. This is the proposition, 'Either God is one or none', which he declares to be the same as 'If God is not none he is one, and if God is not one he is none'.[3] Strictly, it is the second part only of this proposition which defines 'Either God is one or none';

---

[1] Leibniz seems sometimes to count this as a hypothetical proposition (C 262: an example of a hypothetical proposition is 'A is B, therefore C is D'). In modern logic this would be called an 'inference', and distinguished sharply from a hypothetical proposition.

[2] Though it is to be found in the *Logica Hamburgensis* of Jungius, which Leibniz had read. Jungius states (p. 105) that the distinction is to be found in the Jurisconsults, who would be known to Leibniz through his legal studies. (On Jungius, see also § 2.3 below.)   [3] C 238.

the first part defines the equivalent proposition 'Either God is none or one'.

Something has now been seen of what Leibniz means by the statement that in every proposition the predicate is said to be included in the subject, or the concept of the predicate in that of the subject; or at least, that this is true of categorical propositions, which are the basis of all others. Despite the length of the discussion there is still more to be said in explanation of Leibniz's theory of the structure of the proposition. However, what remains can best be introduced in answer to some of the criticisms to which Leibniz's views have been subjected.

II

The Limitations of Leibniz's Account

§ 2.1. There is no doubt that there would be general agreement among contemporary philosophers that Leibniz's account of the proposition is incomplete. Russell argued[1] that it is unable to explain either relational propositions or 'propositions which employ mathematical ideas', and it is widely held that Russell was right. In the chapter which follows, however, reasons will be given for supposing that Leibniz's account of the proposition, although far from perfect, is not as defective as Russell believed.

By 'propositions which employ mathematical ideas' Russell understands such propositions as 'There are three men'.[1] His argument is that such propositions do not assert a predicate of a subject, but assert plurality of subjects. From this it follows that if Leibniz wishes to maintain the view that all propositions are of the subject-predicate form he must adopt a monistic position, and say that all propositions have one and the same subject. For if there were two subjects, 'the proposition that there were two would not ascribe a predicate to either'.[2] Sentences such as 'There are three men' must, presumably, be regarded as meaningless, or else as a highly misleading way of ascribing a predicate to the one subject. Such, according to Russell, is the metaphysics which Leibniz should logically have adopted. Instead of this, Leibniz rejected monism, and so failed to draw the full consequences of his logical views.[3]

Leibniz would have answered that his logical views do not entail monism. His reply to Russell's argument is to be found

[1] Russell, p. 12.
[2] Russell, *Our Knowledge of the External World* (2nd ed., London, 1926), p. 48. Cf. pp. 115-17 of *A Critical Exposition of the Philosophy of Leibniz*.
[3] Cf. Introduction, p. 3.

in two related papers,[1] in the course of which he investigates
'what one and many are'.[2] During this investigation he gives,
in subject-predicate terms,[3] an explanation of what it is to say
'There are three m'. He begins by defining the term 'disparate', saying that a and b will be called 'disparate' if a is not
b and b is not a.[4] Although Leibniz says[5] that 'a' is to be taken
as meaning *every a*, the propositions which he gives as examples
have individuals as their subjects. There is no inconsistency
here, since (as already noted) Leibniz regards a singular proposition as a kind of universal proposition.[6] One may therefore replace 'a' and 'b' by (say) 'a man' and 'a stone', and take
Leibniz to mean that a man and a stone are disparate, since a
man is not a stone and a stone is not a man.[7] Now if a and b are
disparate, and a is m and b is m, this is the same as saying that
there are two m;[8] similarly, if a, b, and c are disparate and a is m
and b is m and c is m, there are three m; and so on. The need for
a and b, etc., to be disparate is this. Suppose that a is m and b is
m, but that a and b are not disparate: then it may be that a is b
and b is a, which means that a and b are identical, so that there
is only one m, not two. For example,[8] Octavian is a Caesar
and Augustus is a Caesar; but Octavian and Augustus are the
same, so that only one Caesar is enumerated.

In some respects, what Leibniz has said here does not differ
much from the account of the same propositions which would
be given by modern symbolic logicians. A typical modern

---

[1] *Specimen Calculi Universalis*, G vii. 218–21 (L 370 ff.) and C 239–42;
Ad Specimen Calculi Universalis Addenda, G vii. 221–7 (L 373 ff.). The former
is conjectured by Couturat to have been written in about 1679 (C. L.,
p. 336).   [2] C 239.
[3] The formulae which he uses—e.g. 'a is b'—might be thought to stand
for identities, 'is' having the force of 'is identical with'. However, it becomes
clear in the course of the argument that this is not so. It may be mentioned
here that Leibniz says explicitly that in 'a is b' the first symbol may stand for
'man', the second for 'animal', which gives a proposition which is not an
identity (G vii. 223).
[4] C 239; G vii. 225 (L 378).
[5] G vii. 218 (L 370); G vii. 223 (L 376).   [6] § 1.4.
[7] G vii. 225 (L 378).   [8] G vii. 225 and C 239.

account[1] of the proposition that there are three things having the predicate f could be put in verbal form as follows: 'For some x, x is f; for some y, y is f; for some z, z is f; and x is not identical with y and y is not identical with z and x is not identical with z; and whatever u may be, if u is f then either u is identical with x or u is identical with y or u is identical with z.' This differs from Leibniz's account in that it does not take the singular proposition as a form of universal proposition, but uses instead what may roughly be described as the notion of at least one thing and at most one thing having a certain predicate. Once this difference is allowed for, the similarity between the two accounts becomes striking.[2]

It is not clear, however, exactly how all this is to be applied to Russell's argument. Leibniz might mean that 'There are three men' is a *sentence* which expresses the proposition that a is a man and b is a man and c is a man, and a, b, and c are disparate. Or he might mean that one may indeed speak of the *proposition* that there are three men, but that since this proposition can be shown, in the way just described, to be equivalent to a proposition all of whose constituent propositions are of the subject-predicate form, it is *as if* all propositions were of the latter sort. Of the two interpretations, the latter seems the more probable. It has already been seen[3] that Leibniz seems prepared to say that there are certain propositions—namely, hypothetical propositions—which are not of the subject-predicate form but

---

[1] H. Reichenbach, *Elements of Symbolic Logic* (New York, 1948), p. 247.

[2] It is an interesting side-light on Russell's philosophical development that in his book on Leibniz he argues against such an account, saying that the proposition that there are three men 'cannot be regarded as a mere sum of subject-predicate propositions, since the number only results from the singleness of the proposition, and would be absent if three propositions, each asserting the presence of one man, were juxtaposed' (Russell, p. 12). This is reminiscent of Kant's argument for the synthetic character of the proposition '$7 + 5 = 12$' (*Critique of Pure Reason*, B 15-16); and indeed, when Russell first wrote about Leibniz he believed that the propositions of arithmetic were synthetic (Russell, p. 21). Later he came to abandon this view, moving away from Kant and towards Leibniz, for whom mathematical propositions were analytic.   [3] § 1.6, pp. 32 ff.

can be reduced to propositions which are of that form, and there seems no reason why he should not give the same account of propositions about aggregates. Nor, again, does he give any indication here of making the sharp distinction between a proposition and its linguistic expression which the first interpretation demands. It may be said, then, that Leibniz believes propositions about aggregates to be 'reducible'[1] to propositions of the subject-predicate form.

§ 2.2. Russell's second point against Leibniz was that anyone who says that every proposition is of the subject-predicate form cannot account for relational propositions.[2] This objection is generally, and rightly, thought to be justified. Nevertheless, Russell has to some extent misunderstood Leibniz's arguments which, although invalid, are less inept than he supposes. Clearly, then, the first task must be to make clear what Leibniz did think about relational propositions.

The first step towards completing this task is to note a further ambiguity in the word 'predicate'. When Russell speaks of a 'predicate', he uses the word in a sense which is now widely accepted; it is a usage which has several variations,[3] but the common factor is that a distinction is drawn between, on the one hand, propositions such as those expressed by the sentences 'John is pale' and 'John runs', and, on the other, by 'John is paler than Peter' and 'John runs faster than Paul'. Propositions of the first sort are said to be of the subject-predicate form, whilst those of the second sort are said to be not of the subject-predicate but of the relational form. There is, however, another sense of the word 'predicate', in which it means anything which

---

[1] Cf. § 1.6, p. 33.

[2] § 2.1, p. 36.

[3] Sometimes the predicate is regarded as a characteristic or attribute (Stebbing, pp. 34–35), sometimes as the word or phrase used to speak of this attribute (Russell, *Logic and Knowledge* (London, 1956), p. 205), sometimes as the concept of this attribute (Russell, *The Principles of Mathematics* (Cambridge, 1900), p. 45). It will be noticed that these ambiguities correspond to those in Leibniz's use of the words for 'predicate' (§ 1.1, pp. 6 ff.).

can be said of a subject.[1] Since one can say of a term that it has such and such relations, just as much as one can say that it is of a certain quality, one may count relations as predicates, in this sense of the word 'predicate'. Understood in this way, predicates are not opposed to relations, but include them.

The latter sense of the word 'predicate' will be called the 'wide', and the former the 'narrow' sense.[2] It seems unlikely that Leibniz would say that the word 'predicate' cannot properly be used in the wide sense,[3] and if he had the wide sense in mind when saying that all propositions have a subject and predicate, it could not be said that he fails to take account of relational propositions. Russell would probably not deny the truth of this implication as a whole, but he would say that the antecedent is false, in that what Leibniz says about the proposition involves the narrow sense of the word 'predicate'. It will be argued later that Russell would be right in this, though whether all that he says about Leibniz's account of relations is correct is another matter.

A starting-point for a discussion of Leibniz's views about

[1] Also the concept of anything which can be said of a subject, or the words by which this can be said. We shall continue to use the convention adopted in § 1.1, and refer to these as the concept of the predicate and the predicate expression respectively. What is said here of predicates can easily be applied to concepts and to predicate expressions.

[2] The word is sometimes used in the wide sense by contemporary logicians. For example, Hilbert and Ackermann distinguish between monadic, dyadic, triadic etc. predicates, the first-named being predicates in the narrow sense, and the rest relations. See *Principles of Mathematical Logic* (New York, 1950), pp. 45, 57; a translation of *Grundzüge der theoretischen Logik* (2nd ed., Berlin, 1938).

[3] A passage in his fifth paper to Clarke, though not referring explicitly to predicates, seems to imply the wide sense of the term. In this passage (*To Clarke*, § 5.47) Leibniz discusses the relation between two lines, one of which is longer than the other, and says that each may be called 'the subject of that accident which philosophers call *relation*'. He does not normally speak of subject and accident, but rather of substance and accident (e.g. G iv. 364; C 19–21, 245, 512), and in his view a line is not a substance (cf. § 5.7 below). However, the passage is most naturally taken to mean that a relation can be predicated of a line; that is, it implies the wide sense of the term 'predicate'.

relational propositions may be provided by a passage from his fifth paper to Clarke, declared by Russell to be 'of capital importance for a comprehension of Leibniz's philosophy'.[1] In Clarke's translation, the passage begins:

> The ratio or proportion between two lines L and M, may be conceived three several ways: as a ratio of the greater L, to the lesser M; as a ratio of the lesser M, to the greater L; and lastly, as something abstracted from both, that is, as the ratio between L and M, without considering which is the antecedent, or which the consequent; which the subject, and which the object. And thus it is, that proportions are considered in music.

All this is quite clear. One may say, for example, that a line L is twice as long as a line M, or that M is half as long as L, or that the lengths of L and M are in a ratio of two to one—just as in musical theory the interval of the octave can be spoken of as the ratio of two to one, or that of the fifth as three to two, and so on. So far, Leibniz has said nothing extraordinary; the passage which follows is the one which Russell stresses. In the first case, Leibniz says, L is 'the subject of that accident which philosophers call *relation*', and in the second case M is the subject. In the third case, however, it cannot be said that L and M together are the subjects of that accident which is the ratio of two to one; this is simply not the way in which the word 'accident' is used. 'It cannot be said that both of them, L and M together, are the subject of such an accident; for if so, we should have an accident in two subjects, with one leg in one, and the other in the other; which is contrary to the notion of accidents.' Leibniz concludes that the ratio, being neither substance nor accident, must be a 'mere ideal thing', or, as he says elsewhere, an 'entity of reason'.[2]

---

[1] Russell, p. 13. The passage is from par. 47 of Leibniz's fifth paper.

[2] For the ideality of relations, cf. G ii. 486 (L 992); NE, 2. 12. 3, 2. 25. 1; relations as entities of reason, NE, 2. 25. 1. The term 'entity of reason' (*ens rationis*) was in general philosophical use from the Middle Ages onwards to refer to what does not strictly speaking exist, but is 'apprehended by the

Russell argues[1] that in this passage Leibniz almost realizes that 'relation is something distinct from and independent of subject and accident', but that he 'thrusts aside the awkward discovery, by condemning the third of the above meanings as "a mere ideal thing"'. But this appears to be a misunderstanding. Leibniz is not thinking about the question, whether to talk of relations is to talk of predicates, in the narrow sense of that term; what he has in mind is the status of a relation, considered as a certain kind of entity. He is saying that the ratio of two to one is clearly not an 'accident', in the sense in which 'twice as large as M' is an accident—that is, it is not a predicate in the wide sense of the term.[2] Equally, it is not a substance; it must therefore be a mental construction, an 'ideal thing' or 'entity of reason'. This is not to say that a term such as 'the ratio of two to one' is without meaning; Leibniz says explicitly that, although relations are entities of reason, 'they have their basis in things',[3] which may be taken to mean that although the relation of two to one is not a real thing, to talk about such a ratio is a way of talking about things.[4] This is a perfectly defensible point of view, though it can hardly be called fundamental to an understanding of Leibniz.

Much more important for an understanding of Leibniz's views about relational propositions is a thesis which he himself called one of his fundamental propositions[5]—namely, that there are no 'purely extrinsic denominations'.[6] This thesis, it will be seen shortly, is about the question whether relational propositions can be regarded as propositions in which a subject is said to have a predicate or predicates, in the narrow sense

reason' (Aquinas, *Summa Theologica*, i, Qu. 16, Art. 3, ad 2). Cf. Jungius, pp. 54–55, Gilson, *Index Scolastico-Cartésien* (Paris, 1913), pp. 106–7, and the author's *Spinoza's Theory of Knowledge* (Oxford, 1954), pp. 151–6.

[1] Russell, p. 13.   [2] Cf. p. 40, n. 3.

[3] *NE*, 2. 25. 1. Cf. G ii. 486 (L 992).

[4] In the same way, it will be seen later (§ 5.7) that when Leibniz says that unextended substances are the basis of what is extended, he does not mean that assertions about the latter are nonsensical.

[5] G ii. 240 (L 857).

[6] G vii. 311; *NE*, 2. 25. 5; C 8, 520–1 (L 413–14).

of the term. Before going further, however, it will be convenient to introduce a change in terminology. As the predicates mentioned in the rest of this chapter will be predicates in the narrow sense, these may conveniently be referred to as 'predicates' simply.

Leibniz does not define the term 'extrinsic denomination', nor its opposite, 'intrinsic denomination', but it appears from his usage that he takes them in their accepted Scholastic sense, an extrinsic denomination being a relation, and an intrinsic denomination a predicate.[1] The point of saying that there are no *purely* extrinsic denominations seems to be that every extrinsic denomination is held by Leibniz to have a basis (*fundamentum*) in an intrinsic denomination.[2] What this means, however, is not immediately clear. Leibniz might perhaps mean that whenever a proposition expressed by a relational sentence is true of something, some subject-predicate proposition is, by that very fact, necessarily true of the thing also. For example, he might mean that X cannot be father of Y unless X is male, or that X cannot be redder than Y unless X is coloured, and so on. This may be plausible as a philosophical thesis,[3] but it does not seem to be what Leibniz meant. He says,[4] for example, that quantity and position are 'mere results which, through themselves, constitute no intrinsic denomination, and so are merely relations which demand a basis derived from the category of quality; that is, from an intrinsic accidental denomination'. This passage mentions only some relations, and does not of itself show that Leibniz regarded all relations as 'mere results'; elsewhere, however, he says of any relation that it 'results from the state of things'.[5] He seems to believe, then, that to talk in relational terms is meaningful, but unnecessary,

---

[1] On extrinsic denominations, see C 8–9, 244; *NE*, 2. 25. 5; on intrinsic denominations, see C 9. On the Scholastic use of *denominatio* see Gilson, op. cit., s.v. 'Dénomination'.

[2] G ii. 240 (L 857); G vii. 321 (L 606); C 9, 520; Grua, pp. 387, 547.

[3] Cf. G. E. Moore, *Philosophical Studies* (London, 1922), p. 309.

[4] C 9.

[5] Grua, p. 547.

being another way of putting what could have been said in subject-predicate terms.

It is now possible to state the relations between Leibniz's thesis that there are no purely extrinsic denominations and his view that a relation such as the ratio of two to one is an 'entity of reason', which has a basis in things. The latter is not logically dependent on the former; it was seen above that, in discussing the ideality of a ratio, Leibniz does not assume that phrases such as 'twice as long as M' are capable of analysis in subject-predicate terms. Similarly, in arguing that space is an 'ideal thing',[1] he proceeds by defining space in terms of the spatial relations of objects. It may be said, then, that even if Leibniz had believed that terms such as 'twice as long as M' or 'half as long as L' were logically indispensable, he would doubtless still have said that a ratio is an entity of reason, on the grounds that to talk about a ratio is really to talk about things in certain relations. In saying that there are no purely extrinsic denominations, however, Leibniz is saying that to talk of things as being in certain relations is itself logically unnecessary. It is his view, then, that the basis of the ratio of two to one, and of the extrinsic denomination 'twice as long as M', is ultimately describable in the same terms: that is, in subject-predicate terms.

One point remains to be clarified. It has not yet been asked whether Leibniz would regard the term 'relational proposition' as, strictly speaking, a misnomer; whether he would wish to say that all propositions are of the subject-predicate form, but that only some of these are expressed by subject-predicate sentences, others being expressed by relational sentences. This would be consistent with the views discussed in this section; so also, however, would be the view that there are relational propositions, but that these can always be replaced by equivalent subject-predicate propositions—that is, that they are 'reducible'[2] to subject-predicate propositions. In view of the

---

[1] *To Clarke,* § 5.47.

[2] Cf. § 1.6. It is also stated by Russell that Leibniz held relational propositions to be 'reducible' to subject-predicate propositions (Russell, pp. 13,

arguments brought at the end of the last section, the latter inter-pretation seems the more probable.

§ 2.3. What has been said so far does not exhaust what Leibniz means by saying that there are no purely extrinsic denomina-tions. The view which has been described is that when one says that A has a certain relation to B, the proposition asserted is reducible to subject-predicate propositions whose subjects are A and B respectively. Similarly, a three-termed relational proposition, whose terms are A, B, and C, is reducible to subject-predicate propositions whose subjects are A, B, and C respectively; and so on. However, Leibniz also takes the state-ment that there are no purely extrinsic denominations to mean that in order to assert a relational proposition about (say) A and B, it is in principle enough to know either the predicates of A alone or the predicates of B alone. This may be called Leibniz's 'stronger' thesis about extrinsic denominations; it is not entailed by the other, which may be called the 'weaker' thesis, though it can only be true if the weaker thesis is true. An examination of the stronger thesis must be deferred[1] until Leibniz's views about the completeness of the concept of a substance have been discussed; meanwhile, let us consider the weaker thesis.

In one of his philosophical works[2] Russell argues that the statement that all relational propositions are reducible to pro-positions of the subject-predicate form can easily be refuted by a reference to asymmetrical relations. By an 'asymmetrical relation' is meant a relation such that, when A has it to B, B never has it to A—for example, relations such as 'husband of', 'greater than'. A symmetrical relation, on the other hand, is one

15). What Russell means by this, however, is not clear, since he also says that, for Leibniz, 'relational propositions must be strictly meaningless' (p. 14); that a relational proposition 'must be no proposition' (p. 15). It has been argued above that this is neither what Leibniz thought, nor what he should consistently have thought.

[1] The subject is taken up again in § 5.4.
[2] *Our Knowledge of the External World*, p. 56.

such as 'equal to', 'similar to'; that is, it is a relation such that, when A has it to B, B has it to A. Russell says that it can plausibly be argued that symmetrical relations are reducible to predicates; for example, when it is said that A and B are unequal, this can be regarded as reducible to the proposition that A and B have different magnitudes. But one cannot give the sense of the proposition that A is greater than B by saying that A and B are of different magnitudes, since they would have been of different magnitudes had B been greater than A. The relation 'greater than' cannot, therefore, be reduced to predicates, and the same is true of all other asymmetrical relations.[1]

It now has to be asked what Leibniz would say about this. The arguments discussed in the last section show that it is unlikely that he would have tried to reduce symmetrical relations in the way suggested by Russell. That A and B have different magnitudes can only be said of A and B together, from which it follows that having different magnitudes would (in Leibniz's phrase) be an accident which has a leg in two subjects, and so would be no accident.[2] So much, then, can be inferred about what Leibniz would not say; to see what he would say about the reduction of relations, it is necessary to examine another part of his logic, a part which concerns arguments rather than propositions.

One of the chief reasons for distinguishing relational from subject-predicate propositions[3] is based on the fact that there are deductive arguments which depend for their validity on the logical properties of relations—for example, 'If A is equal to B, B is equal to A', or 'If A is greater than B, B is less than A'. It is pointed out that the validity of such arguments cannot be shown by a logic which is restricted to propositions of the subject-predicate form, which indicates that relational propositions are irreducible to subject-predicate propositions. To put this in another way: a relational proposition can generate arguments

---

[1] Op. cit., pp. 58–59.   [2] Cf. § 2.2, p. 41.
[3] It should be remembered (cf. § 2.2, p. 43) that the word 'predicate' is being used in its narrow sense.

of a type which a subject-predicate proposition cannot, and so the two propositions are not of the same logical form.

Leibniz was well aware of the existence of relational arguments, which were discussed in the *Logica Hamburgensis* of Joachim Jungius; it was, indeed, this discussion which was partly responsible for his interest in Jungius.[1] In the *Logica Hamburgensis* relational arguments are divided into two main types, called 'oblique inference' (*consequentia a rectis ad obliqua*) and 'inversion of a relation' (*inversio relationis*).[2] Oblique inferences are of two kinds. The first is the 'affirmative direct', of which an example is 'A circle is a figure, therefore he who describes a circle describes a figure'.[3] This is similar to the well-known argument 'Because a horse is an animal, the head of a horse is the head of an animal', instanced by the nineteenth-century logician de Morgan as unprovable by the methods of syllogistic logic.[4] The second kind is the 'affirmative inverse'—for example, 'Every reptile is an animal, therefore He who created every animal created every reptile'.[5] By the 'inversion of a relation' is meant, for example, 'David is the father of Solomon and Solomon is the son of David', and 'A perfect number is equal to all its parts taken together, and all the parts of a perfect number taken together are equal to the perfect number'.[6] Jungius, it will be noticed, does not distinguish here between asymmetrical and symmetrical relations.

In the *Logica Hamburgensis*, Jungius does no more than classify such arguments and give examples of them. Leibniz

---

[1] A ii. 1, 498. For Leibniz's interest in Jungius, see e.g. G vii. 186 (L 343); C 345, 428. See also C. *L.*, p. 73, n. 4, and A. Meyer-Abich, in *Beiträge zur Leibniz-Forschung*, ed. by G. Schischkoff (Reutlingen, 1947), pp. 138 ff.

[2] Jungius, p. 391. This is a table copied by Leibniz, C 426–8.

[3] Jungius, p. 123.

[4] Cf. Jevons, *The Principles of Science* (2nd ed., London, 1877), p. 18. The similarity is made clearer if Jungius' example is changed to 'A circle is a figure, therefore the describer of a circle is the describer of a figure'.

[5] Jungius, p. 268.

[6] Jungius, p. 89. These examples are not arguments, but it is easy to turn them into argument form. For further examples of such arguments, see Jungius, pp. 192–4, 258–9, 261.

accepted this classification,[1] but what chiefly interested him was whether Jungius had given any formal proofs of these arguments.[2] Johann Vagetius, Jungius' editor, was unable to produce any such proofs for Leibniz, who therefore had to provide his own, or at any rate suggest a way in which they might be given. He admits that such arguments cannot, as they stand, be handled by the methods of traditional logic. Unlike Jungius, however,[3] he does not say that this means that traditional logic must be expanded; instead he says that it must be supplemented. This supplementation is to come from 'rational' or 'philosophical' grammar, which will show how the recalcitrant arguments can be translated into forms which traditional logic can handle.[4] Although Leibniz is here concerned with the transformation of sentences, what he says may also be regarded as an indication of the way in which, in his opinion, relational propositions can be reduced to subject-predicate propositions.

The argument 'Peter is similar to Paul, therefore Paul is similar to Peter', which is an example of what Leibniz would call the inversion of a relation, is based on the symmetrical relation of similarity. This argument, according to Leibniz, is to be reduced to the propositions 'Peter is A now and Paul is A now'.[5] He does not explain how the argument is to be reduced to these propositions, but he may have had in mind something of the following sort. Each of the propositions 'Peter is similar to Paul' and 'Paul is similar to Peter' is equivalent to 'Peter is A now and Paul is A now'. On substituting this proposition for each, the argument becomes 'Peter is A now and Paul is A now, therefore Peter is A now and Paul is A now', whose validity is obvious.[6]

---

[1] Inversion of a relation: C 244, 284; NE, 4. 17. 4. Oblique inference: NE, 4.17. 4. It must be added that Leibniz sometimes uses the term 'oblique inference' to cover arguments based on the inversion of relations, as in C 244.   [2] A ii. 1, 498.   [3] C 287.

[4] C 36, 244, 286–7, 406.   [5] C 244.

[6] This analysis of a symmetrical relation may be compared with Russell's, cited on p. 46.

Leibniz's account of asymmetrical relations may be discussed in connexion with the argument 'David is the father of Solomon, therefore Solomon is the son of David',[1] which is another instance of what Leibniz calls the inversion of a relation. In grammatical terms, Leibniz has to give an analysis of the genitive case; in fact he gives two, using respectively the particles *eo ipso* and *quatenus*.[2] In the first of these the example which he uses is an instance of a non-symmetrical relation,[3] but his method of analysis can be applied to asymmetrical relations also. 'Paris is the lover of Helen', Leibniz says, can be regarded as saying 'Paris loves, and by that very fact (*eo ipso*) Helen is loved', or 'Paris is a lover, and by that very fact Helen is a loved one'. In Leibniz's other analysis the relation discussed is the asymmetrical relation of ownership, Leibniz arguing that to say of something that it is the sword of Evander is to say that it is an article of property in so far as (*quatenus*) Evander is an owner.[4] It is easy to see how these analyses could be used to show the validity of the relational argument about David and Solomon by following the line of reasoning suggested in the last paragraph, and regarding 'David is the father of Solomon' and 'Solomon is the son of David' as reducible either to 'David is a father, and by that very fact Solomon is a son' or to 'David is a cause in so far as Solomon is an effect'.[5]

Leibniz's method of proving the validity of oblique inferences is to be found in a paper written in 1687 for Vagetius.[6] Translated literally, the argument which Leibniz examines is

---

[1] *NE*, 4. 17. 4; cf. C 284. It is hardly necessary to point out that the argument assumes that it is known that Solomon is male.

[2] C 286–7.

[3] A relation is non-symmetrical when, if *A* has it to *B*, *B* sometimes has it to *A*, but sometimes has not.

[4] Strictly, the analyses which Leibniz gives are of *a* lover of Helen, *a* sword of Evander, although what is to be analysed seems to be about *the* lover and *the* sword; had he wished to speak of *a* lover, he would have added a qualifying word such as *quidam*. However, the correction is easily made, and in any case does not affect Leibniz's analysis of the genitive.

[5] The latter version is suggested by C 245.

[6] Dutens, vi. 1, pp. 38–39.

'Painting is an art, therefore he who studies painting, studies an art', but its oblique character is brought out more clearly if it is rendered as 'Painting is an art, therefore the student of painting is the student of an art'. Leibniz's proof proceeds, as he himself notes, by the substitution of equivalents.[1] He begins by asserting, on grammatical grounds, that the student of painting is the student of a thing which is painting. Next he substitutes 'a thing which is an art' for 'a thing which is painting', since (by hypothesis) painting is an art. Finally he substitutes, again on grammatical grounds, 'an art' for 'a thing which is an art', giving 'The student of painting is the student of an art'.[2]

Such are the ways in which Leibniz treated, or would probably have treated, deductive arguments which depend on relations. Couturat regards all this as the story of a lost opportunity. In his view, Leibniz had all the materials for a logic of relations which was far more comprehensive than classical logic. But[3] 'he systematically neglected them; or rather, he excluded them from pure logic and turned them over to grammar, thus depriving logic of its proper matter and its richest content'. This, however, is by no means just. It is true that Leibniz had almost no conception of a logical calculus dealing with relations,[4] but his concern in these grammatical analyses is with a logically perfect language rather than with pure logic. A calculus of relations would not, in his view, be an adequate way of treating relational arguments. For example, the formal logician can tell us about the logical properties of transitive relations, but he cannot, as a formal logician, say that

[1] Dutens, op. cit., p. 32.

[2] Leibniz's proof may be compared with Jevons's treatment of the argument 'Because a horse is an animal, the head of a horse is the head of an animal'. This, said Jevons, 'amounts merely to replacing in the complete notion *head of a horse*, the term "horse" by its equivalent *some animal* or *an animal*' (op. cit., p. 18).   [3] C. L., p. 437.

[4] The only hints of such a conception are given by the *Analysis Didactica* (C 424–6), a series of notes on a symbolism for relations proposed by an unknown author, and by a brief reference in C 327 (a note on logical symbolism).

a given relation is transitive. To be able to say this he needs other sources of information, and it was to have been the function of Leibniz's 'rational grammar' to provide such information.

More important here, however, are the questions whether Leibniz intended his translations of relational propositions to be a reduction of them to the subject-predicate form, in the sense of giving a complete analysis of them, and if so, whether he succeeded. His analysis of symmetrical relations may be accepted, but it is not these relations on which Russell rests his case. The question is, whether Leibniz can reduce propositions about asymmetrical relations to propositions of the subject-predicate form. Certainly, if he thought that the passages just discussed provide such a reduction, he was mistaken. Take, for example, the proposition 'David is a father, and by that very fact Solomon is a son', which renders 'David is the father of Solomon'. First, the relational proposition is not reduced simply to the two propositions 'David is a father' and 'Solomon is a son'; to omit 'by that very fact' from the sentence 'David is a father, and by that very fact Solomon is a son' changes its sense. Much the same can be said if the relational proposition is rendered as 'David is a cause in so far as Solomon is an effect'; to omit the words 'in so far as' would give a sentence which expresses two propositions which, taken together, are not equivalent to the proposition that David is the father of Solomon. Second, and more important, relational terms occur in the very propositions which to be substituted for relational propositions; to call someone a father or a son, or a cause or an effect, is to say that he is related to someone else.

It is possible that Leibniz did not believe that in the passages just discussed he was reducing relational to subject-predicate propositions. In a letter of 1679[1] he says that his purpose in giving these translations was 'to make all reasonings reducible to a certain and indubitable form'. It may be, then, that he regards his analyses of relational propositions not as complete, but only as complete enough to permit relational arguments to be transformed into arguments of a kind generally regarded as valid by his contemporaries. But if this is so, it is not clear what Leibniz would regard as a complete reduction of a proposition involving an asymmetrical relation to a subject-predicate proposition. He seems, then, to have no adequate answer to Russell, so that his weaker thesis about extrinsic denominations fails; a fortiori, his stronger thesis fails also.[1]

§ 2.4. It is now time to leave Leibniz's account of relational propositions, and to discuss some of the other criticisms which can be brought against his theory of the structure of the proposition in general. Perhaps the most important of these concern hypothetical and existential propositions respectively. It was mentioned earlier[2] that Leibniz argues that every hypothetical proposition can be reduced to a proposition in which is asserted the inclusion of the predicate in the subject, by which he seems to have meant the inclusion of the *concept* of the predicate in that of the subject. The feature of this view which is criticized is precisely the fact that it is put forward as an account of *all* hypothetical propositions, whereas it has been recognized since the time of Kant that there is an important difference between hypothetical propositions which assert a causal relation and the hypothetical propositions of pure logic, in that the denial of true propositions of the former kind does not involve a contradiction, whereas the denial of true propositions of the latter kind does. Leibniz's account may fit some (though perhaps not all) propositions of the latter kind; it does not fit any of the former kind—that is, of those which assert a causal relation.

This objection cannot conveniently be discussed at present,[3] since Leibniz's answer to it involves his account of truth, and in particular his method of distinguishing between necessary and contingent truths. However, the objection that Leibniz has given the same account of all hypothetical propositions

[1] Cf. p. 45.   [2] § 1.6.   [3] Though see below, § 3.4.

can be given another form which does not involve his views about truth, and which can be discussed here. It may be conceded (a critic may say) that the account which Leibniz gives is sometimes plausible; namely, when the antecedent and consequent of the hypothetical proposition have the same subject. To say, for example, 'If anyone is a man, he is rational' is to say that all men are rational, which Leibniz can plausibly render as 'The concept of humanity contains that of rationality'. Similarly, 'If Socrates is a man, Socrates is rational' can be regarded as a shortened form of 'If Socrates is a man, and if, if anyone is a man, he is rational, then Socrates is rational', which can be taken as saying that the concept of Socrates contains that of humanity and the concept of humanity contains that of rationality, from which it follows that the concept of Socrates contains that of rationality. But what of cases in which the antecedent and consequent have different subjects? Take, for example, a hypothetical proposition cited earlier, 'If Caesar is victorious, then Pompey will be angry'.[1] It is just not true that the concept of the victoriousness of Caesar contains that of the future angriness of Pompey; that is, that if one considers all that it means to talk about the victoriousness of Caesar, the concept of the future angriness of Pompey will be found to be a part of this.

Leibniz would probably reply that this may be true of our concept of the victoriousness of Caesar, or rather (since victoriousness is predicated of Caesar) of our concept of Caesar. But, he would add, he understands by 'the concept of Caesar' the concept which an omniscient being, such as God, has of Caesar;[2] and in his concept of Caesar God sees, not only the concept of Caesar's future victoriousness, but that of Pompey's future anger. The objection to this is that, although what Leibniz says may be true, no good reason has so far been given to suppose that it is. It may well be that anyone who wishes to say that all propositions are of or are reducible to the subject-predicate form must talk much as Leibniz has just been

[1] § 1.6.   [2] Cf. § 1.2.

represented as talking. But it is not obvious that all propositions are of this form, and the fact that, if they are, such a forced account has to be given of some hypothetical propositions may be held to be a reason for thinking that they are not.

The other objection mentioned earlier was that Leibniz's theory of the structure of the proposition cannot account for existential propositions, by which are meant propositions whose subjects are asserted, or at any rate assumed, to exist. This is another objection which cannot be fully discussed at present, but enough must be said to make its nature clear. It is directed not so much against Leibniz's subject-predicate bias, as against his preference for the intensional treatment of the proposition. In the last chapter it was argued[1] that Leibniz interpreted universal propositions in intensional terms in order that a proposition such as 'All perfectly wise men are happy' could be true even if there are no perfectly wise men. But one might wish to use the sentence 'All perfectly wise men are happy' to assert that there are perfectly wise men, all of whom are happy; and the question is, how Leibniz can account for the proposition which this sentence expresses. The same difficulty occurs in the case of 'Some perfectly wise men are happy' and 'Socrates, who is perfectly wise, is happy'; indeed, it has often been pointed out that to say that some perfectly wise men are happy implies that there are perfectly wise men. A similar problem is provided for Leibniz by the use of words such as 'so' and 'therefore'. For example, even if it is granted that Leibniz has explained in conceptual terms 'If Caesar is victorious, Pompey will be angry', this is not the same as explaining 'Caesar is victorious, therefore Pompey will be angry', which implies that there is a Caesar who is victorious and a Pompey who will be angry.

There might seem to be an obvious solution: to interpret the proposition 'x exists' as saying that the concept of existence is contained in that of x. This, however, would raise further difficulties for Leibniz. These difficulties, and Leibniz's answer

[1] § 1.3.

to them, involve his views about the existence and nature of God, and are best discussed in a later chapter.[1] Meanwhile, it is time to sum up the account which has so far been given of Leibniz's theory of the proposition. The argument has been twofold. First, it has been argued that, although the theory does not account for all types of propositions, it is not as inept as is often supposed. Second, it has been argued that it is not true that Leibniz failed to draw from the theory its full metaphysical consequences, and avoided monism only at the expense of inconsistency. Indeed, it has not been seen that the theory has of itself any consequences which relate to metaphysics, in the sense that it entails propositions which state what the world must be like, if there is a world.[2] It is clear, then, that if Leibniz's logic has any consequences relating to metaphysics, these must be derived from a part of his logic which is other than that which has just been studied.

[1] Cf. § 4.4, p. 92, and § 4.7, p. 107.   [2] Cf. Introduction, p. 3.

III

Truth and Sufficient Reason

§ 3.1. It will be remembered that when we speak here of the relations between Leibniz's logic and his metaphysics, the term 'logic' is taken to mean his views about the structure of the proposition and about truth.[1] Of this logic, there now remain for consideration his views about truth. Leibniz says that truth is the predicate's being in the subject,[2] a thesis which he also expresses by saying that the nature of truth consists in the fact that the predicate is in the subject, or that a true proposition is that whose predicate is contained in the subject.[3] Two things are immediately clear about these assertions. First, in claiming to say what truth is, or what its nature is, Leibniz is putting forward a *definition* of truth. Second, his definition is phrased in terms which indicate that he is here regarding every proposition as stating that a predicate is in the subject, negative propositions being taken to affirm the inclusion of a negative predicate.[4] The words 'subject' and 'predicate' themselves, however, again raise difficulties. It has already been mentioned[5] that Leibniz sometimes speaks of 'subject' and 'predicate' where 'concept of the subject' and 'concept of the predicate' would be a clearer way of expressing his meaning. What he has said about truth, then, may mean either that a true proposition is one the concept of whose predicate is included in that of the subject, or that it is one whose predicate is in the subject, where 'subject' means that which is talked about and 'predicate' means that which is said of it. These two definitions of truth are not inconsistent, and Leibniz may intend to give both, though it will be argued later that he seems to think of truth primarily in terms of the inclusion of concepts.

[1] Cf. § 1.1.   [2] C 1.   [3] C 68, 401, 518 (L 412).
[4] Cf. § 1.4 above.   [5] § 1.1, pp. 6 ff.

Besides defining truth in terms of inclusion Leibniz also says that a true proposition is one which is either an identical proposition or reducible to one.[1] This definition may seem quite clear, but it again requires some explanation. The term 'identical proposition' would probably now be understood to refer to propositions of the form 'A is A', 'Every A is A', or 'Everything is what it is', and indeed Leibniz often uses it in this sense.[2] He makes it clear, however, that when he speaks of an identical proposition in the present context he has in mind, not only propositions such as 'A man is a man', but also propositions such as 'A white man is white'.[3] In effect, he is using the term 'identical' as a synonym for 'tautologous', as he himself implies when he remarks that he calls certain truths 'identical' because 'it seems that they do nothing but repeat the same thing, without teaching us anything'.[4] In saying, then, that a true proposition is one which is either an identical proposition or reducible to one, Leibniz means that a true proposition either is or is reducible to a tautology.

Leibniz relates his two accounts of truth, that in terms of identity and that in terms of inclusion, by saying that in an identical proposition the predicate is in the subject manifestly or expressly, whilst in all other true propositions it is present in the subject in a concealed form (tecte), or implicitly or virtually.[5] Alternatively he says that in a true proposition the concept of the predicate is in the concept of the subject, either expressly or virtually.[6] Once again it has to be asked whether Leibniz distinguishes here between subject and predicate on the one hand, and their concepts on the other. The answer seems to be that he does not; that is, that by 'subject' and 'predicate' he means what we have called the *concepts* of subject and predicate.

[1] C 513. Cf. G vii. 296 (L 356); C 519 (L 412–13).
[2] 'A is A': G vii. 299; NE, 4. 2. 1; C 186, 518 (L 411). 'Every A is A': NE, 4. 2. 1; C 416. 'Each thing is what it is': NE, 4. 2. 1; C 518.
[3] C 11; cf. C 272, 369; NE, 4. 2. 1; FC, p. 182 (L 407).
[4] NE, 4. 2. 1.
[5] C 11, 519; DM, par. 8; G vii. 309; Grua, p. 303.
[6] C 402.

Take, for example, the true proposition 'Every man is rational'. This is clearly not an identical proposition, even in Leibniz's wide sense of the term, so that the inclusion of the predicate in the subject must be concealed, virtual or implicit. But it is hard to see what this can mean, if 'subject' and 'predicate' have the sense which we have given them. It was argued earlier[1] that the only meaning which can be given to the statement that the predicate is in the subject is that the predicate is a predicate *of* the subject; in the present case, what must be meant is that rationality is a predicate of every man. But there is nothing concealed, virtual or implicit about this predicate. What Leibniz must surely mean is that the inclusion of the *concept* of rationality in the *concept* of man is implicit. This inclusion can, as he remarks, be made explicit by analysis of the concepts or terms of the proposition;[2] in this case, by replacing the term 'man' by the term 'rational animal', giving the proposition 'Every rational animal is rational', which Leibniz would call an identical proposition.

In giving his definition of truth, Leibniz is not saying 'This is how I propose to use such words as "true" and "truth", regardless of the way in which other people use them'. He is claiming to give a correct account of the way in which these words are generally used; to say 'what it is to be truly attributed to a certain subject'.[3] Consequently it can properly be asked whether (given his views about the structure of the proposition) his account of the nature of truth is justifiable. This question can most conveniently be answered by breaking up Leibniz's definition into its constituent propositions. A definition can always be represented as an equivalence;[4] that is, as a proposition

---

[1] § 1.5.

[2] C 11, 519; G vii. 309. It should be added that when Leibniz speaks of 'virtual' inclusion he does not mean that the concept of the predicate of a true proposition is sometimes not actually in that of the subject. 'Virtual' is contrasted not with 'actual' but with 'express' (C 402; *DM*, par. 8); Leibniz means that what is sometimes virtual is the exhibition of the hitherto concealed presence of the concept of the predicate in that of the subject.

[3] *DM*, par. 8.   [4] Cf. C 242, 258, 406.

of the form 'If and only if p, then q', which in turn is the same as saying 'If p then q, and if q then p'.[1] Leibniz, then, must be able to show that a proposition is true if and only if it is an expressly or implicitly identical proposition; that is, he must be able to show, first, that if a proposition is true it is expressly or implicitly identical, and second, that if a proposition is expressly or implicitly identical it is true. The same tasks can of course be formulated in terms of subjects and predicates, or of their concepts.

§ 3.2. The view that every expressly or implicitly identical proposition is true, or more simply that every identical proposition is true, is related by Leibniz to what he calls the 'principle of contradiction', which he declares to be one of the 'two great principles' used in reasoning.[2] This relation, however, is not easily stated, because of the many ways in which Leibniz formulates the principle.

Traditionally the principle of contradiction is taken as saying that the same proposition cannot be at once true and false,[3] or (doing without the terms 'true' and 'false') that A is not both B and not B.[4] Leibniz, too, says that he understands by the principle of contradiction the statement that a proposition cannot be true and false at the same time.[5] He also states the principle in a form which does not involve the terms 'true' and 'false' when he says that it asserts that the same thing cannot at the same time be and not be.[6] Another related formulation of the principle says that what implies or contains a contradiction is false,[7] understanding by a 'contradiction' something which says that 'at the same time the same thing is and is not'.[8] Here, instead of saying that at the same time the same thing cannot both be and not be, Leibniz has said that the proposition

---

[1] Cf. C 406.   [2] *Mon.*, par. 31; G vi. 127, 413.
[3] H. W. B. Joseph, *Introduction to Logic* (Oxford, 1906), p. 360, n. 1.
[4] Stebbing, p. 469. Cf. Aristotle, *Metaphysics*, 996^{b}26–30, 1005^{b}19–23.
[5] *To Clarke*, § 2.1.   [6] Grua, pp. 20–21.
[7] *Mon.*, par. 31; G vii. 199; Grua, p. 287.
[8] G vii. 295.

that the same thing at the same time both is and is not is false, as is any other proposition in which this is contained.

So much Leibniz might reasonably be expected to say; it may seem strange, however, that he should sometimes state the principle of contradiction as 'A proposition is either true or false',[1] or as asserting that of two contradictory propositions the one is true and the other false.[2] These are formulations of what is now usually called the principle of bivalence, which is equivalent to the law of excluded middle, usually formulated as 'Either p or not-p', where 'p' is as it were a 'placeholder' for any sentence which is used to express a proposition.[3] Leibniz says that the principle of contradiction, taken in this sense, 'contains' the true proposition that a proposition cannot be true and false at the same time[4]—that is, that it contains what is more usually called the principle of contradiction. He is right in saying that what is usually called the principle of contradiction can be derived from the principle of bivalence;[5] this does not mean, however, that the principle of bivalence is logically more basic, since it in its turn can be derived from the principle of contradiction, so that the two principles are equivalent. It is possible that Leibniz realised this, and for that reason used the term 'principle of contradiction' to refer to the principle of bivalence as well as in its more usual sense.

It may be asked what all this has to do with the assertion that every identical proposition is true, which is presupposed by Leibniz's definition of truth. The answer is that just as the principles of contradiction and bivalence tend to coalesce for Leibniz, so do the principles of contradiction and identity.

---

[1] *NE*, 4. 2. 1; cf. G vii. 299 (L 347).

[2] G ii. 62; G vi. 127, 413; *Mon.*, par. 31. It may be assumed that Leibniz is here using 'contradictory' in the usual sense, in which (subject and predicate being the same) a universal affirmative and a particular negative proposition are contradictory, as are a universal negative and a particular affirmative. He also expresses what seems to be the same principle as 'If an affirmation is true, the negation is false; . . . if a negation is true, the affirmation is false' (G vii. 299).   [3] Cf. Kneale, p. 47.

[4] *NE*, 4. 2. 1.   [5] Cf. § 3.4, p. 74, n. 5.

The latter principle is usually stated as 'A is A', or 'Every-thing is what it is', a usage which agrees with that of Leib-niz.[1] He seems to suggest that the principle of contradiction can as well be called that of identity, when he speaks of 'the principle of contradiction or of identity',[2] and says that the principle of identity is the same as that of contradiction, or that the two come to the same.[3] This is also implied by his assertion that direct and indirect proof—that is, the method of proof which reduces the proposition to be proved to identi-cal propositions, and that which shows that its contradictory implies a contradiction—coincide.[4]

If this is so, one would expect each principle to be derivable from the other. All that Leibniz seems to mention, however, is the derivability of the principle of identity from that of contra-diction, when he speaks of 'the principle of contradiction or identity' as saying that 'A proposition cannot be true and false at the same time and therefore A is A and cannot be not-A'.[5] Presumably the argument is that to say that A is not-A would commit one to saying that the proposition 'Something is A' is both true and false; it is, therefore, false that A is not-A and true that A is A. There is no reason to suppose, however, that Leibniz would not also have regarded the propositions that it is false that A is not-A and that a proposition cannot be true and false at the same time as derivable from 'A is A', that is, from the principle of identity. Certainly, there is no sug-gestion in his writings that he believed that what is commonly called the principle of contradiction is logically prior to the

---

[1] Stebbing, p. 469; Joseph, op. cit., p. 378; *To Clarke*, § 2.1, cf. *NE*, I. I. 4.   [2] *To Clarke*, § 2.1; G vi. 413; C 1.

[3] G v. 14 (A vi. 6, 4): 'My view is, therefore, that one should take for a primitive principle nothing but experiences and the axiom of identity, or (what is the same thing) the principle of contradiction.' G iv. 357 (L 633): 'Of the truths of reason, the first is the principle of contradiction or, what comes to the same thing, of identity (*identicorum*), as Aristotle also has rightly remarked.' The same may be meant when Leibniz formulates the principle of contradiction as 'Every identical proposition is true and its contradictory is false' (G vii. 309).

[4] G vii. 295 (L 356).   [5] *To Clarke*, § 2.1.

principle of identity in the sense that it cannot be derived from the latter, which is, however, derivable from it. Leibniz says explicitly that 'identical propositions, whose opposite contains an express contradiction, cannot be proved and do not need to be proved'.[1] They alone are *per se notae*, 'self-evident';[2] they are the primary truths (*primae veritates*) which cannot be reduced to any others.[3] The principles of contradiction and identity, then, seem after all to coincide for Leibniz. From this it follows that the proposition that every identical proposition is true, the truth of which is required by Leibniz's definition of truth, is a form of the principle of contradiction. As such, Leibniz believes that its truth does not require proof.

§ 3.3. It was mentioned earlier[4] that for Leibniz's definition of truth to be justified he must be able to show, not only that if a proposition is expressly or implicitly identical it is true, but also that if a proposition is true it is expressly or implicitly identical. Leibniz often makes assertions which are equivalent to the latter, saying that in every true proposition the predicate is in the subject,[5] or the concept of the predicate is in that of the subject.[6] The question is, with what right he says this. Couturat argues[7] that this assertion is one of Leibniz's basic principles; to be exact, it is the principle of sufficient reason, the second of the 'two great principles' which Leibniz declares

[1] *Mon.* par. 35.
[2] G vii. 309. Cf. G vii. 300 (L 348); C 365; A ii. 1, 398 (L 286); FC, p. 181 (L 407); *NE*, 1. 1. 18.
[3] C 518 (L 411); G vii. 300. Also called 'veritates originariae', FC, p. 181.
[4] § 3.1, p. 59.
[5] G ii. 43, 56 (L 517); G vii. 300 (L 348), 309; C 11, 272, 388; Grua, pp. 304, 305, 536; FC, p. 179 (L 405). G ii. 56 and FC, p. 179 are restricted to affirmative propositions, G vii. 309 and Grua, p. 305 to universal affirmative propositions. This springs from Leibniz's uncertainty (cf. § 1.4) as to whether to say that in every proposition the predicate is said to be in the subject, etc., or that this is stated in affirmative propositions only.
[6] G ii. 56; G vii. 199, 300; C 388, 402; FC, p. 179.
[7] C. L., pp. 214-15; *RMM*, 1908, p. 8.

to be used in reasoning.[1] To see if this is so, it will be necessary to examine the principle in question.

Like the principle of contradiction, the principle of sufficient reason is related to Leibniz's definition of truth; like that principle, again, it is stated by him in a number of ways. In one common formulation, the principle of sufficient reason states that there must be a sufficient reason for anything which exists or happens.[2] Leibniz defines a sufficient reason as 'that on the assumption of which a thing exists',[3] and distinguishes it from a 'requisite' (*requisitum*), which is 'that without the assumption of which a thing does not exist'.[4] In other words, the former is a sufficient condition, the latter is a *sine qua non* or necessary condition.[5] The adjective 'sufficient', then, shows the extent of Leibniz's claim. He is saying, not only that it is possible to state a necessary condition of the existence of any given thing, or state of affairs, or event, but also that it is always possible to give a full explanation of it. It must be added that Leibniz often drops the adjective 'sufficient' and speaks simply of 'the principle of the need for giving a reason',[6] or of the principle that 'there is nothing without a reason'.[7] However, when he does so it is often clear that he has in mind what he

[1] *Mon.*, par. 32; G vi. 127, 413. Cf. § 3.2, p. 59.

[2] *To Clarke*, § 5.125. Cf. *To Clarke*, § 2.1; *PNC*, par. 7; *Mon.*, par. 32. A similar definition is given of what Leibniz calls the 'principle of determining reason' (G vi. 127).

[3] Bodemann, Theol. xx, p. 223. Published by R. Zocher in *Leibniz' Erkenntnislehre* (Berlin, 1952).

[4] Ibid. Cf. Grua, p. 267.

[5] Cf. C 471; Grua, p. 267. The meaning of the term 'sufficient reason' was correctly explained by E. Boutroux, in *Leibniz: La Monadologie* (Paris, 1881: p. 158, n. 2 of the 1956 edition). R. Latta, on the other hand, is quite wrong in saying of the principle of sufficient reason that 'the name has a makeshift sound—as if one should say, "We must be content with a sufficient reason in cases where a perfect reason is not to be found"' (*Leibniz: The Monadology* (Oxford, 1898), p. 62). From what has been said above it is clear that a sufficient reason *is* a perfect reason.

[6] G vii. 309; C 525.

[7] G ii. 56 (L 413); G iv. 232 (L 222); G vii. 109, 289, 300–1 (L 349); *NE*, 2. 2. 13; G. *M.* vii, Supp. 113; C 11, 25, 515, 618, 622, 625; Grua, pp. 13, 267, 268, 287; FC, p. 182 (L 408); Bodemann, p. 58.

calls elsewhere the 'principle of sufficient reason',[1] and there is never any indication that some other principle is meant; the dropping of the adjective, then, seems to have no philosophical significance.

Leibniz also formulates the principle of sufficient reason as saying something about truth; namely, that there is no true proposition 'whose reason could not be seen by a man who had all the knowledge necessary to understand it perfectly'.[2] In modern English, the statement that a reason can be seen (or, as Leibniz often says, can be given)[3] for every truth has a strange sound. One speaks, for example, of being able to give a reason for Caesar's crossing of the Rubicon, but not of giving a reason for the true proposition that Caesar crossed the Rubicon. Leibniz makes it clear, however, that when he uses phrases which we translate literally as 'giving a reason for the truth of a proposition', what he means is 'providing an *a priori* proof of the truth of a proposition'.[4] The principle of sufficient reason, then, states that every true proposition is provable. One might ask whether this is not a different principle from that which was described earlier, according to which there must be a sufficient reason for anything which exists or happens. Leibniz clearly does not think so, but regards himself as putting forward alternative formulations of one principle.[5] How he can do so can be seen from an example. The equality of the angles at the base of an isosceles triangle has, according to Leibniz, a sufficient reason; but to say this is the same as saying that the true proposition that the angles at the base of an isosceles triangle are equal can be proved.

[1] Compare e.g. the remark that physics requires the 'principle of the need for giving a reason' (G vii. 309) with the statement that it requires the 'principle of the need for a sufficient reason' (*To Clarke*, § 2.1). In this last passage, again, God's existence is deduced from the 'principle of sufficient reason', but elsewhere from the principle that there is nothing without a reason (C 533–4; G vii. 300–1; Grua, p. 13).

[2] G vi. 413; cf. *Mon.*, par. 32; *To Clarke*, § 5.125.

[3] e.g. G vii. 309; Grua, p. 303.

[4] G ii. 62; G vii. 301 (L 349), 309; *DM*, par. 13; C 402, 519 (L 413).

[5] e.g. *Mon.*, par. 32; *To Clarke*, § 5.125.

The principle of sufficient reason also appears in the form of the assertion that nothing happens without a cause, or that there is nothing without a cause.[1] Leibniz does not seem to intend to say anything new by this, but appears simply to be using 'cause' as a synonym for 'sufficient reason'.[2] In this sense, a correct answer to the question 'Why is S, P?' always states a cause of S's being P, whether the question is 'Why does this figure have interior angles which are equal to two right angles?' or 'Why is this triangle on the blackboard?' It is obvious that this sense of the word 'cause' is wider than that which is now generally given to the word. The question about the interior angles of a figure requires a geometrical answer, and geometers are not now regarded as stating the causes of the properties which figures have; one might, on the other hand, ask for the cause of there being a triangle on the blackboard. To put this in more general terms, the word 'cause' (as Hume and Kant saw) is normally used to refer to something which precedes its effect in time, and what the geometer gives as a reason for a figure's having a certain property is not of this sort.

Although Leibniz's use of the word 'cause' is different from what is now its normal use, this does not mean that it is wrong. Leibniz was using the word in a widely accepted sense, that of Aristotle and the Scholastics, for whom any answer to the question 'Why?' stated a cause. For example, somebody who asks 'Why is this triangle on the blackboard?' might be asking for an 'efficient cause' ('Who put it there?'), or for a 'final cause' ('For what purpose was it put there?'); the geometer, on the other hand, seeks the 'formal cause' of the properties of triangles and other figures.[3] But although Leibniz's usage cannot be called wrong, it can be called obsolete; indeed, passages from his own writings indicate that even in his own time the meaning of the word 'cause' was changing from the medieval

[1] A ii. 1, 248 (L 238); G ii. 40; G iii. 168; G vii. 301; C 519; Grua, p. 263.
[2] e.g. G vii. 301, 309; C 519; G. M. vii, Supp. 113.
[3] Cf. Grua, p. 269, where Leibniz indicates that when he says that there is nothing without a reason he has in mind the four Aristotelian causes.

to the modern sense. In these passages he distinguishes between a 'cause' and a 'reason', saying, for example, that 'nothing ever happens without a cause, or at least a determining reason'.[1] Again, he says that what is eternal may have no cause, but it must have a reason,[2] which may be taken to mean that although it may have no cause in the sense that nothing can precede it, it must be possible to explain it, that is, to give a reason for its existence.[3]

It now has to be asked why Leibniz should suppose all this to be true. In 1716, the last year of his life, he said in a paper addressed to Clarke that the principle of sufficient reason does not require proof.[4] This remark, however, was made in some exasperation at what proved to be the end of a long controversy, and is not typical of Leibniz. More typical is the assertion, made only six years earlier, that the principle of sufficient reason is 'contained in the definition of truth and falsity'.[5] There are many passages in which Leibniz explains what this means,[6] but one will suffice. After saying that in every true proposition the concept of the predicate is contained in that of the subject, he continues:[7]

It is evident, therefore, that all truths—even the most contingent —have an *a priori* proof, or some reason why they are truths rather than not. And this is just what is meant when it is commonly said (*hoc ipsum est quod vulgo dicunt*) that nothing happens without a cause, or, that there is nothing without a reason.

The argument is fairly clear. Leibniz is saying that to give a reason for a truth, to prove that a proposition is true, is to

[1] G vi. 127.   [2] G vii. 302 (L 790).
[3] The same, restricted sense of the word 'cause' may be in Leibniz's mind when he says that a cause is a reason for a thing which is outside the thing (Grua, p. 13), i.e. that it is not a 'formal' or 'material' cause, and perhaps not a 'final cause', which may be 'immanent in' the thing whose end it is. Cf. G vii. 289: a cause is a 'real reason'.
[4] *To Clarke*, § 5.125.   [5] G vi. 414.
[6] *DM*, par. 13; G ii. 56 (L 517), 62; G vii. 199, 295 (L 356), 301 (L 349); C 11, 402, 513, 519 (L 413); Grua, p. 287.
[7] G vii. 301.

show how the concept of the predicate is included in that of the subject.[1] Now, in every true proposition the concept of the predicate is included in that of the subject, therefore every true proposition can be proved. The only obscurity is provided by the fact that Leibniz sometimes says that an *a priori* proof can be given, not of all true propositions, but only of those which are not self-evident, that is, are not expressly identical propositions.[2] This can hardly mean that an expressly identical proposition has no reason for its truth, in view of the many passages in which the principle of sufficient reason is stated by Leibniz to apply to all truths without exception.[3] Perhaps what is meant is that an expressly identical proposition cannot be proved,[4] if by 'proof' is understood the reduction of a proposition to one which is expressly identical. But it has a reason for its truth—namely, the very fact that it is expressly identical —and in a broad sense of the word 'proof' may be said to be provable.

In sum, a proposition which Leibniz calls 'the principle of sufficient reason' is part of his logic, in that it follows, and was seen by Leibniz to follow, from his definition of truth. To suppose that this is all that Leibniz ever meant by the term 'principle of sufficient reason' would be a mistake,[5] but there can be no reasonable doubt that it is part of what he meant. It is now time to relate all this to what was said at the beginning of the present section. It was pointed out then that if Leibniz is to justify his definition of truth, he must show that if a proposition is true it is expressly or implicitly identical, and it was mentioned that Couturat had said that this proposition is asserted by Leibniz as a fundamental principle, the principle of sufficient reason. Our enquiry has shown, however, that the principle of sufficient reason does not state this. What it says

---

[1] e.g. G vii. 295–6; C 402, 513, 519; *DM*, par. 13.

[2] G vii. 199, 309; C 513.

[3] G ii. 62; G vi. 413; G vii. 295, 301; *To Clarke*, § 5.125; C 402; Grua, p. 287. Cf. C 387, which says that a true proposition is one which can be proved.   [4] Cf. § 3.2, p. 62.   [5] Cf. § 4.7.

is that every true proposition can be proved; as such, it is derived from Leibniz's definition of truth,[1] and so cannot be used to justify that definition. In defence of Couturat's interpretation, it must be allowed that Leibniz sometimes writes as if the principle of sufficient reason were identical with the assertion that in every true proposition the concept of the predicate is in that of the subject. He says, for example,[2] that one of the two principles which he uses in reasoning is that 'A reason can be given for every truth which is not immediate or identical; that is (*hoc est*) the concept of the predicate is always in the concept of its subject, either expressly or implicitly'. But Leibniz cannot be speaking accurately here; it has already been seen that these two propositions are not equivalent, but that the first is entailed by the second taken in conjunction with one other proposition—namely, that every proposition in which the concept of the predicate is contained in that of the subject can be proved.

Meanwhile, Leibniz's definition of truth has still not been justified; it has still not been explained why he should say that every truth is, or is reducible to, an identical proposition. Perhaps the answer is to be found in his views about the proposition as such, together with a suppressed premiss which has some similarity to Aristotle's statement[3] that 'to say of what is that it is, and of what is not that it is not, is true'. Leibniz has argued that to assert any proposition is to say that the concept of the predicate is included in that of the subject, and he may have thought it obvious (and so did not state explicitly) that whenever one asserts a true proposition one is saying that the concept of the subject includes that of the predicate when the concept of the subject does include that of the predicate. The

---

[1] More exactly, it is derived from the premiss that every true proposition is a proposition which is or is reducible to an identical proposition, in conjunction with the premiss that every proposition which is or is reducible to an identical proposition can be proved. From these it follows syllogistically that every true proposition can be proved.

[2] G vii. 199; cf. Grua, p. 287.

[3] *Metaphysics*, 1011ᵇ25 ff. (trans. Ross).

distinguishing mark of a true proposition, then, is the inclusion
of the concept of the predicate in that of the subject; in other
words, in every true proposition the concept of the subject
includes that of the predicate, or, what for Leibniz is the same,
every true proposition is or is reducible to an identical proposition.

§ 3.4. So far, this chapter has been devoted to the exposition of
Leibniz's views, and it is now time to consider some criticisms.
As the principle of sufficient reason is so closely related to
Leibniz's definition of truth, it follows that an objection to one
will be an objection to the other. It has already been said,[1]
against that theory of truth, that it is a mistake to think that all
true hypothetical propositions are necessary truths, and it
could similarly be argued that it is not true that, whenever one
says something of the form 'q, because p' what is inferred follows with logical necessity. This objection could also be put
in the form that it is wrong to say that all proof is *a priori*
proof. Leibniz saw the force of this objection, and tried to meet
it. He tried to show that there is room in his logic both for
truths which are necessary and for truths which are not, i.e.
for 'contingent' truths;[2] with what success, we must now try to
determine.

It is immediately noticeable that Leibniz's account of necessary truths is given in the same terms as those in which he states
his views about truth in general. He has said that a true proposition is one which either is or is reducible to an identical
proposition, and he says the same about a proposition which is
necessarily true.[3] Alternatively, he defines a necessary truth as

[1] § 2.4.
[2] G iii. 400; G vii. 108; C 17; Schmidt, p. 480.
[3] Necessary truths as identical propositions: FC, p. 181 (L 407). As
reducible to identical propositions: G vii. 300 (L 348); C 17; FC, p. 181;
Grua, p. 303. Sometimes (e.g. G vii. 300; C 17; Grua, p. 303) Leibniz
writes as though only those propositions which are reducible to identical
propositions are necessary truths, but this can hardly be what he means, for
as he says elsewhere (FC, p. 181) expressly identical propositions are also
necessary truths.

a proposition whose contrary implies a contradiction.[1] It is reasonable to assume that he is here using the word 'contrary' in its traditional sense, in which a universal affirmative and a universal negative proposition which have the same subject are contraries. If so, he may have in mind the fact that (for example) the identical proposition 'A is A' is one whose contrary is a self-contradiction, 'No A is A', so that he is only stating in other words his thesis that a necessary truth either is or is reducible to an identical proposition.

Leibniz also says that a necessary truth is a proposition whose 'opposite' implies a contradiction.[2] Traditionally, to speak of propositions which are 'opposites' is to speak, not only of contrary propositions, but of contradictory, subcontrary, and subaltern propositions also. Leibniz may here be thinking of contrary propositions alone, but it is also possible that he has in mind contradictory propositions—that is (subject and predicate being the same) the universal affirmative and particular negative, and the universal negative and particular affirmative.[3] For example, 'Some A is not A' is the contradictory of 'Every A is A', and is a contradiction; so also is 'Some A is not-A', which is the contradictory of 'No A is not-A'.[4] It is probable, however, that Leibniz has contradictory propositions alone in mind when he says that necessary truths depend on the principle of contradiction.[5] His argument is that if someone denies that a necessary truth is true, he can be refuted by pointing out that

---

[1] A ii. 1, 398 (L 285–6); C 186; Grua, p. 287; FC, p. 181. Cf. G vi. 413–14.

[2] G iii. 400; G vii. 300; C 17, 374.

[3] In C 76, C 369–70, and G vii. 211 Leibniz uses the term 'opposite' to *mean* 'contradictory'; cf. *Mon.*, par. 31, 'that which is opposed to or contradictory of the false'.

[4] In speaking of 'opposite' propositions in this context, Leibniz cannot mean subaltern propositions. For example, 'Some triangles are four-sided' is the subaltern of 'Every triangle is four-sided', but Leibniz could hardly wish to say that either is necessarily true if the other implies a contradiction. Nor is he likely to have in mind subcontraries—that is (subject and predicate being the same) the particular affirmative and particular negative—since, as Kant was to point out, it is the mark of a necessary truth that it is universal.

[5] G vi. 413–14; Grua, pp. 287–8, 303.

to say that the proposition in question is false implies a contradiction, and (by the principle of contradiction) what implies
a contradiction is false.[1] For this argument to be valid, the
assertion of the falsity of the necessary truth must be the assertion of its contradictory, not of its contrary.[2] For example,
suppose that the proposition whose truth is denied is 'Every
A is A'. It is not enough to point out that its contrary, 'No A is
A', is a contradiction, since from the falsity of 'No A is A' it
does not follow that 'Every A is A' is true; both might be false.
Instead it must be pointed out that its contradictory, 'Some A
is not A', is a contradiction, and therefore false, from which
it follows that 'Every A is A' is true.

What Leibniz says about the nature of necessary truths will
not be criticized at this stage; at present the question is how,
given his definitions of necessary truth and of truth in general,
Leibniz can account for the difference between necessary and
contingent truths, and for the difference between the ways in
which propositions are proved to be true. Leibniz's answer is
complicated, and the whole of it cannot be given at once. First,
if the words 'necessary truth' are taken in the sense so far given
to them, then Leibniz admits that not all truths are necessary
truths. From this it also follows that he would agree that not
all proof is *a priori* proof. But Leibniz also says that there is
a sense in which all truths are necessary; however, to see what
this sense is one must go some way into his metaphysics. Let us
leave this aside for the moment,[3] and continue to use the words
'necessary truth' in the sense which has already been discussed.
Although Leibniz denies that all truths are necessary in this
sense, he does not abandon his belief that all true propositions
are implicitly or expressly identical. He reconciles the two
views by saying that to speak of necessary and contingent
truths is to speak of our ability or inability to prove that a
true proposition is identical. Briefly, every truth is an identical

---

[1] Grua, p. 287.
[2] Despite what Leibniz says in Grua, p. 287.
[3] The topic will be resumed later, in § 4.7.

proposition, or reducible to one; a truth is necessary if it is either an identical proposition, or human beings can demonstrate that it is an identical proposition; it is contingent if they cannot, but know its truth by other, non-deductive means.[1]

Here the word 'cannot' needs explanation. To say that human beings 'cannot demonstrate' a certain proposition might be taken to mean that they do not at present know how to prove it, just as a schoolboy sometimes cannot demonstrate a mathematical proposition which his teacher knows how to prove. If this were what Leibniz meant, it would follow that a truth might be contingent for a time, and later become necessary on the discovery of a way in which it can be proved. For Leibniz, however, a contingent truth can never be proved by us. 'Cannot', as he uses it here, is a logical 'cannot'; we cannot demonstrate a contingent truth because its demonstration would involve an infinite number of operations.[2] In other words, the indemonstrability of a contingent truth is itself a necessary truth, given that no human being can perform a task which involves an infinite number of steps.

What Leibniz means by saying that a proof may require an infinite number of operations can best be shown by one of his examples.[3] Suppose that the sun is now shining; that is, that the proposition that the sun is now shining is true. This, says Leibniz, is not a necessary truth. It might indeed be said that the sun is shining at this time in our hemisphere because its previous motion was such that, granted that it continues, this result will certainly follow. But it is not necessary that the sun should have continued its motion, that is, the non-continuance of its motion does not imply a contradiction; nor, again, is it a necessary truth that it moved previously in the way that it did. To understand why the sun and the planets move as they do requires a knowledge of all the parts of an infinite universe.[4]

---

[1] C 17, 272, 388, 405; Grua, p. 303.
[2] Leibniz probably reached this conclusion in 1686: cf. C 388–9, and Grua, p. 302, n. 128. See also G vii. 200; C 1–2, 17–18, 272–3; Grua, p. 303; FC, p. 182 (L 407).   [3] C 18.   [4] C 19.

In other words, only if the concept of the subject of the true proposition 'The sun is now shining' is analysed into a concept of infinite complexity, describing everything in the universe, can it be seen how the concept of the subject includes that of the predicate. But such an analysis is possible only to God;[1] human beings can know the truth of such propositions only by means of sense-experience.[2] It emerges, then, that when Leibniz speaks of a necessary truth as reducible to an identical proposition, he means 'reducible in a finite number of operations'. All truths, in his view, are either identical propositions or reducible to them; but those which are either identical propositions or reducible to such propositions in a finite number of operations we call 'necessary', and those which require an infinite number of operations for their reduction we call 'contingent'.

By making use of the notion of an infinite analysis of certain concepts, Leibniz has succeeded in reconciling his view that every truth is either an expressly or an implicitly identical proposition with his view that not all truths are necessary. It might seem, however, that he has had to pay for this success. In the last paragraph reference was made to the propositions that the universe is of infinite complexity, and that each part of it is connected with all others, in such a way that it cannot be fully understood apart from the rest. These are metaphysical propositions, so it may seem that Leibniz has had to introduce metaphysics into his logic.[3] However, this is not so. The metaphysical propositions in question were only introduced to show the type of infinite analysis Leibniz has in mind; but to explain the possibility of contingent truths Leibniz need only say, without being more specific, that there are certain true propositions whose analysis is infinite.

What Leibniz has said about the nature of necessary truth

[1] C 2, 272; Grua, p. 303; FC, p. 182; G vii. 200.

[2] FC, p. 182; G iii. 259; G vii. 44. Cf. NE, 4. 8. 4; Grua, p. 304.

[3] Leibniz's defence of these propositions will be examined later: his view that there is an infinity of substances in § 5.3, and that each substance is connected with all others in § 5.4.

may hardly seem to require criticism here; it is obvious that his account must be unsatisfactory, in so far as it assumes all propositions to be of the subject-predicate form. However, another weakness in it[1] is worth mention, since it has a bearing on Leibniz's views about the way in which a derivative concept is composed of other concepts.[2] Leibniz has said that a proposition is a necessary truth if it is either an identical proposition or can be reduced to an identical proposition in a finite number of operations; and a proposition is 'reduced' by means of the analysis of concepts, i.e. by substitutions made on the basis of definitions.[3] This analysis of concepts, it may be remembered, is analogous to spelling out the letters of a word; another analogy which Leibniz uses is the factorization of a number.[4] The objection to this is that there are necessary truths, incidentally of a quite familiar kind, whose necessity cannot be shown in this way. Take, for example, the necessary truth that a proposition is true if, and only if, it is not not true, or its equivalent, 'p if and only if not-not-p'.[5] This can hardly be said to be reducible to an identical proposition on the basis of a definition,[6] and it is interesting that Leibniz himself seems to realize this, and says that 'Not-not-A is A' is 'the definition, i.e. the use of the sign "not"'.[7] Here he may be suggesting that 'not' has what

[1] It is not implied that this is the only other weakness. For further criticisms of Leibniz's theory of necessary truth see, e.g., A. Pap, *Semantics and Necessary Truth* (Yale, 1958), chap. 1, and Kneale, pp. 333–4.

[2] Cf. § 1.3.

[3] Cf. A ii. 1, 398 (L 286); A vi. 1, 460–1 (L 206–7); G ii. 239 (L 856); G vii. 191 (L 280); FC, p. 181 (L 407).   [4] G vii. 292 (L 352).

[5] It may be added that this would have to be used in deriving from the principle of bivalence the principle of contradiction, which Leibniz declares to follow from it (cf. § 3.2, p. 60). Replacing the principle of bivalence by its equivalent, the law of excluded middle—i.e. 'Either p or not-p'—and taking the principle of contradiction as 'Not both p and not-p', the derivation may be made as follows: (1) Either p or not-p (law of excluded middle). (2) Not both not-p and not-not-p (by de Morgan's law: p or q, if, and only if, not both not-p and not-q). (3) Not both not-p and p (by the law of double negation: p if, and only if, not-not-p). (4) Not both p and not-p (by the law of the commutativity of 'and': p and q, if, and only if, q and p).   [6] Cf. Pap, op. cit., p. 8.   [7] C 230; cf. C 252, 259.

is now called an 'implicit definition', i.e. that it is defined by
an axiom or set of axioms in which it occurs. This, however,
is quite a different type of definition from the analysis of a concept into its component concepts, which is what Leibniz usually
understands by a definition.

This concludes our account of Leibniz's logic, as far as it is
relevant to his metaphysics. Our aim has been to make clear
just what are the logical doctrines from which Leibniz derived
consequences which relate to metaphysics, and to evaluate those
doctrines. It is now time to turn to the second main part of this
inquiry, and to consider the consequences which Leibniz
believed to be derivable from his logic.

IV

Logic and Theism

§ 4.1. In discussing the derivation from Leibniz's logic of propositions which relate to metaphysics, the first problem which
arises is one of order. It is well known that there is no Leibnizian *magnum opus*, in which an attempt is made to present, in
strictly deductive form, all the propositions relating to metaphysics which Leibniz believes to be derivable from his logic.
When Leibniz does derive such consequences from his logic
he does so piecemeal and in relatively short works, which often
take for granted propositions for which arguments could have
been brought. For example, in the *Discourse on Metaphysics* he
derives from his views about truth certain propositions about
the nature of individual substances, and this is doubtless one
reason why the nature of substance is the first metaphysical
topic discussed in Russell's book on Leibniz. The *Discourse on
Metaphysics*, however, takes for granted the existence of an
absolutely perfect being, God. This is a topic which Russell
does not examine until the chapter before his last; yet Leibniz's
logic is involved in some of his arguments for the existence of
God, and it can be argued that the existence and nature of God,
the being upon whom all others are said to depend, has a claim
to be discussed first—as it is by Spinoza in his deductive pre-
sentation of his metaphysics in the *Ethics*, and sometimes by
Leibniz himself.[1] For this reason, the present chapter will begin
with the relevant arguments for the existence of God which
are advanced by Leibniz, and will then discuss certain views
about the nature of God which can be derived, if not from

---

[1] See, e.g., *Specimen inventorum de admirandis naturae generalis arcanis*
(G vii. 309–18), where the existence of God is the first metaphysical topic
discussed after a brief preface on logical principles.

Leibniz's logic, at any rate logically, in the sense of following from definitions which Leibniz gives. The next chapter will be concerned with Leibniz's account of the nature of individual substances, or rather of individual substances other than God.

The arguments for the existence of God which involve Leibniz's logic are two, commonly referred to as the ontological and cosmological arguments. In the former, Leibniz uses his logic to derive from a definition or definitions of God the conclusion that God exists; the latter is based partly upon logic and partly upon experience, which provides Leibniz with a justification of the proposition that contingent things exist. The logical basis of the ontological argument is stated by Leibniz in the words, 'Whatever can be proved from the concept of a thing, can be attributed to the thing'.[1] In other words, if the concept of the subject S can be shown to include the concept of the predicate P, then the proposition that S is P is true. From this point, Leibniz formulates the ontological argument in two ways. In one, the way already followed by Anselm and Descartes,[2] he says that the concept of God is that of the most perfect being, by which he understands a being which contains all perfections;[3] now, existence is a perfection, from which it follows that the most perfect being must exist.[4] Often, however, Leibniz expresses a preference for another formulation of the argument, which is derived (though he does not mention the fact) from Spinoza. This, he says, is more concise and is free from obscure phrases (*ambagibus*)[5] about the most perfect being. It begins[6] with a definition of a 'necessary being', or *Ens a se*,

[1] G iv. 359 (L 635).

[2] Anselm, *Proslogion*; Descartes, e.g. *Discourse on Method*, Part iv (Haldane and Ross, i, p. 104); *Meditations*, Part v.

[3] A ii. 1, 272 (L 260), 312, 323, 435; G iii. 442; G iv. 359, 405, 424; G vii. 490; *DM*, par. 23.

[4] G i. 385; G iii. 442–3; G iv. 359 (L 635), 401–2, 405, 424 (L 451); G vii. 294, 310, 490; *NE*, 4. 10. 7; *DM*, par. 23; A ii. 1, 271–2, 312, 323–4, 435–6, 476, 478.

[5] G iv. 359, 405; G vii. 490; A ii. 1, 312.

[6] Besides the passages quoted in the preceding note, cf. G iv. 402; G vii. 310; *Mon.*, pars. 44–45; G. M. i. 85 (L 257); A ii. 1, 323–4.

as a being to whose essence existence belongs.[1] This is the same
as what Spinoza calls *causa sui*, on the definition of which he
bases his first proof of the existence of God in the *Ethics*.[2]
Leibniz does not make explicit what he means by 'essence' here,
but the context shows that to say that existence belongs to the
essence of a necessary being is to say that such a being is one
which must be thought of as existing,[3] and that it must be
thought of as existing because it is defined as something which
exists.[4] He then declares that it is evident from the very terms
used that such a being exists.[5] No doubt he means that if a thing
must be thought of as existing, then it does exist; or, as he
expresses himself elsewhere,[6] what *necessarily* exists certainly
exists. Now, God is by definition a necessary being, therefore
God exists.[7]

Besides following Spinoza in formulating the ontological
argument, Leibniz also agrees with him in his definition of
eternity. This might seem to have nothing to do with the
matter now at issue, but in fact it is simply a paraphrase of what
has already been said. God, Leibniz has argued, exists necessarily; and for Leibniz, as for Spinoza, the term 'eternity' *means*
necessary existence.[8] To call something eternal is not to say
that it is everlasting; eternity has nothing to do with endless
duration, or indeed with duration at all, but differs from it in
nature.[9] Although at first sight this may seem obscure, Leibniz's
meaning is not difficult to grasp. He is arguing that if a property

---

[1] G iv. 359. For the definition of an *Ens a se* cf. A ii. 1, 312; G iv. 402,
405; *DM*, par. 23. Cf. also the definition of an *ens per se*, Grua, p. 274.

[2] *Ethics*, Part I, Def. 1 and Prop. 11.

[3] For the connexion between essence and necessity, cf. Grua, pp. 311, 383.

[4] Cf. G. iv. 359, which implies that the essence of God is the definition
of God.   [5] G iv. 359.   [6] A ii. 1, 323.

[7] G iv. 359; G vii. 490.

[8] Dutens, i, p. 18; G i. 140 (a note on Definition 8 of Book I of Spinoza's
Ethics); G iii. 588.

[9] *To Clarke*, § 5.106; G iii. 588; *NE*, 2. 17. 8. Cf. Spinoza, Ep. 12 (Gebhardt, iv, p. 55); *Ethics*, Part V, Prop. 23 Sch. and Prop. 34 Sch. Leibniz is
not always consistent in this usage, sometimes speaking of 'eternity' or
'eternal' when he means endless duration. See, e.g., A vi. 1, 490 (L 170);
G vii. 302 (L 790).

belongs necessarily to something, then it is logically inappropriate to say that the property belongs to it at a certain time, or over a certain period. For example, a Euclidean triangle has interior angles which are necessarily equal to two right angles, and to say of such a triangle that its interior angles equal two right angles at a certain time is not so much false as inappropriate. One can of course say of a three-sided field that its interior angles at a certain time equalled two right angles, but that since then its boundary lines have bulged outwards, so that its interior angles are now equal to more than two right angles. This, however, is merely to say that at a certain time the field had the shape of a Euclidean triangle; it is not to say that at that time the interior angles of a Euclidean triangle equalled two right angles. In the same way, God has been said to exist necessarily, so that it would be inappropriate to say of God that he exists at a certain time, or has existed for a certain period, no matter how long.

§ 4.2. So far Leibniz has said nothing original. In formulating the ontological argument he has followed the lines laid down by Anselm and Descartes on the one hand and by Spinoza on the other, whilst he follows Spinoza in what he says about the eternity of God. His originality lies in his insistence that all previous formulations of the ontological argument are incomplete.[1] As early as 1672 he remarked:[2] 'St. Thomas refutes this argument; but I think that it is not to be refuted, but needs supplementation. For it supposes that a Being which cannot not be, and also the greatest or most perfect Being, are possible.' In other words, before it can be validly inferred from the concept of God that God exists it must be shown that God, or the concept of God, is possible—that is, does not imply a contradiction.[3] Leibniz explains this further. If something does imply

---

[1] This point is made in all the passages cited in p. 77, nn. 4–6, and p. 78, n. 1.

[2] *Leibnitiana: Elementa Philosophiae Arcanae*, ed. by I. Jagodinsky (Kazan, 1913), p. 112. Cf. A. Rivaud, *RMM*, 1914, p. 98.

[3] A thing possible if it does not imply a contradiction—G ii. 55; G vii.

a contradiction, then whatever one infers concerning it, one can with equal justice infer the opposite.[1] Although, then, one may have deduced from the concept of God the proposition that God exists, one cannot know that God's non-existence is not also deducible, until it has been shown that the concept of God is possible. This can be put in other Leibnizian terms by saying[2] that, for the ontological argument to be valid, it is not sufficient to have only a 'nominal' definition of God—that is, a definition which does no more than enable what is defined to be distinguished from other things.[3] What is required is a 'real' definition, by which Leibniz understands a definition which shows that what is defined is possible.[4]

What Leibniz is saying here has a parallel in modern logic. The axioms of a deductive system must be consistent, since a conjunction of inconsistent propositions implies absolutely all propositions.[5] One of the aims of the modern logician, therefore, is to prove the consistency of the axioms with which he operates, just as Leibniz tries to prove that the concept of God is possible, that is, self-consistent. Modern proofs of consistency are very different from Leibniz's, but of Leibniz's proof it may at least be said that it is a deductive argument, based on definitions of God and of perfection, and so is relevant to an examination of his logic and metaphysics. It also has a bearing on his idea of an 'alphabet of human thoughts',[6] in that the concepts which belong to this alphabet, the primitive concepts from

310; Grua, p. 390; G. *M*, iii. 574 (L 833): possible if its concept does not imply a contradiction—G iv. 425: a term or concept possible if it does not imply a contradiction—C 261, 513.

[1] G iv. 294; G vii. 294, 310.

[2] G vii. 310.

[3] G ii. 63; G iv. 424-5 (L 452); G vii. 293 (L 353); *DM*, par. 24; *NE*, 3. 3. 18; C 220.

[4] G iv. 425; G vii. 293-4, 310; *NE*, 3. 3. 18; C 220. These passages state that a real definition of a thing must show the possibility of the thing; Leibniz sometimes says merely that real definitions, or definitions simply, must be possible (G vii. 293; G i. 337; C 372).

[5] See, e.g., Kneale, p. 387.

[6] Cf. § 1.3, p. 15.

which all others are derived, are regarded by Leibniz as the concepts of the attributes of God.[1]

Leibniz's proof is stated most fully in a paper written in 1676, and submitted to Spinoza.[2] Although this is a comparatively early work, Leibniz continued to think the argument sound, stating it in a condensed form in the *Monadology* of 1714.[3] The proof is based on the definition of God as the most perfect being, and begins with a definition of a 'perfection' as 'every simple quality which is positive and absolute, that is, which expresses without any limits whatever it does express'. In calling any such quality 'positive' Leibniz probably has in mind the view which is summed up in Spinoza's phrase that 'determination is negation',[4] and is in effect saying that anything which has limits, and so is not a perfection, 'will be understood through the negation of further progress'.[5] Such simple qualities are by definition unanalysable, and Leibniz argues that it follows from this that they are all compatible, i.e. can all exist in the same subject. Suppose, he says, that any two such qualities, A and B, are incompatible, that is, that they cannot be in the same subject. This is a necessary truth—it is being said that something *cannot* be the case, not simply that it is not—and as such must be either self-evident or demonstrable. Leibniz claims, without any discussion of the matter, that the incompatibility of A and B is not self-evident. He does not define the term 'self-evident' (*per se nota*), but it would be consistent with his views about necessary truth and self-contradiction if he were to say that, for the incompatibility of A and B to be self-evident, the proposition which ascribes them to a single subject must be an express contradiction, such as 'X is A and not-A',

---

[1] Leibniz actually says that the primitive concepts *are* the attributes of God (G iv. 425; cf. G v. 15 (A vi. 6, 5) and A ii. 1, 437–8). This, however, must be an inaccurate expression: God's attributes can hardly be called concepts, though we may be said to have concepts of them.

[2] A ii. 1, 271–2 (L 259–60).

[3] *Mon.*, par. 45. Cf. Grua, p. 325 (dated by Grua, 1683–1694?); also published in Schmidt, p. 480.

[4] Spinoza, Ep. 50 (Gebhardt, iv, p. 240).   [5] A ii. 1, 272.

or 'X is B and not-B'. Clearly, the proposition 'X is A and B' is not of this type, so that if A and B are incompatible, their incompatibility must be demonstrable. But this entails the analysis of either A or B, or of both; for[1] 'otherwise their nature would not enter the reasoning, and incompatibility could be proved of any other things equally well as of them'. This appears to mean that if A and B are to be proved incompatible, it must be shown wherein their incompatibility lies. But this can only be done by analysing them, and it has been assumed that they are incapable of analysis.

All this is true, as has been admitted by critics as diverse as Kant and Russell.[2] The weakness of the proof is that it is analytically true, and so gives no information about matters of fact. It says only that all God's perfections (defined as a certain type of simple quality) are compatible, but it gives no indication of what these perfections are. In particular, it does not show the compatibility of what many, including Leibniz, have regarded as the perfections of God—for example, perfect wisdom, goodness, and power.[3] For the concepts of these are certainly analysable.

Besides this weakness, Leibniz's proof of the possibility of God raises an obvious difficulty. Leibniz has said that there are primitive concepts, from which all others are derived, and also that all primitive concepts are positive; that is, they have in them no element of limit, or negation. This means that no proposition all of whose terms are primitive concepts can be negative; but since all concepts are either primitive or reducible to primitive concepts, it is hard to see how any negative proposition can be true.[4] For example, it is difficult to see how one concept can exclude another; that is, how a universal negative proposition can ever be true.[5]

---

[1] A ii. 1, 272.   [2] Russell, p. 174; Kant, *Critique of Pure Reason*, B 630.
[3] Cf. Grua, p. 126.
[4] Cf. Kauppi, pp. 113–14; Russell, p. 19; Kneale, pp. 334–5.
[5] Cf. §1.4, p. 23. It may indeed be asked whether a sentence expressed in negative terms can even be meaningful, if words have meaning only when they are the signs of concepts (§1.1), and all concepts either are or are

This is a difficulty which affects not only Leibniz's logic, but his metaphysics also.[1] It is an important thesis of Leibniz's metaphysics that it is possible to think of a number of universes, each of which is self-consistent but which is such that its existence would be incompatible with the existence of any other. Leibniz expresses this by saying that there are various 'possible worlds', which are not, however, 'compossible',[2] and he says that of these possible worlds, God creates the best. But if no negative proposition can be true, no proposition which asserts the incompatibility of two concepts can be true. Consequently, there can be no non-compossible worlds between which God can choose, from which it follows further that if God is to create anything he must create everything possible, which Leibniz emphatically denies.[3]

Leibniz faces the problem of negative propositions when he considers the nature of finite things, that is, of things which are limited, and whose concepts therefore involve negation.[4] He declares that such things derive their perfections from God, and that the source of their imperfections is nothing;[5] or he says that everything follows from 'pure Being', namely God, and nothing.[6] In this sense, God and nothing are 'the two first principles'.[7] Leibniz is fond of illustrating this by the analogy of the binary system of numerals, saying that just as all numbers can be represented by the symbols 1 and 0, so everything follows from God and from nothing.[8]

reducible to primitive, positive concepts. Leibniz might perhaps reply that what is reducible to primitive concepts is *the* concept of such and such; this does not prevent us from having *a* concept of the same (cf. § 1.2), and so saying something meaningful, but false.

[1] Cf. C. L., p. 219, n. 2.   [2] Cf. § 4.5, p. 97; § 4.7, p. 104.
[3] G vii. 289 (C 534); C 530 (L 262).   [4] Cf. p. 81.
[5] To Bouvet, Feb. 1701. Quoted by R. F. Merkel, *Leibniz und China* (Berlin, 1952), pp. 18-19. This is also one of Leibniz's explanations of evil (G vi. 120; *DM*, par. 30; Grua, pp. 364-5)—a conscious following of Platonic and Augustinian tradition.
[6] C 430-1.   [7] Merkel, loc. cit. Cf. Grua, p. 364.
[8] C 430-1; Grua, pp. 126, 364, 371; Merkel, loc. cit. Cf. *Von der wahren Theologia Mystica*, Guhrauer, *Leibniz's deutsche Schriften* (Berlin, 1838-40), i, pp. 410 ff. (L 608 ff.).

This answer might seem to say either too much or too little. Too little, in that one may ask how nothing can be responsible for anything, and what difference there is between God and nothing on the one hand, and God alone on the other. Too much, in that it might seem to set up a principle which is contrary to God, like the Manichean concept of Satan. It occurred to Leibniz that he might be understood in the latter sense, and he expressly denied that his theory was Manichean; to speak of nothing in this context, he says, is not to speak of a principle which opposes God.[1] This leaves open the question of the sense in which God and nothing can be called two principles. The answer seems to be that Leibniz is thinking here of not-being, and not-being in the sense of not being such and such. So, for example, instead of 'nothing' he sometimes writes 'the privative', 'privation', or 'limitation'.[2] In other terms, the second of Leibniz's two principles could be called the principle of limit, as this was understood by the Pythagoreans and by Plato. Yet to recognize this as a principle seems to say no more than that certain things have *limits*; that one can say that they are *not* such and such. The origin of limitation remains obscure, as Leibniz himself seems to recognize when he says that the source of the incompatibility of concepts 'is not yet known to men'.[3]

In sum, not only is Leibniz's attempted proof of the possibility of God empty, in the sense that it has no application to what is commonly called 'God', but the concept of God whose possibility has been shown is one from which Leibniz cannot derive the concepts of finite things, nor is it clear how there can be any incompatible possible worlds between which God can choose. The emptiness of Leibniz's proof also means that, if he is right in saying that the ontological argument depends for its validity on a proof of the possibility of God, then the ontological argument has not been shown to be valid.

Most philosophers would go further, and say that even if the possibility of God could be shown, the ontological argument

[1] Grua, p. 364.   [2] Grua, pp. 126, 371; C 430.   [3] G vii. 195.

would still be unsound. It is unnecessary to recount here all the familiar objections to the argument, but one which is directly relevant to Leibniz's logic is worth mention. It will be remembered that Leibniz argued that if the concept of P is included in the concept of S, then the proposition that S is P is true; consequently, if the concept of existence is included in the concept of God, then it is true that God exists.[1] Here one may cite against Leibniz his own logical views. He has taken singular propositions, such as 'God exists', as a type of universal proposition,[2] and he has argued that 'Every S is P' is to be interpreted as 'The concept of S includes that of P' precisely because in this way the existence of S is not assumed.[3] In other words, he has taken 'Every S is P' to mean 'Every S (if there is any S) is P'. Applying this to what he says about God, one reaches the conclusion that to say that the concept of existence is contained in that of the most perfect being is to say that the most perfect being (if there is such a being) exists—in short, that if there is a God, there is a God. This is undoubtedly true, but it is not what Leibniz wishes to prove.

It will be seen later that this has further consequences for Leibniz's logic. If his account of the proposition is to be complete, it must of course cover existential propositions. Now it has just been argued that, if what he says about the nature of the proposition is correct, it is not clear how it can be said that God exists; all that Leibniz's account seems to allow is the hypothetical proposition that if there is a God, there is a God. This difficulty also affects his account of propositions about the existence of contingent things; for this account depends in part upon the proposition that there is a God.[4] If, therefore, it is not clear how Leibniz's logic permits one to say that God exists, it is not clear how it can permit the assertion of any existential proposition whatsoever.

§ 4.3. It was said at the beginning of this chapter that another of Leibniz's arguments for the existence of God, the so-called

[1] § 4.1.   [2] § 1.4.   [3] § 1.3.   [4] § 4.7, pp. 107 f.

'cosmological argument',[1] is partly derived from his logic. Strictly, this assertion needs qualification. Leibniz claims that the existence of a 'necessary being' can be proved with the help of the principle of sufficient reason, and it is clear that by the latter he understands the principle which was shown in the last chapter to be related to his definition of truth—namely, that a reason can be given for every true proposition by showing the inclusion of the concept of the predicate in that of the subject, or, that there must be a sufficient reason for everything which exists or happens.[2] He also claims, however, that there is only one necessary being,[3] and that this being is what is usually called 'God'; to support this claim he has to produce quite different arguments.[4] The question is, therefore, whether the term 'cosmological argument' is to be understood to refer only to the argument, based on the principle of sufficient reason, for the existence of a necessary being, or whether it is to be taken to refer to a more complex argument which is designed to show, not only that a necessary being exists, but that this necessary being is what is usually called 'God'. This is simply a question of terminology, which can be settled by an arbitrary decision; however, if confusion is to be avoided a decision must be made. In what follows, then, the term 'cosmological argument' will be taken in the first sense, as referring to an attempt at proving the existence of a necessary being.

Briefly, the argument is as follows. It begins with the assertion that there exist 'contingent things'.[5] The term 'contingent'

[1] For this argument, see G i. 138, n. 23; G vi. 106, 542 (L 957); G vii. 301 (L 349), 302 (L 789), 310; A ii. 1, 117; A vi. 1, 490 (L 170); C 13; PNG, par. 8; Mon., pars. 36–38; Grua, p. 268.

[2] Compare C 13 with C 11, G vii. 310 with G vii. 309, and G vii. 301 with G vii. 300.

[3] G vi. 107; G vii. 305 (L 794); A vi. 1, 492 (L 173); Mon., par. 39.

[4] It could also be objected to that version of the ontological argument which is based on the notion of a necessary being that even if it were valid it would not prove the existence of what is commonly called 'God'. Leibniz would no doubt reply to this by using the same arguments as those mentioned above.

[5] G vi. 106; C 13; PNG, par. 8; cf. G vii. 310. Leibniz also refers to 'things'

has already been explained as meaning 'non-necessary',[1] and
Leibniz shows that by speaking of 'things' in this context he
means not only physical objects[2] but also minds.[3] He asserts
further that a thing may be called contingent with respect
either to its existence or to its nature; for example, it is not
necessary that Leibniz should have existed at all, nor is it necessary that the Leibniz who did exist should have met Spinoza.
Now, on the basis of the principle of sufficient reason it can be
said that there must be a reason why anything contingent exists
at all, and why contingent things are as they are. This reason
must be a necessary being, which contains within itself the
reason for its own existence.

It is not necessary to discuss at equal length what Leibniz
says about the reason why contingent things are as they are,
and why there are any contingent things at all. The line of
argument is essentially the same in each case, and is displayed
clearly in what he says about the reason for the nature of contingent things; when this has been discussed in detail it will then
be necessary to make only the briefest mention of what he says
about the reason for the mere fact that contingent things exist.
Let us, then, begin a detailed exposition of the cosmological
argument, as it concerns the nature of contingent things.

Leibniz begins by saying that one must be able to give some
reason for the world's determinate characteristics;[4] one must
be able to state, not only why the world is temporal and spatial,
but why the things in it are of the shape and size that they are,
and why they move as they do. Now, any true proposition
about the shape, size, or movement of such things cannot be
a necessary proposition, for things could have had quite different shapes, sizes, or movements.[5] Further, the reason which
is sought cannot be found solely in space, time, or what Leibniz

---

simply (*Mon.*, par. 36; Grua, p. 268), to 'contingents' (G vii. 310), and to
'mutables' or 'individuals' (G vii. 302; G i. 138 n.).

[1] § 3.4, p. 69, n. 2.
[2] *PNG*, par. 8; *Mon.*, par. 36; Grua, p. 268; cf. A vi. 1, p. 490.
[3] *PNG*, par. 8; *Mon.*, par. 36.   [4] C 13.   [5] G vi. 106.

calls 'bare matter', by which he understands matter regarded solely as extension and resistance to impact.[1] These admit of any size, shape, or motion, and so cannot be used to explain why a body is of a particular shape or size, or moves as it does.[2]

It might be argued that a particular body has its shape—say, that of a cube—because it always had it. Leibniz replies that this does not give an adequate reason for its shape, since we can still ask why it did not always have some other shape.[3] If it is said that it was made cubical by the motion of another body, it is still necessary to explain the shape which it had before that motion, and if another motion is postulated to explain this, one still has to account for the shape it had before that motion, and so on.[4] Similarly, a reason has to be given for motion. It has already been argued that this reason cannot be found in 'bare matter',[5] and to postulate the eternity of motion is again no answer. It is true that a present motion may come from one which precedes it, and that from another, and so on. But however far one goes, there always remain the questions, 'Why motion at all?' and 'Why this motion and not some other?'[6]

In sum, the sufficient reason for the determinate characteristics of the world must be found outside contingent things, in a 'necessary being, carrying the reason for its existence with it',[7] which may be taken to mean that the concept of such a thing, unlike the concept of a contingent thing, contains the concept of existence. Similarly, just as there is a reason for the fact that contingent things are as they are, there must also be a reason for the fact that they exist at all, and this reason, too, must be a necessary being.[8]

---

[1] C 13. Leibniz's word for resistance to impact is 'antitypia': see, e.g., A ii. 1, 16 (L 148); G vii. 328, 501, 529; G ii. 171.

[2] C 13; A vi. 1, 490 (L 170); G vi. 542; PNG, par. 8.

[3] A vi. 1, 490; cf. C 519 (L 413).

[4] A vi. 1, 490.

[5] Cf. nn. 1 and 2 above.

[6] PNG, par. 8.   [7] Ibid.; cf. C 13; G vi. 106.

[8] G i. 138, n. 23; Grua, p. 288; G vii. 310; A ii. 1, 117.

Leibniz asserts that this ultimate reason for things, this necessary being, is what is usually called 'God'. It is clear, however, that this does not follow from the argument which has just been expounded. If valid, this would only show that there exists at least one necessary being, whereas to say that this is what is usually called 'God' is to say that there exists one and only one such being. Further, God is usually regarded as the most perfect being, the creator of the universe, and the preceding argument does not show that either of these attributes belongs to the necessary being. As mentioned earlier in this section, Leibniz does bring arguments to show that the necessary being is properly called 'God', but these are quite different from the argument by which he tries to show that there is a necessary being, and which we have termed the 'cosmological argument'. Before these supplementary arguments are discussed, some comments will be made on the cosmological argument itself.

§ 4.4. It has been seen that the argument is based on the existence and nature of contingent things, and that Leibniz cites physical objects as examples of such things, arguing, for example, from the shapes or movements which they have. Here, however, a complication arises, since it is well known that Leibniz believed that any physical object is only an appearance or appearances presented to us by immaterial substances.[1] It seems likely that he argues from physical things because these are observable, whereas substances are not, and because it will readily be admitted that the existence and nature of observable things is contingent. This does not affect the rigour of the cosmological argument; Leibniz does not predicate contingency of material things alone, but counts them as the appearances of substances whose existence and nature is similarly contingent.[2] It has also been seen earlier that he uses the term 'contingent thing' in such a way as to include minds,[3] and he regards minds as substances.[4] However, the topic of substance must be reserved

[1] Cf. § 5.7.   [2] Cf. § 5.3.   [3] § 4.3, p. 87.   [4] Cf. § 5.8.

for the next chapter; for the moment we shall continue to discuss the cosmological argument in Leibniz's own terms, that is, in terms of 'contingent things'.

The first question to be asked is why Leibniz should think that there are any contingent things.[1] He gives different answers to this question, depending upon the type of contingent thing. He says that we know by 'immediate internal experience'[2] that it is true that there is an 'I' which thinks; this truth, moreover, is not a necessary truth, but is a primitive truth of fact.[3] With regard to the existence and nature of physical objects, Leibniz argues that when we say, for example, that we see that the sun is shining, the reason which we can bring in support of this utterance is that there is a certain coherence among phenomena,[4] that is, among the appearances each of which exists in a mind.[5] He rightly points out that this does not amount to a demonstrative proof; it does not entitle us to say that we are 'metaphysically certain' of the truth of the proposition in question—that is, that to suppose the contrary would imply a contradiction.[6] Nevertheless, Leibniz insists that this coherence 'is to be counted as the truth';[7] it has what he calls 'the greatest probability', or what was commonly called 'moral certainty', a term used by Descartes to refer to 'a certainty which is sufficient for the conduct of life'.[8] As Leibniz puts it,[9] one cannot seriously doubt that Constantinople is in the world, or that Constantine, Alexander the Great, and Julius

---

[1] It is not strictly necessary for the cosmological argument that there should exist more than one contingent thing; however, Leibniz never formulates the argument in a way which allows explicitly for this.

[2] G iv. 329; NE, 4. 2. 1, 4. 7. 7.

[3] G iv. 327, 357 (L 632–3); G vii. 296 (L 357); G vii. 319 (L 603).

[4] G vii. 320 (L 604); NE, 4. 2. 14. Cf. G ii. 516; G vii. 296; A ii. 1, 248–9 (L 239).

[5] G vii. 319. Cf. G ii. 70 and C 14 (phenomena as 'thoughts' and 'perceptions' respectively).

[6] G vii. 320; cf. G vii. 296.

[7] G vii. 296.

[8] G vii. 320. Cf. Descartes, *Principles of Philosophy*, iv. 205, and *Discourse on Method*, Part iv (Haldane and Ross, i, p. 104).

[9] NE, 4. 11. 1–10.

Caesar have lived, if 'serious doubt' is taken to mean a doubt which has relation to practice.

We cannot reasonably doubt, then, that there are physical objects; similarly, we cannot reasonably doubt that they are contingent. Borrowing an argument brought against Spinoza by Bayle, Leibniz says that to suppose that all things are necessary would be absurd—not logically absurd, but contrary to common sense. For example,[1] it is absurd to suppose that 'it is impossible, from all eternity, that Spinoza should not die at The Hague'. Leibniz supports this by an argument from unfulfilled possibilities, saying that if all existent things exist necessarily, then it is impossible that what does not exist should exist.[2] But certain non-existent things could have existed, from which it follows that not all existent things exist necessarily.[3] That there are unfulfilled possibilities Leibniz again seems to regard as a matter of common sense. Everyone will agree, he says, that at least some of the events described in historical romances are possible, but that they did not happen and never will happen.[4]

Nothing has so far been said of Leibniz's views about our knowledge of other minds, which happens to be a topic on which he has little to say. What he says is that 'our experience teaches us', not only that each of us is a particular being, which thinks, is aware of itself, and wills,[5] but also that each of us is distinguished from other beings which think and will something

[1] G vi. 217.

[2] FC, p. 178 (L 405).

[3] G ii. 181; G vi. 217; A ii. 1, 505-6 (L 420); FC, pp. 178-9; Grua, pp. 16, 288, 305, 391.

[4] G ii. 181; G vi. 217; FC, p. 179; Grua, pp. 16, 305.

[5] Leibniz sometimes uses the words rendered as 'think' in a wide sense, to cover not only what would now be called thinking, but perception and dreaming as well. For example, G vii. 319 (L 603) suggests that dreaming is a form of 'thinking', whilst DM, par. 28, takes seeing the sun as an example of 'thinking'. In these cases Leibniz seems close to Descartes's use of such words as cogitare and penser, which is similarly wide (cf. Anscombe and Geach, Descartes: Philosophical Writings (London, 1954), pp. xlvii-xlviii). In the passage cited above, however, 'think' has a narrower sense, as it also has in DM, par. 14, which speaks of our thoughts and perceptions.

else.[1] He does not explain what he means by saying that experience teaches us this; it may be, however, that he means
that our belief that there are other minds rests on the fact that
our views are sometimes contradicted, which suggests that there
are others who think, and that our will is sometimes thwarted
in ways which suggest that there are other wills. If so, his point
is surely a good one.[2]

As already mentioned, Leibniz regards minds as substances,
and what he says about their contingency is best considered in
connexion with the topic of substance.[3] Meanwhile, it is time
to comment on the arguments which have been brought
forward. No one is likely to deny that there are contingent
things; the question is, whether Leibniz can consistently say
that there are.[4] Take, for example, any true proposition which
would normally be called contingent, such as 'There is in
Athens a building called the Parthenon'. This proposition says
(amongst other things) that a building called the Parthenon
exists, and as the proposition is true it seems that the concept of
existence must be contained in that of the subject, since Leibniz
has said that in every true proposition the concept of the subject contains that of the predicate. But if so, the Parthenon must
be a necessary being—unless, of course, Leibniz's theory of
truth is false. Leibniz claims that there is a way through the
horns of the dilemma, since he is not faced with the sole alterna-
tives of either abandoning his theory of truth, or of accepting
the Parthenon—and, indeed, any other so-called contingent
thing—as a necessary being. However, his way of escape cannot be discussed until more has been seen of his views about

---

[1] G vi. 537 (L 908). Leibniz in fact writes of our distinction from another
being, but his arguments are clearly applicable to other beings.

[2] For a similar argument, cf. H. H. Price, 'Our Knowledge of Other
Minds', *Proceedings of the Aristotelian Society*, 1931–2, pp. 53 ff. In G vii.
321–2 (L 606) Leibniz offers what seems to be another argument for the
existence of other minds, but the passage is extremely confused and the
nature of the argument quite obscure.

[3] See below, § 5.3.

[4] Cf. Russell, p. 185.

the nature of God.[1] Meanwhile there are further objections to the cosmological argument which demand consideration.

It might be argued against Leibniz that he has made the very mistake which he claimed to find in Anselm and Descartes—that of arguing for the existence of something, in this case, of a necessary being, before showing that that whose existence is argued for is possible. He has indeed argued that a most perfect being is possible;[2] but is this the same as a necessary being? Leibniz would reply that it is, but that in any case the cosmological argument itself provides a means of establishing the possibility of the necessary being. It has been shown, he claims, that contingent things exist if and only if there is a necessary being; consequently, if the necessary being is not possible, nothing else is.[3] Presumably we are to add that contingent things are possible, since they exist,[4] from which it follows that the necessary being is possible also.

Perhaps, however, a more obvious and a more telling objection to the cosmological argument is that one contingent thing might depend on another, and that upon another, and so on to infinity. Whatever contingent thing is considered, it is always in theory possible to point to another on which it depends; there is, therefore, no need to postulate a necessary being as the ultimate reason of contingent things. The argument, often referred to as the argument from the infinite regress of causes, is a familiar one, and did not escape Leibniz's attention. It has already been mentioned[5] that he thought it to be invalid, and it is now time to examine his reasons for rejecting it. Broadly, his thesis is that even if there were such an infinite regress, his argument for the existence of a necessary being would be unaffected. It follows that he is not affirming what Kant called 'the impossibility of an infinite series of causes, given one after the other, in the sensible world',[6] and to that extent his

---

[1] See below, § 4.7.   [2] § 4.2.
[3] G iii. 444; G iv. 406; G vii. 310.
[4] On the argument from *esse* to *posse*, cf. G iv. 425 (L 452); G v. 15 (A vi. 6, 5); G vii. 319 (L 602); C 372; *DM*, par. 24.   [5] § 4.3, p. 88.
[6] *Critique of Pure Reason*, B 638: Kemp Smith translation.

argument differs from what Kant called the 'cosmological argument'. This does not mean that Leibniz thinks that there is such
an infinite series,[1] but only that it would be irrelevant to his
argument, even if it were to exist.

In one paper he explains his meaning by an analogy, which
is reminiscent of one used by Spinoza.[2] Suppose, he says, that
Euclid's *Elements* is eternal,[3] one copy of the book having been
made from another, and that from another, and so on to
infinity.[4] Now,

It is evident that, although a reason for a present book could be
given from a past book from which it has been copied, one will
never reach a complete reason for it, no matter how many books are
assumed in the past. For one may always wonder why such books
have existed from all time, and why books at all, and why written
like this. And what is true of books is also true of the various states
of the world; for a later state is in a way copied from a previous
state, though by fixed laws of change. So, however far back into
previous states you go, you will never find in them a complete
reason why there should be a world at all, and why it should be
as it is.

The argument is, then, that on the supposition considered it
is impossible to give a *complete* reason for any copy of Euclid,
or (by analogy) for any state of the universe, or for the existence
of the universe. For example, we do not in this way explain
why such books—that is, copies of Euclid's *Elements*, and not of
some other book—have existed from all time.[5] To say that it
just happens that the book which has been copied in this way
is Euclid's *Elements* would be a denial of the principle of sufficient reason; there must be some reason why this is the book

[1] He says that he does not deny that there may be a first instant, i.e. that
the world had a beginning in time (G iii. 582 (L 1080); cf. *To Clarke*,
§ 5.74).

[2] Ep. 40 (Gebhardt, iv, p. 198).

[3] Strictly he should say 'has existed from all time', if 'eternal' is taken to
mean that which has no relation to time. (Cf. § 4.1, p. 78, n. 9.)

[4] G vii. 302 (L 790).

[5] Cf. A vi. 1, 490; C 519 (L 413).

which has been copied. If it is said that the existence of such books could be explained, for example, by reference to the existence from all time of successive generations of men with a passion for geometry, Leibniz would ask why such men have existed rather than some other type of men, and if an explanation of this were offered in terms of some other contingent fact, he would ask for an explanation of the fact in question, and so on. In short, he would argue that any explanation in terms of contingent facts must be incomplete.

So far, the analogy with questions about the physical universe has been with the question, 'Why should the universe be as it is?'[1] But one can also ask why there should *be* a physical universe, or, in the analogy, why there should be books at all. Once again, it must either be said that there just happen to be books, or some reason must be given for their existence. The second alternative is the only one which is consistent with the principle of sufficient reason, and Leibniz argues that it again leads to the conclusion that there exists a necessary being.

It may still be doubted, however, whether Leibniz has given a satisfactory answer to the infinite regress argument. It is true that to every answer in contingent terms to the questions 'Why does this contingent thing exist? Why is it as it is?' Leibniz can reply by putting the further question, 'Why is this contingent explanation true?' But the man who asserts that there is an infinite regress of causes has in theory an answer for every such question. Leibniz stresses the fact that he has a question for every answer; his opponent, however, could say that in his turn he has an answer for every question.

§ 4.5. So far the subject of discussion has been Leibniz's argument, based on the existence and nature of contingent things,

[1] In the analogy the question was, 'Why have such books existed?' Leibniz also asks why there should exist books which have been written like this. It is not clear how this question differs from the first, unless by 'sic scripti' Leibniz means 'sic descripti', and the question is 'Why should one book have been copied from another?' inviting such answers as 'Because books wear out in time'.

for the existence of a necessary being. It is now time to consider the arguments by which he tries to show that this necessary being is properly called 'God'.[1] These are not derived from his logic, but they serve to make clearer his concept of God, and a grasp of this concept is vital to an understanding of his metaphysics.

First, Leibniz has to show that there is only one necessary being. He has already argued that there are contingent things; he now adds that all contingent things are connected, so that a reason for one is a reason for all.[2] A rough analogy might be provided by picturing contingent things as a chain; to hang up the chain only one hook, i.e. only one necessary being, is required. The analogy breaks down, however, in that Leibniz does not think of God as a metaphysical hook, attached to nothing. To see how he does think of the dependence of contingent things upon the necessary being it is necessary to inquire further into his views about the kind of sufficient reason which God is.

It is obvious that this reason must be one which will permit things to be contingent—that is, to have been other than what they are, or not to have existed at all. Now, Leibniz believes that when one chooses to do something one could have chosen to do something else—'could have', in the sense that to suppose that some other choice had been made, and some other action performed, does not imply a contradiction.[3] In his phraseology, motives for action 'incline without necessitating'.[4] If someone chose to create contingent things, then, he would be the reason for their existence and nature, whilst at the same time they might have had some other nature, or not have existed at all. Leibniz therefore asserts that the reason for the existence and nature of contingent things is a voluntary agent,[5] who chose to create or produce the world,[6] making actual one out of

[1] Cf. § 4.3.   [2] G vi. 107; G vii. 305 (L 794); A vi. 1, 492 (L 173).
[3] e.g. Grua, pp. 300, 383, 479; To Clarke, § 5.8.
[4] e.g. To Clarke, § 5.9.   [5] G vi. 106.
[6] God as 'creator', G vi. 233, 364. God as 'producer', G vi. 107; Mon., par. 55. Cf. G vii. 302 (L 789): God 'fabricates or makes' the universe.

series of possible worlds.[1] This is why he says that the reason for a contingent truth inclines but does not necessitate,[2] in this case taking the 'reason' as not so much the necessary being as the motive which the necessary being had in creating contingent things.

In saying that there is only one necessary being, and that this is the creator of the universe, Leibniz has gone a long way towards the conclusion that this being is properly called 'God'. It remains for him to show that the necessary being has the other attributes commonly ascribed to God, those of omniscience, omnipotence, and perfect goodness. He tries to do this by using a Scholastic argument. The creator, he says, must have 'in more eminent form' all the perfections which are possessed by created things.[3] The creator will therefore have perfect wisdom, power, and goodness; that is, will be omniscient, omnipotent, and perfectly good.

Before these arguments can profitably be criticized, a good deal needs to be made clear. Leibniz has said that the sufficient reason for the existence and nature of contingent things is their creator, who has 'produced' or 'made' them,[4] and it seems to be God's creativity which Leibniz has in mind when he calls God the 'cause' of the universe.[5] But what is meant by calling God a 'cause' in this way; what is meant by saying that he 'produced' or 'made' the universe? Let us compare, for example, the statements that God made the world, and that a certain man made a marble statue. What the man has done can be

[1] G vi. 107-8, 233, 252, 364; G vii. 306 (L 794); *Mon.*, par. 53; *PNG*, par. 10; Grua, pp. 16, 285-6, 390.

[2] G iii. 168; G vii. 301 (L 349), 302 (L 790); C 402, 405; Grua, p. 303. Cf. C 402 and Grua, p. 287, in which contingent truths are said to depend upon the divine will.

[3] *PNG*, par. 9. Cf., e.g., Aquinas, *Summa Theologica*, i, Qu. 4, Art. 2.

[4] Cf. p. 96, n. 6.

[5] e.g. G vi. 106; *PNG*, par. 8. It was remarked earlier (§ 3.3, p. 65) that Leibniz sometimes takes 'cause' and 'reason' to be equivalent terms; when he says, however, that the sufficient reason for the series of contingent things is outside this series *and is its cause* (*PNG*, par. 8), he seems to mean to say something about the nature of the reason for contingent things which God is, and this must surely be that he is their creator.

described in Aristotelian language by saying that he has given a new form to pre-existent matter. He has made a statue *out of* marble; he has not made the marble itself. When, on the other hand, God is said to have created the world, he is regarded as having produced both the form and the matter. This is an obvious difference; Leibniz, however, also argues that there is another, which is not so obvious.

Once the statue has been made, it is not dependent on its maker for the continuation of its existence; marble statues are durable things, and can safely be left to themselves. God, however, is regarded by Leibniz as not only the maker but the pre-server or 'conserving cause' of contingent things.[1] Leibniz lays much stress on God's conservation of the universe; indeed, in one formulation of the cosmological argument[2] he remarks that if it were admitted that the world could exist, perhaps for millions of years, without God's assistance, then it would be hard to explain to the atheist why it should not always have existed without God. Here again one may ask what is meant. There is no difficulty in understanding the assertion that what Leibniz would call one created thing conserves or preserves another. For example, a man may preserve a piece of timber by applying a coat of paint to protect it from the weather; he preserves his own existence by means of food, clothing, and the other necessaries. None of this, however, is comparable with conservation by God. Using Aristotelian language again, one may say that to preserve a piece of timber is to preserve a certain form which matter has; it is to prevent that which is now sound timber from becoming, say, rotten wood. God, on the other hand, seems to be regarded as preserving the matter itself. If his conservation is withdrawn, the piece of timber will not become some other material substance, it will be annihilated. The question is, what is to be understood by this type of conservation.

---

[1] *DM*, pars. 14, 28, 30, 35; *To Clarke*, § 2.5, 8, 11; ibid., § 3.16; Grua, p. 315.
[2] Grua, p. 315.

For a pantheist there would be no difficulty. He could say that God is the conserving cause of things inasmuch as God *is* things; in other words, he conserves them by being them. But Leibniz, in saying that God has created the universe, has rejected pantheism, and his answer to the problem is that God conserves a created thing by creating it continually.[1] This is liable to be misunderstood, since the term 'continuous creation' suggests that a contingent thing is re-created at every instant, so that what we call one created thing, existing over a space of time, is really a class of entities each of which is of only momentary duration. Leibniz, however, does not mean this. He rejects Descartes's view that a created thing would be annihilated at each instant, if God did not continually re-create it,[2] and says instead that by continued creation he understands 'the continuation of the initial dependence' of the created thing.[3] Creation and conservation, he says, are the same operation; 'creation is incomplete conservation, just as conservation is continued creation'.[4] The difference between them is only 'extrinsic', that is, relative, in the sense that to speak of creation is to say that the operation is new, while to speak of conservation is to say that it is not.[5] Here, then, is another difference between divine creation, as Leibniz understands it, and the making of something by a human being. Divine creation is also conservation; the making of something by a human being is not.

§ 4.6. We have now seen the arguments by which Leibniz tries to show that the necessary being is properly called 'God', since it is the only necessary being, is the creator of the universe, and is omniscient, omnipotent, and perfectly good; we have also tried to understand what the term 'creator' means to Leibniz. It is obvious that the arguments just described depend for their validity upon a number of assumptions—that the perfections

[1] *DM*, par. 30; G vi. 118–19, 343–4, 440; G vii. 564; *To Clarke*, § 2.5; Grua, p. 330.

[2] G vi. 343. Cf. Descartes, *Principles of Philosophy*, i. 21.

[3] G iii. 558.

[4] FC, p. 150. Cf. Grua, p. 307.   [5] FC, loc. cit. Cf. G vi. 343–4.

of created things exist 'more eminently' in their creator, that all contingent things are connected, and that the will is free. Leibniz does not argue for the first of these, though it will be seen later that he produces arguments for the second.[1] As for the last assumption, it would take us too far out of our way to try to discuss all that he has to say about free will. It can however be said that what he means when he says that the will is free is relatively modest, and that it is quite likely that it would be generally accepted. He is not an indeterminist, in the sense of asserting that choice is unpredictable and without reason. Such an assertion would obviously clash with the principle of sufficient reason, and it is not surprising that Leibniz should say that a free act is none the less determined,[2] and that that to which a man's motives 'incline' him follows certainly and 'infallibly'.[3] All that he says is that it does not follow 'necessarily', by which he means that to suppose that some other choice had been made does not imply a contradiction.[4] In other words, in saying that the will is free Leibniz seems chiefly concerned to deny the truth of Spinozistic determinism; and in so far as this is what he means, many will agree with him.

It may be argued, however, that these assumptions are insufficient to show that a necessary being is properly called God, since they do not entail the consequence that there is only one necessary being. The proposition that all contingent things are connected would, if true, only show that one necessary being would be sufficient, not that there exists only one such being. Leibniz could reply that all that is still required to show the uniqueness of the necessary being is a use of Occam's razor. One necessary being, he might say, has been admitted to be sufficient; but entities (and therefore necessary beings) are not to be multiplied superfluously, and so he is justified in saying that there is only one necessary being. There *may* be more than one such being, but there is no *reason* to say that there is.

---

[1] Cf. § 5.4.   [2] G iii. 168; *NE*, 2. 21. 13; Grua, p. 274.
[3] G vi. 414; *To Clarke*, § 5.9; Grua, pp. 300, 383.
[4] Besides the references cited in the two preceding notes, cf. G vi. 123-4.

More serious than this are the objections which can be made, not to the propriety of calling a necessary being 'God', but to the Leibnizian concept of a creative deity itself. It has already been pointed out that Leibniz says that there are close connexions between creation and conservation;[1] but his views about God's conservation of the universe are far from clear. When he tries to explain his meaning, he speaks of God creating continually by a kind of emanation, 'as we produce our thoughts'; or he says that continued creation is like a ray coming continuously from the sun, or that it is a series of continual flashes (*fulgurations continuelles*).[2] All this suggests a continued repetition of events, and so seems to imply that any one contingent thing is perpetually re-created from instant to instant. But this would be the same as Descartes's view, and Leibniz is emphatic that such a view is not his. What he does mean, then, remains obscure.

The chief objection to Leibniz's account of creation, however, is that which Kant brought to what he called the cosmological argument,[3] and it is this objection to which a modern philosopher is most likely to require an answer. Leibniz has argued[4] that God is the cause of the universe, to which Kant replies that such a statement is a misuse of the word 'cause'. If X is to be called the cause of Y, then X must be such that it

---

[1] § 4.5, p. 99.

[2] See *DM*, par. 14, G vi. 440, and *Mon.*, par. 47, respectively. That the last passage refers to continual creation is shown by the reference to *Theodicy*, pars. 382–91 (G vi. 342–7), in which this topic is discussed. In *La Théorie leibnizienne de la substance* (Paris, 1947), p. 173, J. Jalabert tries to explain away this passage on the basis of G vii. 564, in which Leibniz says that 'the duration of things, or the multitude of momentary states, is the aggregate (*amas*) of an infinity of flashes (*éclats*) of the Divinity, each of which is at each instant a creation or reproduction of all things, having strictly speaking no continual passage from one state to the next'. Jalabert argues that Leibniz is referring here, not to substances, but to sensible things regarded as phenomena. It is not certain that this is so; Leibniz does not seem to mean that continued creation has reference only to phenomena, but rather that *duration* is phenomenal. In any case it is clear that in *Mon.*, par. 47, he is referring, not to phenomena, but to created or derivative *monads*—i.e. to substances.   [3] *Critique of Pure Reason*, B 637.   [4] Cf. § 4.5, p. 97.

can be, or at least could have been, an object of sense-experience. God, however, is admitted to be outside the range of sense-experience; consequently, to say that God is the cause of the universe is a misuse of terms. Essentially the same point can be made in terms of time. Leibniz has said[1] that God is eternal; that is, that it cannot properly be said of God that he exists now, or has existed, or will exist. The same must presumably be said of God's acts, so that it is strictly speaking incorrect to say that at a given time God created the universe. Leibniz would agree with this; he held a relational and not an absolute theory of time, saying that[2] time is an order of succession, so that there was no time before there were contingent things.[3] But the language which Leibniz uses in speaking about creation (like, Kant would say, all language about causes) implies a reference to time. Making something (in this case, making it in preference to others, or in preference to making nothing at all) is a temporal act, which precedes in time the existence of the finished article.

Leibniz's answer to these objections can only be conjectured, but it seems likely that it would have involved some reference to the miraculous nature of creation. For reasons to be discussed later, Leibniz believed that the creation of a contingent substance, in the sense of its production from nothing, is not a natural event but a miracle.[4] By this he means, not that the creation of a contingent substance cannot be understood by any intelligence whatsoever, but only that it cannot be understood by human beings.[5] Leibniz could say, then, that Kant's account is true of causation in the natural world; that in the sense in which the word 'cause' is used in the natural sciences and in everyday life, it is indeed true that the cause of an event must be such that it can be, or could have been, an object of

---

[1] Cf. § 4.1, p. 78.

[2] *To Clarke*, §§ 3.4, 5.105. Cf. G ii. 253 (L 865), 269 (L 874), 450 (L 983); G iv. 394, 523 (L 806); G. *M*, vii. 18 (L 1083).

[3] *To Clarke*, § 3.6.

[4] *PNG*, par. 2; *Mon.*, pars. 4–6; G ii. 76; G iv. 479 (L 742). See below, § 5.6.   [5] *DM*, pars. 7, 16; G iii. 353.

sense-experience. But, Leibniz might say, when we assert God
to be the cause of the universe we are not using the word
'cause' in this way; we are talking about a miracle, which is
not and cannot be a part of the natural sciences. A similar reply
would perhaps be made to the objection based on the relations
between creation and time.

If this were to be Leibniz's answer, it could hardly be called
satisfactory. He seems to begin his argument by regarding God
as a cause in the ordinary sense; God makes the world much as
(though not exactly as) a man makes some artefact. Then,
when difficulties are pointed out, it appears that the word 'cause'
has some other sense; but what this sense is, remains obscure.

§ 4.7. To complete our survey of Leibniz's theism we must
follow further what he says about God's creation of the universe. This will introduce a number of topics which at first
sight might appear quite unrelated. These are: Leibniz's belief
that this is the best of all possible worlds; his account of a principle to which he sometimes gives the name of the principle of
sufficient reason, but which is different from that which has already been considered; his explanation of contingent existential propositions; and part at any rate of what he believes can be
known *a priori* about the nature of created things.

The universe, Leibniz has argued, exists because God chose
to create it. Like everything else, a choice has a reason,[1] and it
must therefore be possible to say why God chose to create a
universe at all, and why he chose to create the universe which
was created and not some other. Many theists might think that
although these questions can be answered, the answer is known
to God alone. Leibniz, however, would not agree. He answers
the first question by saying that the reason why God chose to
create at all is to be found in his goodness. It is goodness, he
says, 'which leads God to create, in order to communicate
itself'.[2] Here he is echoing the Scholastic tag *omne bonum est
diffusivum sui*, and is using an argument which goes back to

[1] Cf. § 4.5, p. 97.   [2] G vi. 253; cf. G vi. 144.

Plato.[1] To the second question, which concerned God's reason for choosing to create the universe which he did create, Leibniz's answer is a little more complicated.

It was mentioned earlier[2] that he believes God to choose between a number of possible worlds—different conceptual universes, none of which implies a contradiction in itself, but which are not 'compossible', that is, compatible with each other.[3] According to Leibniz, the reason which determines God to create one rather than another can be found only in the degree of perfection which these worlds have.[4] Since God is the most perfect being, and since to choose anything other than the most perfect possible world would be a sign of imperfection,[5] it follows that God must choose to create the most perfect, that is, the best possible world.[6] Further, the universe in which we live was not only intended as the best possible, but actually is the best possible. This is because God's perfections include omnipotence and omniscience,[7] so that God not only chooses to create the best possible world, but knows which possible world is the best, and not only knows it, but has the power required to create it. 'And it is this which is the cause of the existence of the best, which wisdom makes God know, his goodness makes him choose, and his power makes him produce.'[8] This makes it clear that Leibniz's 'optimism', his belief that this is the best possible world, is not simply the expression of a mood, but is a logical consequence of his theism. He is saying that, given the existence of a God of the kind in whom theists believe, then, whatever the appearances, this world *must be* the best possible.

---

[1] Cf. Aquinas, *Summa contra Gentiles*, 1. 93. 6, on the 'liberality' of God. On this, and on its Platonic antecedents, see e.g. A. O. Lovejoy, *The Great Chain of Being* (Harvard, 1936), pp. 49 ff.   [2] § 4.5.

[3] G iii. 573; G vii. 289 (C 534); *NE*, 3. 6. 12; C 530 (L 262); Grua, p. 325.

[4] *Mon.*, par. 54; Grua, p. 16.   [5] Cf. G vi. 236.

[6] *PNG*, par. 10; *Mon.*, pars. 53–55; G vi. 107–8, 233, 252, 364; G vii. 306 (L 794); Grua, p. 390. For the equivalence of 'best' and 'most perfect' see *PNG*, par. 10; *Mon.*, pars. 54–55; G vi. 236.

[7] Cf. § 4.5.   [8] *Mon.*, par. 55. Cf. G iv. 507 (L 813).

Leibniz often makes this point by the use of legal metaphor, saying that every possible world claims existence, or has the right to claim it, in proportion to its perfection.[1] Here God is viewed as a judge or arbiter, whose business it is to make an award—that of existence—to the most perfect claimant. Sometimes God seems to be left wholly out of account, and the metaphor becomes physical rather than legal. This is when Leibniz says that possibles tend to existence, or demand it, or that they strive to or have a propensity to exist,[2] and that from a conflict of possibles there results the existence of the most perfect.[3] But it would be wrong to suppose that the emergence of the existent from the possible is, as has been suggested, 'the result of a quasi-mechanical process'.[4] Leibniz says explicitly that the contending possibles exist only in the mind of God; as he puts it, the conflict 'can only be ideal, i.e. can only be a conflict of reasons in the most perfect understanding'.[5]

All this shows what Leibniz means when he describes the sufficient reason for contingent things as 'the principle of the best'.[6] It is clear that this principle is not derived from his logic, for although it is partly established by deductive reasoning, it starts from the non-logical premisses that wisdom, power, and goodness are perfections of man, and that any perfection of man exists in a 'more eminent' form in God. It is therefore unfortunate that Leibniz sometimes refers to this principle as 'the principle of sufficient reason', since it has already been seen that a principle of this name does follow from his logic.[7]

There are several passages in which Leibniz gives this name to what he calls elsewhere 'the principle of the best'. He says, for example, that whereas the basis of mathematics is the

---

[1] Mon., par. 54; PNG, par. 10; G vi. 236; G vii. 304 (L 792).
[2] G vii. 195 n., 289-90 (C 534), 303 (L 791), 310 n.; Grua, p. 324.
[3] G vii. 290.   [4] Lovejoy, op. cit., p. 178.
[5] G vi. 236. Cf. G vii. 305 (L 793); PNG, par. 10; Grua, p. 286.
[6] To Clarke, § 5.9; G vi. 44. Also referred to as 'the principle of fitness' (convenance, convenientia—Mon., par. 46; PNG, par. 11; C 528) and as 'the principle of perfection' (Grua, p. 288).
[7] On the ambiguity, cf. Russell, p. 30, and C. L., p. 216.

principle of contradiction or identity, physics requires another principle, that of sufficient reason.[1] This would be a puzzling remark, if Leibniz meant by this principle the proposition that every truth has an *a priori* proof, in that every truth is or is reducible to an identical proposition. The physicist does not, in so far as he is a physicist, use such a principle. If he did—that is, if his method of procedure were the reduction to identical propositions of the propositions whose truth he is trying to prove—then his methods would be those of the mathematician or logician, and Leibniz has just insisted that these methods are not enough for him. This shows, then, that the 'principle of sufficient reason' which physics uses is not the logical principle which was discussed in an earlier chapter; other passages indicate that the principle in question is what has just been called 'the principle of the best'. Laws of movement, for example, are said to depend on the latter principle;[2] again, Leibniz says of inferences in physics that they do not necessitate, but only 'incline',[3] which must mean that they involve some reference to the motives of God. There is no genuine inconsistency here, but the terminology is confusing; to avoid such confusion, the expression 'principle of sufficient reason' will henceforward be used to refer only to the proposition that every truth has an *a priori* proof, whilst the proposition that the world is as it is because God chose to create the best possible world, and had the power and knowledge necessary to create it, will be called only 'the principle of the best'.

The principle of the best has been defined in terms of the creation of a world or universe—that is, *all* contingent things. From this principle there obviously follows the consequence that any part of the world, that is, any particular contingent thing, has the nature which it has because it is a part of the best possible world. This makes it possible to state the answer which Leibniz would have given to an objection made earlier in this

[1] *To Clarke,* § 2.1; G vii. 301, 309; G. M. vii. Supp. 113.
[2] G vi. 44; C 528. See also below, § 4.8.
[3] *NE,* 2. 21. 13.

chapter.[1] The objection was that when it is true that there exists
a certain contingent thing—say, the Parthenon—the concept of
existence must be contained in that of the thing, which therefore turns out to be a necessary being. Leibniz's answer would
be that what is contained in the concept of the thing is the concept of being part of the best possible world.[2] The concept of
the thing, he might say, contains the concept of being existence-
worthy, but not the concept of existence, and the thing will
exist only if there is a God who creates the best possible world.
This also provides the answer to the question, asked at the end
of Chapter II,[3] how Leibniz can account for existential propositions in terms of his view that in every proposition one
concept is said to be included in another, a view which he
seems to have adopted precisely because it does not commit
him to asserting the existence of the subject of a proposition.
What might seem to be the obvious solution—to say that, in
an existential proposition, the concept of existence is asserted
to be in that of the subject—is inadequate, since propositions
of this type are said by Leibniz to assert necessary existence only.
For contingent existential propositions, then, some other solution must be found, and it has now been seen what this would
be. Leibniz would say that such a proposition is complex, being
partly hypothetical and partly categorical; that it says in effect,
'If, and only if, there is such and such a contingent thing, there
exists the best possible world; if there is a God, the best possible
world exists; and there is a God.'

There are two weaknesses in this answer. The first is that
it involves a reference to the existence of God, and it has already
been argued[4] that it is not clear how, if propositions are regarded intensionally, it can be said that God exists. The second

[1] § 4.4.
[2] It will be seen later (§ 5.4) that Leibniz also argues that the concept of
the whole world can in theory be derived from the concept of any individual
thing, so that the concept of the best possible world is contained in the concept of that thing. However, his answer to the present objection does not
depend on this view.
[3] § 2.4, p. 54.   [4] § 4.2, p. 85.

weakness[1] is that it does not seem that Leibniz has, after all, been able to account for contingent existential propositions in terms of his view that in every proposition the concept of the predicate is said to be included in that of the subject. For example, it has been seen that he would probably say, of the proposition about the existence of the Parthenon, that the concept of the predicate is not the concept of existence, but is the concept of being existence-worthy; and since to say this of the concept of the Parthenon is not the same as saying that the Parthenon exists, he has to add that there is a God who creates all that is existence-worthy. But it is hard to see how, on Leibniz's premisses, the proposition that God exists could be derived from, or, as he would say, contained in, the concept of a contingent thing such as the Parthenon. It might be thought that the cosmological argument for the existence of a necessary being would be relevant here; but this is an argument from the *existence* of contingent things, not from their concepts. From the mere concept of a contingent thing Leibniz could only argue to the possible existence of a necessary being; that is, he could only say that *if* there is a contingent thing, then there is a necessary being, whereas his analysis of a contingent existential proposition requires the existence of a necessary being, indeed the existence of God. When it is said, therefore, that a contingent thing exists, more is being said than that a certain concept is contained in that of the subject; that is, Leibniz's method of avoiding the conclusion that everything which exists is a necessary being involves the abandonment of a fundamental thesis of his logic.

It might be thought that there is another reason why Leibniz should think that everything which exists, exists necessarily. He has defined God as the most perfect being, possessed of perfect wisdom, power, and goodness, and he seems also to think that it follows logically from this that God must create the best possible world. But this surely means that the existence of any world other than that which does exist is inconceivable, so

[1] Cf. Russell, p. 27.

that if Leibniz were consistent he would have to agree with
Spinoza, for whom everything which exists or happens, exists
or happens necessarily.[1] Leibniz saw that this was a possible
objection, and tried to answer it.[2] He agrees that it follows from
the nature of God that he prefers the most perfect state of
things;[3] that, in other words, it is necessary that God chooses
the best.[4] But although God necessarily wills the best, he does
not will the best necessarily.[5] Given that there is a most perfect
being, it is necessary that this being wills the best, but this does
not imply the inconceivability of the existence of some other
world. What does not exist remains possible in its own nature,
even if it is not possible when considered in relation to the
divine will.[6]

Leibniz often expresses this by saying[7] that contingent things
exist with hypothetical necessity, but not with logical necessity.
'Logical' (or 'metaphysical', or 'mathematical') necessity is the
necessity possessed by a truth whose denial would imply a
contradiction.[8] To say, however, that something has 'hypothetical' (or 'moral', or 'consequential') necessity is to say that it is
necessary, *given that* such and such is the case.[9] For example,
the proposition that Judas will sin is one whose opposite does

---

[1] See, e.g., Lovejoy, op. cit., pp. 172–3.

[2] Grua, p. 289. In *Jurisprudence universelle et Théodicée selon Leibniz* (Paris,
1953), pp. 312–15, Grua gives an extensive documentation of Leibniz's
attempts at solving this problem.   [3] Grua, p. 393.

[4] Grua, pp. 276, 289. This might seem to be contradicted by Grua,
p. 301, where Leibniz denies that it can be proved from the nature of God
that he chooses the best. But this does not mean that Leibniz thinks it to be
other than necessary that God chooses the best, since he goes on to say that
this proposition is 'primary or identical'.

[5] Ibid., p. 494.

[6] Ibid., p. 289; G i. 149. This is the sense in which (Grua, p. 279) what does
not exist is impossible.

[7] G vii. 303 (L 790); *DM*, par. 13; C 271; Grua, pp. 271, 288, 300.

[8] G vi. 441; *To Clarke*, § 5.4.

[9] Hypothetical necessity: G ii. 18; G iii. 400; G vii. 303 (L 791–2); *DM*,
par. 13; *To Clarke*, § 5.4; A vi. 1, 541; G. M. iii. 576; Grua, pp. 271, 273, 288,
300. Moral necessity: G ii. 419; G vi. 441. Consequential necessity: G iii.
400; C 271. The term 'hypothetically necessary' is derived from Aristotle,
Physics, 200ª13–14.

not imply a contradiction,[1] but it is hypothetically necessary that Judas will sin, on the assumption that God has foreseen his sin,[2] or in order that the scriptures should be fulfilled.[1] Again, it is impossible that money should be taken from a man, given that he has no money[3]—that is, the proposition that it will not be taken is a hypothetically necessary truth. Similarly, Leibniz would say that it is hypothetically necessary that there is in Athens a building called 'the Parthenon', given that the concept of such a building is a part of the concept of the best possible world, and that there is a God who will create such a world. It is not, however, logically necessary that there should be such a building, so that a Spinozistic determinism is avoided.

§ 4.8. The principle of the best is not only used by Leibniz to explain the nature of contingent truths; he also claims that from it we can obtain a priori knowledge about the universe,[4] by considering what the notion of perfection involves. Not only are the consequences which he draws of intrinsic interest, but one of them is of especial importance to a consideration of Leibniz's logic and metaphysics, since it serves to complete his account of contingent truth.[5] In this section, the subject of discussion will be those consequences of the principle of the best which can be stated without reference to the Leibnizian concept of substance; those which involve this concept will be discussed in the next chapter.

It has already been remarked that the best possible world is also, by definition, the most perfect.[6] By 'perfection' Leibniz understands 'reality' or 'essence';[7] he also defines perfection as

[1] Grua, p. 273.
[2] Ibid., p. 271. This is Leibniz's answer to the medieval problem of future contingents (cf. Grua, p. 493), an answer which is similar to that of Aquinas (*Summa contra Gentiles*, 1. 67. 8; cf. Kneale, p. 237).
[3] C 271.
[4] It must be added that this is not, according to Leibniz, the only way of obtaining such a priori knowledge, as the next chapter will show.
[5] See below, § 5.3.
[6] § 4.7, p. 104.
[7] G vi. 122; G vii. 310 n.; C 22; Grua, pp. 288, 324, 486.

a degree or quantity of these,[1] but it is clear that what he means is (as he sometimes says) that the more perfect a thing is, the more reality or essence it has.[2] From this it follows that the best possible world must be that in which there is the most essence or reality.[3] This may well sound like mere jargon; for what sense can there be in saying that reality admits of more and less? Again, even if it is allowed that what Leibniz says has meaning, it may still be asked with what right it is used to define perfection. The answers to these two questions are linked. The answer to the second is that Leibniz's use of the term 'perfect' was a standard one, going back through the Scholastics to Aristotle. For them, the term 'perfect' meant 'complete', and completeness was viewed teleologically. Roughly speaking,[4] a growing thing was regarded as striving to realize its 'form', its fully developed state; the complete or perfect thing is that which has realized its form. This can also be given a non-teleological interpretation, as it was, for example, by Spinoza.[5] Taken in this way, to say that something is perfectly x is to say that it is in no way limited or incomplete in respect of x.[6] The notion of degrees of reality can now be explained. To say, for example, that one man has more reality than another is to say that he is more really a man; that is, that he is closer to the form of man, or more the complete man.

---

[1] A ii. 1, 327, 329, 363; G vii. 27, 290 (C 534), 303 (L 791), 304 (L 793); G. M. vii, Supp. 172; *Mon.*, par. 41; C 474; Grua, pp. 11, 17, 279, 527, 529.

[2] Grua, pp. 13, 325, 531.

[3] G vii. 303; C 530 (L 262); Grua, p. 17. Leibniz also treats as equivalent the terms 'essence' and 'possibility' (G iii. 573; Grua, p. 390), and so can call the best possible world 'the greatest series of all possibles' (G vii. 290 (C 534); cf. G vii. 304 (L 793)).   [4] See, e.g., Aristotle, *Metaphysics*, 1021^{b}23 ff.

[5] Cf. *Ethics*, Part II, Def. 6, and Ep. 19 (Gebhardt, iv, p. 89).

[6] Cf. the definition of perfection which Leibniz uses to establish the possibility of God (§ 4.2, p. 81). This agrees with the definition above in that it states that a perfection is something which is not limited; it disagrees, however, in stressing the simplicity, by which Leibniz there means the unanalysability of a perfection. For although Leibniz thinks that any created substance (and so, it may be assumed, its form) is indivisible (§ 5.6), he thinks that such a form is analysable (cf. § 5.9, p. 179, on the qualities of a soul or form).

It may be replied that although meaning can be given to the notion of degrees of reality, it is not meaningful to apply this notion, as Leibniz does, to a whole universe. It is possible, for example, to understand what is meant by saying that A is more really a man than B; but what can be meant by saying that the universe is the most real of universes? How can one universe be more really a universe than another—especially as there only is one universe, so that there is nothing with which to compare it? Leibniz would reply to the last point that what are compared are concepts of universes, universes which (if created) would more or less closely approach, and in one case would be identical with, the ideal of the perfect universe. By the perfect, or 'most real', universe Leibniz seems to understand that in which most concepts have instances. For example, he uses the principle of the best to establish the view that each portion of the universe is subdivided to infinity.[1] The same principle is used to show that there can be no vacuum; for to suppose any gap in nature is to suppose it to be less perfect than it might have been, with less than the maximum of reality.[2] Leibniz argues in a similar way about the properties which things have, saying that as far as we can know the nature of gold is more perfect than that of silver, since gold offers more properties for observation.[3] Not only, then, can there be no physical vacuum in the best possible world, but there can be no 'vacuum of forms'.[4] As a result, Leibniz can say that the greatest perfection implies the greatest variety.[5] This does not mean, however, that all possible species exist; Leibniz insists that they do not, since not all possible species are 'compossible', i.e. compatible.[6] He believes, however, that 'all the things

---

[1] *To Clarke*, § 4, P.S. Cf. G iii. 507.

[2] Ibid., § 2.2, 4, P.S.; G vii. 315. Cf. Jagodinsky, op. cit., p. 14; Rivaud, *RMM*, 1914, p. 99.   [3] Grua, p. 529.

[4] G ii. 125 (L 535); G vi. 110; *NE*, 3. 6. 12.

[5] *PNG*, par. 10; *Mon.*, par. 58. This could have been shown in another way, starting from the proposition that there is an infinity of substances, which is also derived from the principle of the best (§ 5.3, p. 140), and then pointing out that, by the identity of indiscernibles (§ 5.2), each substance must differ from every other substance.   [6] *NE*, loc. cit.

which the perfect harmony of the universe can receive, are there'.[1] For example, he argues (contrary to Descartes) that the irrational animals are not mere automata, but are conscious beings, having the faculty of sensation;[2] otherwise, nature would not be as rich as it might be, and there would be a 'vacuum of perfections, or of forms'.[3]

It would be a mistake, however, to think that whenever Leibniz uses the principle of the best to enable him to make *a priori* assertions about the nature of the universe, he is deducing consequences solely from the definition of perfection just stated. It was mentioned earlier[4] that Leibniz claims to derive from the principle of the best certain laws of motion; here, however, he is starting from a principle which states not only that in the best possible world the greatest amount of essence is realized, but also that it is realized 'with, as it were, the least expense',[5] the richest effects being obtained by the simplest means. It is from this principle that he deduces the proposition that, if it is simply assumed that a body is moving from one point to another, then if nothing else determines its route it will travel by the easiest, i.e. the shortest, path.[6] From this principle, again, he infers similar propositions about light, which is sometimes said to travel by the easiest path,[7] sometimes by the 'most determinate', i.e. by a unique path.[8] It is clear that these consequences are not deducible simply from the assertion that the more perfection a thing has, the more essence or reality it has. However, Leibniz could claim that he is here

---

[1] Ibid.   [2] G ii. 117 (L 526); G vii. 529; *PNG*, par. 4; Grua, p. 552.

[3] G ii. 125–6 (L 535); G vi. 543 (L 957); G vii. 531. Leibniz also brings an analogical argument for this conclusion, remarking that the sense-organs of the irrational animals are comparable to ours, and saying that it may be inferred from this that they have sensations which are comparable to ours (G vii. 329).   [4] § 4.7, p. 106.

[5] G vii. 303 (L 791); A ii. 1, 478 (L 323); *DM*, pars. 5 and 6; Grua, p. 285. The combination of richness of effects with simplicity of means seems sometimes to be what Leibniz has in mind when he speaks of the harmony which things display. Cf. Grua, p. 267.   [6] G vii. 304 (L 792).

[7] Dutens, iii, pp. 145 ff.; G iv. 318, 340.

[8] G vii. 275 (L 782); *DM*, par. 22; *NE*, 4. 7. 15.

following a standard use of the terms 'better' and 'best', in that it is commonly said that of two ways of producing identical results, the more economical is the better.

In the *Principles of Nature and of Grace* Leibniz asserts that other physical laws follow from the principle of the best, or 'the principle of fitness', as he calls it there. These are:[1] the conservation of the same quantity of 'total or absolute force, or action', the conservation of the same quantity of 'relative force, or reaction', the conservation of the same quantity of 'directive force', and the law that action is always equal to reaction, or that the entire effect is always equivalent to its full cause. Leibniz does not make clear, however, in what way they depend on the principle of the best. In the *Discourse on Metaphysics*, for example, he says that it is 'very reasonable' that the same force should always be conserved in the universe,[2] but he does not explain why it is best that this should be so.

The consequences of the principle of the best which have been described so far have been quantitative in character; they may be summed up as answers to the questions 'How much?' and 'How economically?' But it would be a serious mistake to suppose, as Couturat does,[3] that the goodness of Leibniz's best possible world is purely quantitative, and has no specifically moral character. This would be to ignore Leibniz's express warning that he is not to be thought to confuse moral perfection with mere magnitude.[4] The world, he says, not only contains the greatest amount of reality—that is, it is not only 'physically' or 'metaphysically' perfect—but it is also most perfect morally. This is because moral perfection is natural (*physica*) to minds. Consequently[5] 'the world is not only the most admirable machine but is also, in so far as it consists of minds, the best commonwealth (*respublica*),[6] through which there is bestowed on minds the greatest happiness or joy, in which their natural perfection consists'. This 'best common-

[1] *PNG*, par. 11.   [2] *DM*, par. 17.
[3] C. L., p. 231; *RMM*, 1902, p. 18.   [4] G vii. 306 (L 794-5).
[5] Ibid.   [6] Not a 'republic', since it has a king, namely God.

wealth' is what Leibniz means by the 'kingdom of grace' as opposed to the 'kingdom of nature'.[1] Couturat's error, then, may be described by saying that he has concentrated on one of Leibniz's two 'kingdoms', to the exclusion of the other. It is easy to see why Couturat should have done this: his concern was with Leibniz's logic and its metaphysical consequences, and although to speak of Leibniz's deductions about the quantitative character of the best possible world is to remain within the field of logic, to talk about its moral nature would be to speak of the ethical rather than the logical aspects of Leibniz's metaphysics. But although this explains Couturat's neglect of the concept of the kingdom of grace, it does not justify him in writing as if Leibniz had no such concept.

It remains to make some comments about Leibniz's use of the principle of the best to establish scientific propositions. Obviously, this is a respect in which Leibniz is very much a man of his time: no one would now think seriously of using such a principle to prove scientific propositions. To say nothing of the many who reject outright the concept of a purposive deity, even those who believe in such a deity are much more reluctant than Leibniz was to make *a priori* assertions about the means that such a deity must adopt. There would probably be general agreement that if the notion of divine purpose has any use in the sciences, it is only as a heuristic principle—not, that is, as a means of proof, but as a way of suggesting hypotheses which can be tested empirically. If it is used in this way, then it does not matter that God's purposes should really be as supposed, or even that God can properly be said to have any purposes at all: it is enough that it should be *as if* there were a purposive God.[2] All this is very different from Leibniz's use of the principle of the best.

It is certain that the attempt to match one's knowledge

---

[1] See, e.g., *Mon.*, pars. 84–90; *PNG*, par. 15; *DM*, pars. 35–36; G ii. 124–5 (L 534–5); G ii. 136; G iv. 392 (L 676), 485–6 (L 748–9); G vi. 196–7, 545(L 960); G. *M.* vi. 243 (L 723).

[2] Compare Kant on the regulative use of the idea of the wise purposes of God, *Critique of Pure Reason*, B 714 ff.

against that of omniscience, in saying how such a being would act, is an undertaking which can lead to ludicrous results. Such an outcome, it might be thought, is Leibniz's assertion that in the best possible world there can be no vacuum. Here Leibniz seems to be indulging in *a priori* dogmatism about what is, for us at any rate, an empirical matter; he may remind us of those Italian professors who refused to look through Galileo's telescope, on the grounds that things could not be as Galileo saw that they were.[1] In fact, however, the issue is not quite so clearcut. In Leibniz's time, the assertion that there was a vacuum was not made primarily on empirical grounds. It is true that air pumps had been invented, and that Guericke had used such pumps to give dramatic evidence of the pressure of the atmosphere; but not only was Leibniz right in saying that Guericke had not made a complete vacuum,[2] but the chief reasons for which his contemporaries asserted the existence of a vacuum had nothing to do with air pumps. They asserted it as part of an atomic theory, a theory which was still a long way from being satisfactorily verified. More important, it was a metaphysical theory: it was put forward, not as a model to be justified by the extent to which deductions from it agreed with observations, but as an account of the nature of real but unobservable entities. Really, the theory said, everything consisted of what Newton called[3] 'solid, massy, hard particles', moving about in a vacuum, though these particles could not be observed. In so far as this was a metaphysical view, Leibniz was justified in answering it with a metaphysical argument.

It is also worth noting that Leibniz is not proposing that the concept of God's purposes, or of what he calls 'the way of final causes',[4] shall be used in the sciences without check or control. He is well aware of the importance of the concept of explanation in mechanistic terms, or 'the way of efficient causes',[4] but thinks that the other method is sometimes easier to use. He

---

[1] E. A. Burtt, *The Metaphysical Foundations of Modern Science* (2nd ed., London, 1932), pp. 66–67.   [2] *To Clarke*, § 5.34.

[3] *Opticks*, 1704; Burtt, op. cit., p. 229.   [4] *DM*, par. 22.

says, for example, that he believes that Snell used the concept of
God's purposes to discover the law of optics which bears his
name,[1] and that he would have waited a long time for his discovery if he had used some other, 'more physical' route.[2]
Similar examples, Leibniz claims, can be found in the science
of anatomy.[3] All this seems to imply that the slower, but what
Leibniz calls the 'more profound',[4] method of explanation in
mechanistic terms will act as a check on explanations which
use the concept of the purposes of God.

Before leaving the subject of Leibniz's views about God,
there is a further topic on which something must be said.
Throughout this chapter, Leibniz's assertions about God have
been taken at their face value; that is, it has been assumed that
he means what he says. This may seem a reasonable assumption
to make, but it is one which needs justification in view of
Russell's thesis that Leibniz had two philosophies—the one,
which he proclaimed, being orthodox and shallow, and the
other, which he kept to himself, being profound, logical, and
largely Spinozistic.[5] Clearly, the views about God which have
just been expounded belong to what Russell would call Leibniz's
orthodox philosophy; whether they are shallow is a matter of
opinion, but whether they were genuinely held by Leibniz is
a matter of fact on which at any rate a probable decision can
be reached.

As a man may usually be assumed to mean what he says, the
burden of proof falls on those who say that Leibniz did not.
The evidence brought forward to support the theory of
Leibniz's duplicity seems slender. It is true that Leibniz did, on
at least one occasion, ask a correspondent[6] not to pass on to

---

[1] To be more specific, he says that Snell sought the easiest, or at least the
most determinate, path by which a ray of light might travel from a given
point in one medium to a given point in another (DM, par. 22).

[2] Ibid. Cf. G iv. 317–19, 340; G vii. 270–9; NE, 4. 7. 15.

[3] DM, pars. 19, 22.　　　　　　　　　　　　　[4] Ibid., par. 22.

[5] Russell, p. vi; cf. Russell, History of Western Philosophy (London, 1946),
p. 604.

[6] See his letter to Wedderkopf, May 1671: A ii. 1, 118 (L 228).

others certain remarks of his which were Spinozistic in trend, in that they stated that everything which happens is necessary, so that even sins are necessary. But these remarks were made in 1671, several years before Leibniz's maturity as a philosopher, and Leibniz himself noted[1] that 'I corrected this later; for it is one thing that sins will happen infallibly, another that they will happen necessarily'. It might be replied that this 'correction' was made for the benefit of Leibniz's public, and that the views stated in the letter are his real views. If this thesis is to be sustained there must be other evidence for Leibniz's Spinozism, and it must now be seen what this is.

Mention has already been made[2] of passages in which Leibniz might be thought to mean that the world comes into existence with a kind of mechanistic necessity as a result of a conflict between various possible worlds, a process in which God plays no part. However, it was pointed out that Leibniz is here speaking metaphorically of a conflict between motives in the mind of God; and it may be added that it is hard to see in what other way *possible* worlds could conflict, since, as Leibniz points out, possible worlds have no existence and no power to make themselves exist.[3] There must now be considered two passages from the *Generales Inquisitiones* on which Russell has laid stress.[4] Leibniz says here that ' "Existent" can be defined as that which is compatible with more things than anything else which is incompatible with it',[5] and again, 'I say, therefore, that an existent entity is that which is compatible with most things, i.e. is the most possible entity'.[6] Russell admits that only *criteria* of existence may be in mind here;[7] on the other hand he seems to think that the passages are (as they certainly appear to be) meant as definitions. If this is so, then it follows that Leibniz cannot consistently have believed in any act of

---

[1] A ii. 1, 118.
[2] § 4.7, p. 105.
[3] Grua, p. 286.
[4] Russell, p. vi. On the *Generales Inquisitiones*, cf. § 1.3, p. 19, n. 3.
[5] C 360.   [6] C 376.
[7] *History of Western Philosophy*, p. 617.

creation, and perhaps did not really believe in it. As Russell says:[1]

The relations of essences are among eternal truths, and it is a problem in pure logic to construct that world which contains the greatest number of coexisting essences. This world, it would follow, exists by definition, without the need of any Divine Decree; moreover, it is a part of God, since essences exist in God's mind.[2] Here, as elsewhere, Leibniz fell into Spinozism whenever he allowed himself to be logical.

To see if this view is correct it is necessary to look carefully at the context of the passages quoted. The first is introduced only in parenthesis, and is taken up in a later paragraph, in which there occurs the second passage cited by Russell. It will be worth while to quote the whole of this later paragraph,[3] which may be translated as follows:

But it is asked what 'existent' means: for an existent[4] is an entity, i.e. a possible, and something else besides. All things considered, I do not see what else is conceived in 'existent' than some degree of entity, since it can be applied to various entities. Though I would not wish to say that 'that something exists' is possible, i.e. possible existence. For this is simply essence itself; we, on the other hand, understand actual existence, i.e. something added to possibility or essence, so that in that sense possible existence would be the same as actuality abstracting from actuality (*actualitas praescindens ab actualitate*), which is absurd. I say, therefore, that an existent entity is that which is compatible with most things, i.e. is the most possible entity, and so all co-existents are equally possible. Or, what comes to the same, 'existent' is what pleases something intelligent and powerful; but in this way existence itself is presupposed. However, this definition at least can be given: 'existent' is what would please

[1] Russell, p. vii.
[2] Russell seems to have in mind Leibniz's view that eternal truths exist in the mind of God (G vi. 115; G vii. 305 (L 793), 311; *Mon.*, par. 43; *NE*, 4. 11. 14; cf. Russell, p. 178). See also Leibniz's views about possible worlds, § 4.7, p. 105.   [3] C 375–6.
[4] *Existens* is translated here either as 'existent' or as 'an existent', depending on the context.

some mind, and would not displease another more powerful mind, if minds of any kind were assumed to exist. So it comes to this, that there is said to 'exist' that which would not displease the most power-ful mind, if it should be assumed that a most powerful mind exists. But so that this definition shall be applicable to experience (*experi-mentis*), it must rather be stated as follows: there 'exists' that which pleases some (existent) mind ('existent' must not be added if we seek a definition, and not a simple proposition), and does not dis-please (absolutely) the most powerful mind. But it is pleasing to a mind that there should be made that which has a reason rather than that which does not have a reason. So if there are several things, *A*, *B*, *C*, *D*, and one of these is to be chosen, and if *B*, *C*, and *D* are alike in all respects, *A* alone being distinguished from the rest in some way, then *A* will please any mind which understands this. It is the same if a distinction does not at any rate *appear* between *B*, *C*, and *D*, but does appear between them and *A*, and the mind decides to choose; it will choose *A*. But it chooses freely, for it can still ask whether there is not some distinction between *B*, *C*, and *D*.

This passage is obviously tentative; Leibniz gives the im-pression of feeling his way towards a definition. What is certain is that God's decision is not left out of account, since existence is defined by reference to what pleases the most powerful mind, where the word 'pleases' (*placet*) suggests the approval bestowed by a sovereign on a proposal. The problem concerns the way in which the most powerful mind is regarded. Leibniz begins by defining 'existent' as what would not displease the most powerful mind, if there should be such a mind. God's existence is not postulated here, and Leibniz seems to be de-fining 'existent' in a way which does not distinguish it from 'existence-worthy',[1] which is surely incorrect. He appears to see this, and offers another definition in which he replaces the subjunctive 'would please' by the indicative 'pleases'. 'Exists', he says, must be defined as 'that which pleases some mind', so that the definition 'shall be applicable to experience'. The meaning of the last phrase is not wholly clear, but it seems likely that Leibniz has realized that the question 'Does *X* exist?'

[1] Cf. § 4.7, p. 107.

cannot be answered simply by saying 'X would not displease a God, if there should be a God'; instead we must ask 'Would it displease God?', or, failing an answer to that question, we must ask 'What information about X is provided by our senses?' But whatever the obscurities in this paragraph, if the passage is taken as a whole it seems to offer no support to the suggestion that Leibniz is here advancing Spinozistic views.

The same can be said of a passage which Couturat[1] regards as showing that Leibniz thought that to exist is, by definition, to form part of the system of compossibles which contains the most essence. In this passage Leibniz is opposing the view that existence has nothing in common with essence, and says:

> There must be more in the concept of an existent than of a non-existent thing, that is, existence is a perfection; for 'existence' is only explicable as 'being an ingredient in the most perfect series of things' (*cum revera nihil aliud sit explicabile in existentia, quam perfectissimam seriem rerum ingredi*).

But this only shows that Leibniz thinks that the concept of a thing which exists must differ from the concept of one which does not, in that the former concept is, and the latter concept is not, part of the concept of the best possible world. It does not mean that Leibniz thought that 'existence' can be *defined* as 'forming part of the best possible world'. In his own terms, Leibniz is merely saying that existence has *something* in common with essence. He is not saying that to assert that a contingent thing exists is to speak purely of its essence; all that he means is that to explain why God chose to create a contingent thing it is necessary to refer to its essence, that is, to its concept.

In sum, there seems to be no good reason to suppose that Leibniz had a secret doctrine of the nature of God which was largely Spinozistic, or indeed that he had any secret doctrine at all. The philosophy which Leibniz published and that which he left unpublished do not appear to be completely different; what might be called Leibniz's 'popular philosophy' is what it

---

[1] *RMM*, 1902, p. 13. The reference is to C 9.

may reasonably be expected to be—a simplified version of his more technical doctrines. It is undeniable that Leibniz's theism has its difficulties, but these seem to be difficulties in theism as such; the fact that Leibniz's answers to them may not be thought to be satisfactory does not mean that he did not hold seriously the views which he propounded.

V

Subject and Substance

§ 5.1. The account of the nature of God which has just been discussed contains much that is not distinctively Leibnizian. It is true that the thesis that this is the best possible world is associated primarily with the name of Leibniz, and the proof of the possibility of God is peculiar to him. For the rest, however, his views about the existence and nature of God have been seen to owe much to Scholasticism, with occasional borrowings from Spinoza. On the other hand, there are several typically Leibnizian theses about the nature of substance—that, for example, each substance mirrors the whole universe, is indivisible, acts on no other substance, is exactly like no other, and is in some sense a soul. All these propositions are declared by Leibniz to follow from his logic; more specifically, from his account of the nature of truth. It will be the task of this chapter to examine Leibniz's claim.

Most of the passages to be discussed come from letters written to the logician and theologian Arnauld, or from papers written with him in mind—notably the *Discourse on Metaphysics*. Some critics[1] argue that this limits the importance of these passages. Leibniz, they say, would naturally lay stress on logical considerations when writing for a logician, so that it cannot be inferred from these writings that logic is fundamental to his metaphysics. It can be replied that it has not been proved not to be fundamental; there is no reason why Leibniz should not reveal the bases of his metaphysics when writing to a logician. In any case, the objection can only be damaging to a view such as that of Russell or Couturat—namely, that the only reasons which Leibniz had for his statements about what

---

[1] e.g. H. Heimsoeth, *Die Methode der Erkenntnis bei Descartes und Leibniz* (Giessen, 1914), p. 197.

the world must be like were logical reasons. It has already been pointed out, however, that our concern is with logic as one source of such statements, but not necessarily the only source.[1]

In the *Discourse on Metaphysics* the problem of distinguishing between the actions of God and his creatures leads Leibniz to ask what an individual substance is.[2] It is worth while to consider the nature of this question. 'Individual substance' is a technical term of philosophy, and Leibniz assumes that the reader will be familiar with its use; that he will accept as examples of individual substances Alexander the Great, Julius Caesar, or the sphere on Archimedes' tomb.[3] The terminology is traditional, and goes back to what Aristotle, in the *Categories*, had said about the primary sense of the term 'substance'.[4] Leibniz's problem is to explain the rules according to which this term is used; to explain why, for example, Alexander is called an individual substance, whereas greatness is not.

Aristotle had given his answer by saying that 'when several predicates are attributed to the same subject, and this is not attributed to any other, this is called an individual substance'.[5] Leibniz says that this answer is not satisfactory, and that the explanation given is only 'nominal'. This does not mean that he thought the definition to be worthless; he himself uses it occasionally.[6] What it seems to mean here[7] is that something has been left out—namely, an account of what it is to be truly ascribed to a certain subject. This deficiency Leibniz proceeds

---

[1] Introduction, p. 4. Cf. Russell, p. v; C. L., pp. x–xi, 214 ff.

[2] *DM*, par. 8.   [3] Ibid., pars. 8, 13; G ii. 39.

[4] *Cat.* 2ª11–12. The adjective 'individual' shows that Leibniz is not talking about Aristotle's 'secondary substances', which are genera and species (*Cat.* 2ª14 ff.).

[5] The formulation given here is Leibniz's, *DM*, par. 8. Aristotle's own account, in *Cat.* 2ª11–13, is somewhat different.

[6] C 403; G ii. 457. Cf. Schmidt, p. 477.

[7] Leibniz's language suggests his distinction between 'nominal' and 'real' definitions. (H. W. B. Joseph, *The Philosophy of Leibniz* (Oxford, 1949), pp. 70–71.) In his usage (cf. § 4.2, p. 80) a 'nominal' definition fails to show the possibility of the thing defined. There is no indication, however, that this is why Leibniz finds the Aristotelian definition of substance inadequate.

to remedy, in the way already described.[1] After explaining that in a true proposition the predicate term is contained in the subject term, he continues:[2]

That being so, we can say that the nature of an individual substance, or complete being, is to have a concept so complete that it suffices to comprehend and render deducible from it all the predicates of the subject to which this concept is attributed . . . God, seeing the individual concept or *haecceitas* of Alexander, sees in it at the same time the foundation of and reason for all the predicates which can truly be asserted of him.

In other words, Leibniz is saying that since the concept of the predicate of a true proposition is contained in the concept of the subject of the proposition, then the concept of whatever can truly be predicated of a substance must be contained in the concept of the substance. To say that God sees the reason for all the predicates which can truly be asserted of Alexander is simply to say that an omniscient being, who (by definition) has a complete knowledge of what is involved in being Alexander, sees how the concept of each of Alexander's predicates is included in the concept of Alexander.[3]

This may be summed up by saying that, according to Leibniz, the concept of a substance must be 'complete'. Leibniz also holds that the converse is true; that[4] 'if a concept should be complete, i.e. such that from it a reason can be given for all the predicates of the subject to which this concept can be attributed, this will be the concept of an individual substance'. This may seem strange. It seems obvious that the subject of a proposition can sometimes be an abstraction, such as horse, or man, rather than this horse, or this man; and indeed Leibniz himself sometimes implies this.[5] One might also think that it is

---

[1] Cf. §§ 3.1–3.2.
[2] *DM*, par. 8. Cf. G ii. 42; G vii. 311, 316; C 403, 520 (L 414); Grua, pp. 266, 311, 345, 350, 354, 540.
[3] Cf. the account of the principle of sufficient reason given in § 3.3.
[4] C 403. Cf. Schmidt, pp. 475, 478.
[5] Cf. § 1.5, p. 30, n. 7. It could be argued against this that in a marginal note to a letter to Arnauld (G ii. 49 n.) Leibniz seems to distinguish between

obvious that an abstraction can have a complete concept, in the sense of having a description which contains all that can truly be said of it; but if so, every abstraction will be an individual substance, whereas the point of calling something an individual substance is to distinguish it from what is general or abstract.

Leibniz replies by denying that an abstraction has a complete concept.[1] For example, he calls a concept which includes all that can truly be said of heat a 'full', but not a 'complete', concept; there is, he says, a complete concept of this hot thing, but not of heat.[2] This raises the question of the nature of the difference between a full and a complete concept. Sometimes Leibniz explains the difference by reference to God, saying that the concepts of individual things involve the free decrees of God, but that the concepts of abstractions or 'essences' do not;[3] this is because the former, unlike the concepts of abstractions, involve contingent truths. However, he also gives an explanation in less metaphysical terms. An abstraction, he says, 'is not sufficiently determinate for an individual',[4] in that it does not contain the other qualities of subjects to which it is attributed. What he seems to mean is this. Take, for example,[5] the concept of kingship: even a full knowledge of all that can truly be said about kingship, i.e. the ability to give a full analysis of the concept, will not enable one to say all that can truly be said about the subjects of which kingship can be

a *res* and a *subjectum*, implying that the former can have either a full or a complete concept, but that the latter has only a complete concept. If this is what he means, then 'subject' and 'substance' are equivalent, and in this sense no abstraction is ever a subject. (Cf. Loemker, pp. 42, 561 n. 85, 585 n. 349, and Mahnke, p. 77.) But Leibniz gives no indication elsewhere that this is what he means when he says that every proposition has a subject and a predicate.

[1] G ii. 39. Cf. Schmidt, p. 479.

[2] G ii. 49 n. (L 587, n. 381). In his paper 'Leibniz's Predicate-in-Notion Principle and some of its alleged Consequences' (*Theoria*, 1949), C. D. Broad discusses (pp. 56 ff.) what he calls 'the complete notion of a species'. Leibniz would probably have referred to the 'full' notion or concept of a species.

[3] G ii. 49 (L 509). Cf. § 4.7.

[4] *DM*, par. 8: *assez déterminée à un individu*. Cf. G ii. 49.

[5] Ibid., par. 8; Schmidt, pp. 475–6. Cf. C 375.

predicated, such as Alexander. This is because the concept of
Alexander contains, not only the concept of kingship, but other
concepts also. Suppose, on the other hand, that one knows all
that can truly be said about Alexander, i.e. that one can give
a full analysis of the concept of Alexander. Alexander is a subject which, although it has predicates, is not itself predicable of
anything else; that is, the concept of Alexander is not contained
in any other, more complex concept.[1] Such appears to be
Leibniz's meaning when he says that kingship has only a 'full'
concept, and is therefore an abstraction, whereas the concept of
Alexander is 'complete', and therefore Alexander is an individual substance. In brief, the view suggested here as Leibniz's
is that a concept is complete if, and only if, it cannot form part
of a concept more complex than itself.

To complete the exposition of what Leibniz has said, it will
be useful to give a reminder of a point made in the last chapter:[2]
namely, that the concept of a contingent substance does not
contain the concept of existence. When Leibniz says, therefore,[3] that the complete concept of Alexander contains all the
predicates which can truly be asserted of him, he must not be
taken to mean that the concept of existence is one of those
which are included; what is included is only the concept of
being part of the best possible world. This must be remembered
whenever reference is made in this chapter to all that can truly
be said of a substance.[4]

So far it has been assumed that Leibniz is right in saying that
an individual substance has a single complete concept. However, it may be doubted whether this is so. Consider any true

---

[1] Cf. C 403, which puts this in terms of subjects rather than of concepts,
saying that 'An individual substance is a subject which is not in another subject'. In the passage above, the words 'more complex' might seem to be
otiose, for if a concept A is included in a concept B then it might seem obvious that B must be more complex than A. The reason for inserting them
is to avoid confusion with Leibniz's wide sense of the term 'inclusion', according to which the concept of the predicate of an identical proposition,
such as 'A is A', is said to be included in that of the subject (cf. § 1.3, p. 16).
[2] § 4.7, pp. 106 ff.   [3] Cf. p. 125.   [4] e.g. § 5.5, p. 152.

proposition whose subject is a substance and which states an
event, such as 'Alexander died in Babylon'. Such a proposition,
it may be said, presupposes that the event has occurred;[1] before
the event, the true proposition about the place of Alexander's
death would have been 'Alexander will die in Babylon', and
whilst he was dying the true proposition would have been
'Alexander is dying in Babylon'. If this is so, it may be asked
how there can be *one* complete concept of Alexander. The
answer to this is that the objection confuses the notions of proposition and sentence; that the three sentences 'Alexander died
in Babylon', 'Alexander will die in Babylon', and 'Alexander
is dying in Babylon' all express the same proposition, in which
dying in Babylon is predicated of Alexander. In Leibniz's terms
it could be said that each sentence is a way of saying that the
concept of Alexander contains the concept of dying in Babylon.
For Leibniz, this would be to make an assertion about the
content of a certain timeless concept; it would be to say that
the concept of Alexander which an omniscient being has contains the concept of dying in Babylon.[2]

There seems to be no reason, then, why a substance should
not be said to have a single complete concept. It may also be
asked how, if each substance does have a complete concept,
we can distinguish one substance from another, in view of the
fact that such a concept must be very complex—indeed, is
declared by Leibniz to be of infinite complexity.[3] Leibniz
would reply that to distinguish one substance from another
we do not need to be able to give a complete analysis of their
concepts; that is, we do not need to have what he calls 'adequate'
knowledge.[4] For example, suppose that someone mentions
a person whom he calls 'Alexander', and that we think that he
is talking about Alexander the Great. To discover that he is in

---

[1] It is true that, before Alexander's death, someone might have imagined
a future historian saying 'Alexander died in Babylon'. But it is the historian
who is supposed to be living after the event who is imagined as saying this;
the person who imagines him would not use the past tense if speaking *in
propria persona*.

[2] Cf. § 1.2, pp. 13 ff.   [3] Cf. § 5.4.   [4] Cf. § 1.3, p. 15, n. 8.

fact talking about (say) the son of Priam, it is only necessary to note that some[1] of the predicates which he ascribes to Alexander are predicates of Paris, but not of Alexander the Great, and this can be done without any very lengthy inquiry into what he means by 'Alexander'.

We now reach a much more important, indeed a fundamental question. Leibniz has been saying that a complete concept is one which serves to identify an individual; it does not merely mark off or distinguish one *kind* of thing from another—that would be done by a 'full' concept—it distinguishes one *particular* thing from others. The question is, whether this is so: whether a concept can, in Leibniz's phrase, be 'sufficiently determinate for' an individual; whether there is not an irreducible difference between what may be called 'referring' expressions, such as 'this man' or 'Alexander', which serve to point to or indicate an individual, and descriptive expressions such as 'human' or 'Alexandrian'.

This problem can be approached through a consequence of what Leibniz has said. If a complete concept serves to identify an individual substance, then there cannot be two substances with the same complete concept; in other words, there cannot be two substances which are exactly alike. This proposition is generally known by the name which Leibniz gives to it, that of the principle of the identity of indiscernibles.[2] By calling something 'indiscernible' from another Leibniz seems to mean that the two are exactly alike; a declaration of the identity of indiscernibles is the statement that if (as is not the case) two substances were exactly alike, then they would be identical—

---

[1] It is not possible, *a priori*, to say *how many*. A man who ascribes to Alexander one predicate which belongs to the son of Priam, not to the son of Philip, may mean to talk about Alexander the Great, and may simply have made a mistake. If he continues to talk in this way, however, it becomes increasingly probable that it is the son of Priam who is meant.

[2] *To Clarke*, § 4.5. This principle is often stated by Leibniz: e.g. G ii. 54, 250; G iv. 514 (L 822); *DM*, par. 9; *Mon.*, par. 9; *To Clarke*, § 5.21, 23; *NE*, Pref. (A vi. 6, 58; G v. 50–51), 2. 27. 1, 3; C 8, 519–20 (L 413); Schmidt, p. 476.

not two substances, but one. An examination of this principle will help us to evaluate what Leibniz says about the capacity of the complete concept of a substance to differentiate it from all other substances.

§ 5.2. First it is necessary to be clear about what Leibniz means by the principle of the identity of indiscernibles. It is evidently a proposition about substances; Leibniz does not wish to deny that a geometer, for example, can speak properly of triangles which are exactly alike, but he insists that such triangles are abstractions and not substances.[1] What is not quite clear, however, is whether he wishes to say that to suppose two indiscernible substances is self-contradictory, or whether he means that, although there might be two such substances, in fact there are not. In the last section it was argued that the identity of indiscernibles follows necessarily from what Leibniz says about the completeness of the concept of a substance, and Leibniz himself says that this is so.[2] He has also indicated that by a substance he *means* that which has a complete concept;[3] for him, therefore, the proposition that a substance has a complete concept, able to identify it, is a logically necessary truth, from which it follows that he should regard the identity of indiscernibles as logically necessary.

On the whole, this is what he does seem to mean, but the issue is a complicated one. It is complicated, in the first place, by the fact that Leibniz also says that if there were two substances which are alike in all respects, then it must be possible to give some reason why they are diverse, i.e. why there are two of them.[4] This reason must be sought from some difference in them;[5] but they have been assumed to be exactly alike, from which it follows that there cannot be two such substances. Now if Leibniz, in saying that there must be a reason for the diversity,

[1] C 8, 519.   [2] *DM*, par. 9.
[3] He has said (§ 5.1, pp. 125–6) that every substance has a complete concept and that everything which has a complete concept is a substance; this means that the terms 'being a substance' and 'having a complete concept' are equivalent.   [4] C 519.   [5] C 8, 519; *NE*, 2. 27. 3.

had in mind the principle of the best, then the identity of indiscernibles would be contingent. However, this is probably not what he has in mind. He often indicates that when he says that the diversity between two substances must have a reason he is referring to what we have called the principle of sufficient reason, which is related to the view that in every true proposition the concept of the predicate is contained in that of the subject,[1] from which the proposition that the concept of a substance must be complete is itself derived. When he says, then, that it must be possible to give some reason for a numerical difference between two substances which resemble each other entirely, he must mean that the concept of being numerically different from the other must be included in the concept of each. This is only to put in other words the argument that if one substance differs only numerically from another, then the concept of that difference must be contained in its complete concept, which contains everything which can truly be said of the substance.

Leibniz uses similar reasoning to establish what Couturat calls the 'principle of symmetry', and declares to have a close affinity with the principle of the identity of indiscernibles.[2] The principle states that 'If, in the hypotheses, everything is alike on both sides, there can be no difference in the conclusions'.[3] This is perhaps most clearly explained by a postulate of Archimedes, which Leibniz regards as an instance of the principle. Leibniz says that:[4]

It is assumed by Archimedes as one of the foundations of the whole of statics that two equal weights, *A* and *B*, which are equally distant

---

[1] This is stated explicitly in C 10, which says that the identity of indiscernibles follows from the 'great principle', *praedicatum inest subjecto*. The line of argument in C 519 is clearly the same.

[2] C. L., pp. 227–8.

[3] C 389. Cf. C 519, which is mistranslated by Loemker, L 413.

[4] C 402; cf. G. vii. 301 (L 349-50), 309; *To Clarke*, § 2.1; C 514, 519. It may be added that the argument which Leibniz uses here is by no means obsolete, a similar one being advanced by N. Feather, in *Mass, Length and Time* (London, 1961), pp. 140, 162.

from the centre of motion C, are in equilibrium. This is a corollary of our axiom [sc. the principle of sufficient reason]; for if there should be any diversity, then (by our axiom) some reason can be given for it. But, by hypothesis, this cannot be given; for everything on both sides is assumed to be in the same state, and so it cannot follow from this that they are diverse.

Leibniz also claims that similar reasoning establishes the axiom of Euclid, that 'If equals are added to equals, the wholes are equal'.[1]

Couturat is right in saying that the principles of symmetry and of the identity of indiscernibles resemble each other, to the extent that similar arguments are brought for each. At the same time there is an important difference between them, in that the principle of the identity of indiscernibles has to do with substances, whereas the principle of symmetry has not. The argument just described assumes that there is no difference between two weights; that is, that the two are exactly similar. From the identity of indiscernibles, however, it follows that this can only be true if the weights are not being regarded as substances, but as abstractions. The other use of the principle of symmetry, to establish an axiom of Euclid, clearly has to do with abstractions, from which it follows that if (as is reasonable) one takes metaphysics to be about the nature of what there is, the principle of symmetry does not belong to Leibniz's metaphysics.

To return to the identity of indiscernibles: the evidence so far considered seems to give overwhelming support to the view that Leibniz thought that it is, strictly speaking, self-contradictory to suppose the existence of two indiscernible substances. In his fifth paper to Clarke, however, he says that he means, not that it is absolutely impossible to suppose two indiscernible bodies, but that the existence of two such bodies would be contrary to the divine wisdom, and so is not found.[2] In saying that it would be contrary to the divine wisdom Leibniz seems

---

[1] C 514.   [2] *To Clarke*, § 5.25.

to mean¹ that God would have no reason for creating two exactly similar bodies. Suppose, for example, that in creating the universe God decides to fill one space with one body, *A*, and another with an exactly similar body, *B*. Which body he puts in which space can only be arbitrary, i.e. without reason; but since God does nothing without reason, there can be no such bodies. This is a different view from that described earlier, and to reconcile the two it must be supposed² that the view just mentioned, which makes of the identity of indiscernibles a contingent truth, was adopted by Leibniz for controversial purposes. On this interpretation Leibniz will be saying that, even if it were consistent to say that there are two indiscernible bodies (and it is not), yet it would still be false. It may be added that Leibniz has been speaking of two indiscernible *bodies*, and that he also thinks that a body is not a substance, but is the appearance of a multiplicity of substances.³ All that this argument could show, therefore, is that there are no two indiscernible *classes* of substances.

Mention may be made here of something else that Leibniz says about the identity of indiscernibles, which seems to have been meant to have only a persuasive force. He sometimes remarks that the identity of indiscernibles is confirmed by experience, mentioning the fact that someone who claimed to be able to produce two exactly similar leaves could not do so, and that the microscope shows differences between drops of liquid which look the same to the naked eye.⁴ This is again based on the appearances of substances, no Leibnizian substance being itself visible, even with the help of the most powerful microscope. Further, even if someone did discover two exactly similar leaves, or even if two drops of water looked exactly similar when examined through a microscope, Leibniz's belief in the identity of indiscernibles would not be

¹ Cf. *To Clarke*, §§ 4.3, 5.21.
² Cf. C. D. Broad, *Ethics and the History of Philosophy* (London, 1952), pp. 177–8.   ³ Cf. § 5.7.
⁴ G vii. 563; *NE*, 2. 27. 3; *To Clarke*, § 4.4.

shaken; he would still say that there must be a difference between any two substances, even if this difference is not detect-
able by the senses.

In sum, Leibniz seems to mean by the principle of the
identity of indiscernibles what he should mean if he is to be
consistent: namely, that it is self-contradictory to suppose two
indiscernible substances. It has now to be seen whether Leibniz
has succeeded in showing that this is so. What is at issue here,
it should be remembered, is not simply the necessary truth of
the identity of indiscernibles, but also the proposition from
which its necessary truth follows—that every substance has
a complete concept, which is sufficient to identify it. If the
identity of indiscernibles is not necessarily true—if it is not true
at all, or if its truth is only contingent—then the view which
implies its necessary truth is false. Of course, if the identity
of indiscernibles is necessarily true, this does not mean that
a complete concept can identify a substance; to say this would
be to commit the fallacy of the consequent.[1] In other words,
the necessary truth of the identity of indiscernibles is a necessary,
but not a sufficient, condition of the truth of what Leibniz says
about the completeness of the concept of a substance.

It can be said in answer to these problems that Leibniz's
metaphysics itself implies that the identity of indiscernibles is
not a necessary truth.[2] As is well known, Leibniz argues that
souls are substances;[3] that, indeed, all substances are either
souls or soul-like. But, it has been argued, it is logically possible that two souls should be exactly alike, so that, for example,
whatever perceptions either soul may have, the other has
exactly similar perceptions. However unlikely this supposition
may seem, it is not self-contradictory, from which it follows

[1] If the identity of indiscernibles also implies that the complete concept
of a substance can identify it, then the two propositions will be equivalent
and a proof of the necessary truth of the one will be a proof of the necessary
truth of the other. Leibniz, however, does not seem to argue that this is so,
nor is it obvious what line of argument he could have used.

[2] This is argued by P. F. Strawson, in *Individuals* (London, 1959), p. 125.

[3] G iv. 473, 482 (L 745). Cf. § 5.8.

that Leibniz must either give up his view that souls are substances (and it is almost certain that he would not), or he must
say that the identity of indiscernibles is not a necessary truth.
He might still say that it is true, because God, of his own free
will, decided to create a universe in which no one substance is
exactly like any other; if so, the argument cited earlier from the
fifth paper to Clarke[1] turns out to be of central importance and
not to be merely peripheral, introduced only for controversial
purposes. But though this is an argument for its truth, it is only
an argument for its contingent truth; and, as has already been
seen, the identity of indiscernibles must be necessarily true if
the concept of a substance is to be sufficient to identify it.

There seems to be no way out of this difficulty for Leibniz.
He could make the identity of indiscernibles necessarily true
by identifying a substance with its complete concept, from
which it would follow by definition that a difference between
substances is a difference between concepts.[2] But there is no
indication that he accepts such an identification, and there is
good reason to believe that he would reject it. It seems clear,
in the first place, that to say that a substance is or is like a soul
is not to say that it is a concept; souls may have concepts, but
a soul is not the same as a concept. Second, if a substance were
a complete concept then it would be reasonable to say that it
is an aggregate of its component concepts; but Leibniz denies
that an aggregate can be a substance.[3] Finally, if Leibniz had
identified a substance with a complete concept he would have
solved one difficulty only at the expense of creating another.
It will be seen later that he regards a created substance as having
a temporal existence;[4] but such existence cannot be predicated
of a complete concept.[5] So, for example, although Alexander
the Great had a temporal existence, his complete concept has
not. All this indicates that Leibniz must seek some other
solution.

[1] Cf. p. 132.   [2] Cf. Strawson, op. cit., pp. 126 ff.   [3] § 5.7.
[4] § 5.4: a substance is such that from any one of its states its past and future
states can be inferred. Cf. G ii. 43.   [5] Cf. § 5.1, p. 128.

It might perhaps be thought that the following line of argument is open to him. Suppose, first, that the identity of indiscernibles is necessarily true of physical objects. This seems a reasonable assumption to make, as it certainly seemed to Locke, who remarked that we do not conceive it possible that 'two things of the same kind should exist in the same place at the same time'.[1] Suppose, next, that for every human soul[2] there is necessarily a body. Further, suppose that for any human body there is necessarily no more than one soul, so that two souls cannot (even temporarily) share the same body. Finally, suppose that from the predicates of a soul it is possible to infer the location of its body—not necessarily at all times, but at any rate at some time or times. This means that a man's perceptions—visual, tactual, etc.—are such that he can at least sometimes say 'My body is at this time in such and such a place'. Given all this, now suppose that two souls, A and B, are exactly alike. It follows that their bodies must at some time occupy the same place. But it is impossible that two bodies should do this, since the identity of indiscernibles has been granted to hold of material things; it has also been granted that it is impossible that A and B should, even temporarily, share the same body. It must therefore be said that A and B are not two souls, but that 'A' and 'B' are two names for the same soul; that is, the identity of indiscernibles is true of souls also.

There are, however, fatal weaknesses in what is said here about the relations between souls and bodies. It is not obvious why it should be logically necessary that two souls should never share the same body; nor is it obvious why it should be logically necessary that for every human soul there is a body. Indeed, Leibniz himself would not accept the argument which has just been suggested. He does say that for every created soul there is a body,[3] and he would agree that a body's location can

---

[1] *Essay concerning Human Understanding*, 2. 27. 1.

[2] There is no need for Leibniz to argue for the identity of indiscernibles in the case of God, since for him there is necessarily only one God.

[3] G ii. 253 (L 865); G vi. 545; G vii. 530; C 14.

be inferred from the predicates of its soul,[1] but he regards the former as only a contingent truth. He says, for example, that God can deprive a created substance of what he calls *materia secunda*,[2] i.e. of body,[3] from which it follows that he would say that a created soul without a body is logically conceivable.

It seems, then, that neither of these two solutions to Leibniz's difficulty about the identity of indiscernibles would have been accepted by Leibniz himself. It is not clear what other solution he could offer, so that it must be said that he is unable to establish the necessary truth of the identity of indiscernibles, from which it follows that he cannot maintain his views about the complete concept of a substance. They may still be true, but Leibniz cannot consistently say that they are.

§ 5.3. Although the identity of indiscernibles is by no means the only consequence which, Leibniz claims, follows from his view that the concept of a substance is complete, there is good reason for having considered it first. The other propositions about the nature which substances must have which Leibniz claims to derive from his logic do not in fact follow from his logic alone; the identity of indiscernibles, however, does, so that if it is not a necessary truth neither is the proposition from which it is derived. Now that this has been said, it might seem proper to examine at once these other consequences, with a view to justifying the assertion that they do not follow from Leibniz's logic alone. However, another question has a prior claim on our attention. What has been considered so far has been Leibniz's attempt at explaining the rules in accordance with which the term 'individual substance' is used. Nothing has yet been said about his reasons for supposing that this

---

[1] This follows from his view that each substance 'expresses' the whole universe: cf. § 5.4. The arguments to be discussed in § 5.4 are based on Leibniz's views about the complete concept of a substance, and so cannot be used to justify these views. However, it is sufficient for our present purposes that Leibniz accepted the proposition that a body's location can be inferred from the predicates of its soul.

[2] G ii. 325.   [3] G vii. 529.

terminology is justified—for supposing, in other words, that there are individual substances. These reasons are not derived from his logic, nor does Leibniz say that they are, but they can hardly be left out of a study of his metaphysics.

Leibniz seems to think it obvious that the concept of God is complete—at any rate, he calls God an infinite and eternal substance[1]—and since, as has been seen, he argues that there is a God, it follows that there must be at least one substance. It has also been seen, however, that Leibniz thinks that there are large numbers of created substances, of which Alexander the Great, Julius Caesar, and the sphere on Archimedes' tomb are only three random examples, and it now has to be asked why he believes this.

It might be thought that the answer has already been given, when it was explained in the last chapter[2] why Leibniz asserts that there are contingent things. However, it would be possible to argue that although there is *something* contingent, created by God, what we normally count as things are only forms or 'modes' of one created substance; or it might be said that there are just two created substances, what we call 'minds' being forms of one mental substance and what we call 'bodies' being forms of one corporeal substance. The latter view has some similarities to Spinoza's, with the important difference that what have been called mental and corporeal substances are regarded by Spinoza as attributes of one and the same substance.

Leibniz, it seems, has two main arguments to bring against such views. Sometimes he borrows an argument from Bayle against the view that there is only one mental substance, or (as Spinoza would say) that there is only one attribute of thought, of which minds are the modes. It is, he says, absurd to suppose that God thinks, believes, and wills one thing in me and thinks,

---

[1] G vii. 301 (L 349), 530; *DM*, par. 8; *PNG*, pars. 8–9; *NE*, 3. 3. 18. God is also called a 'monad' (G iii. 636 (L 1072); G vii. 502; Grua, pp. 393, 396, 398–9), and the dominant or primitive unity of the universe (G vii. 302 (L 789); *Mon.*, par. 47; Grua, p. 126); these are alternative names for a Leibnizian substance (cf. § 5.6).

[2] § 4.4.

believes, and wills the contrary in another.[1] In the form in
which Leibniz expresses it this is a superficial argument, which
Spinoza could have answered by pointing out that it rests on
an elementary confusion between the language which is
appropriately used of modes and the language which is appropriately used of God. Spinoza would readily admit that
there are modes of thought which contradict each other, but
he would say that these modes are mere fragments of the divine
understanding, and that if this could be grasped in its entirety
it would be realized that what God thinks is not only self-
consistent, but is also necessarily true.[2]

But although Leibniz's argument is poor, it is directed against
a genuinely weak point in Spinozism. First, as he points out,[3]
Spinoza has not succeeded in proving deductively that there is
only one substance, or that particular things are modes of the
attributes of God. It seems likely, however, that Spinoza had
other reasons for regarding material things at any rate as modes
of what he called the attribute of extension. The science of his
time had made great advances by regarding material things as
temporary forms of a homogeneous matter, and Spinoza's
modal terminology could be a way of expressing this. It would
be justified, not by deductive methods, but on the grounds that
it is a way of expressing established scientific concepts. Leibniz
could reply that even if the modal terminology is justified in
the case of material things (though his mature view was that
it is not), it is only justified there; that there was no comparable
reason to suppose that minds are modes of a single attribute of
thought, and consequently no reason to reject the generally
held view that each mind is an individual and not a mode or
form of something else.[4]

This argument might seem to be limited, in that it can only

[1] G vi. 537 (L 908).
[2] See especially *Ethics*, Book II, Props. 32–35.
[3] G i. 145, 148 (L 309, 312).
[4] Cf. G i. 145 (1678): 'It does not yet seem certain to me that bodies are
substances. It is otherwise with minds.' On bodies as substances, see below,
§ 5.7.

show that the view that there are many substances is one which
there is no reason to reject. To give a reason for supposing that
there are many substances, Leibniz turns to the principle of the
best. The world, he has argued, must be as rich as possible;
consequently there must be, not merely many substances, but
an infinity of substances.[1] This enables him to establish a connexion between his definitions of contingent truth. He has said
that a truth is contingent when the inclusion of the concept of
the predicate in that of the subject can be shown only by an
infinite analysis;[2] he has also said that a contingent truth is one
which depends upon the principle of the best.[3] The connexion
between the two definitions is now clear. God, in creating the
best possible world, *ipso facto* creates a world in which there
is an infinity of substances; and since to give a reason for
a single contingent thing involves a knowledge of all the rest
of the universe,[4] this would be an infinite task.

It must be stressed that, in saying that there is an infinity of
substances, Leibniz does not mean that all possible *kinds* of substances exist;[5] to say this would be to side with Spinoza, and
to deny what Leibniz thinks to be obviously true. He is saying,
then, that although there is an infinity of substances, not only
might there have been a finite number, or indeed no created
substances at all, but the substances which do exist could have
been of other kinds. But although Leibniz thinks that there are
respects in which substances might have been different from
what they are, he also thinks that there are other respects in
which they could not have differed. It has already been mentioned that he seems to argue that the identity of indiscernibles

---

[1] G ii. 460. Leibniz also says here that an infinity of substances is demanded
by 'the order of things, otherwise phenomena would not correspond to all
assignable percipients'. He seems to have in mind his doctrine of 'little
perceptions' (discussed later, § 5.10), according to which each perception
consists of an infinity of 'little perceptions' of which we have no separate
awareness, and the argument appears to be that a substance must correspond
to each of these little perceptions. Usually, however, he argues *from* the fact
that there is an infinity of substances *to* the conclusion that each perception
must consist of an infinity of little perceptions.

[2] § 3.4.   [3] § 4.7.   [4] § 3.4.   [5] Cf. § 4.8.

is logically necessary, in that the concept of a substance must be complete,[1] from which it follows that no two substances can be exactly alike. Similarly he must hold that any other attributes of a substance which are derived from the completeness of its concept must also belong to it necessarily, and not by virtue of having been chosen by God. It is now time to see what Leibniz thinks these attributes are, and how he argues for them. First, however, a word about terminology. As the rest of this chapter will be concerned chiefly with created substances, it will be convenient to refer to these henceforth as 'substances' simply, using the expression 'created substance' only when there would otherwise be some ambiguity.

§ 5.4. Leibniz has said that the complete concept of a substance 'suffices to comprehend and render deducible from it all the predicates of the subject to which this concept is attributed'.[2] But, he continues, all things are connected;[3] consequently, the complete concept of a substance contains relations to the whole series (suite) of things.[4] Since the universe, the 'whole series of things', consists of an infinity of substances, the complete concept of a substance may be said to 'envelop the infinite'.[5] For example, the complete concept of Alexander the Great would have to include Alexander's relations to everything in the universe, and not simply over a limited period of time, but over the whole of time. Such a concept, it is hardly necessary to add, is one which God alone can have.[6] From these premisses Leibniz draws the important conclusion[7] that each substance must 'express' or 'represent' the whole universe.[8]

[1] Cf. § 5.2, p. 130.   [2] DM, par. 8. Cf. § 5.1, p. 125.
[3] Ibid., par. 8.   [4] G ii. 37.   [5] G iv. 475. Cf. C 376.
[6] DM, par. 8.
[7] Ibid., par. 9. Cf. G ii. 57 (L 517); G vii. 316–17, 321–2.
[8] On substance as 'expressing' the whole universe see also G ii. 19; G vii. 311–12; DM, pars. 14, 26, 33; Mon., par. 62. On 'representation' see G iv. 484 (L 747); G vi. 326–7; Mon., par. 62; C 15. In a sense (as Mon., par. 56 and C 15 state) what a substance expresses is the rest of the universe, other than itself. It may be that this is what Leibniz means when he says that

In Leibniz's terminology, one thing 'expresses' another when 'there is a constant and regular relation between what can be said of the one and of the other';[1] that is, when there is 'a certain constant relational law, by which particulars (*singula*) in the one can be referred to corresponding particulars in the other'.[2] For example, an ellipse 'expresses' or 'represents' a circle, in that 'to each point on the circle there corresponds one on the ellipse, and conversely, following a certain relational law'.[3] As will be seen later,[4] the 'particulars' in a substance are not its parts, since a substance has no parts, but are its predicates. When Leibniz says, therefore, that a substance expresses the whole universe, he may be taken to mean that the predicates of any substance, say A, correspond to the predicates of others, in such a way that from the predicates of A alone all the predicates of all other substances can be inferred. This explanation will require some refinement later, but may serve for the present.

It is now clear why Leibniz should say that a substance is a 'mirror of the universe';[5] the point of the metaphor is that just as the whole of a room can be seen in a suitably curved mirror, without looking directly at the room, so the whole universe can in a sense be seen in one substance. The analogy breaks down, however, in that at any one time a mirror can reflect things only as they are at any one time—a window-frame as it now is, a star as it was millions of years ago—whereas a substance at any moment expresses all states of substances at all times, including its own past and future states.[6] To

a substance expresses or represents the whole universe; he may, on the other hand, have in mind his view that the present state of a substance expresses all states of all substances, including the past and future states of the substance itself (see below, p. 143). It is, in any event, hard to see that there is a genuine contradiction here, as is argued by H. W. B. Joseph, *The Philosophy of Leibniz*, pp. 146–7.   [1] G ii. 112 (L 521).   [2] C 15.
   [3] G i. 383; cf. C 15. In G vii. 263–4 (L 318) Leibniz says that what correspond in that which expresses and that which is expressed are relations.
   [4] § 5.6.
   [5] G iv. 557 (L 937); G vi. 626; DM, par. 9; PNG, pars. 3, 12; Mon., pars. 56, 63, 83; To Clarke, § 5.87; C 15.   [6] e.g. DM, par. 9.

call attention to the fact that a substance expresses the past and future, Leibniz says that its present is 'big with the future and laden with the past',[1] or that there are at all times in a substance the residue of what has happened to it and the marks of what will happen to it.[2] The fact that the present state of a substance expresses the substance's past and future states was not allowed for in the provisional explanation of Leibniz's meaning given earlier; this can now be given a more exact form, as follows. Take any substance, say A: for any predicate, say P, of any substance in the universe, there is at any instant of A's history a predicate of A, say Q, such that P can be inferred from Q. P may be some other predicate of A itself, so that the present state of A expresses A's past and future states, as well as all states of all other substances.

All this is claimed by Leibniz to follow from the fact that the complete concept of a substance involves the whole universe. For example, it is because the complete concept of Alexander the Great involves the whole universe that Leibniz says that there are at all times in the soul of Alexander (i.e. in Alexander the substance)[3] traces of all that has happened to him and marks of all that will happen to him, and even traces of all that happens in the universe, though God alone can recognize all these.[4] Leibniz seems to think that the conclusion is obvious, given the premises; yet it is surely not obvious that because the complete concept of Alexander contains the concept of dying in Babylon, Alexander himself must from birth have contained some mark or indication of the place of his future death. Still less is it obvious that if the complete concept of Alexander contains the concepts of all that ever happens in the universe, Alexander must contain the marks or traces of everything that happens. Leibniz, one may think, has been misled by his failure to

---

[1] PNG, par. 13; NE, Pref. (G v. 48; A vi. 6, 55); cf. G ii. 282 (L 879), 503 (L 999); G iv. 563 (L 943); G vi. 329; Mon., par. 22.
[2] DM, par. 8.   [3] Cf. § 5.8.
[4] DM, par. 8. The nature of these marks and traces does not concern us at present; it will be seen later that they are the appetitions and perceptions of Alexander (§§ 5.8 and 5.9).

distinguish clearly between what were called earlier[1] the subject of a proposition and the concept of the subject, and the
predicate and the concept of the predicate.

It is possible, however, that Leibniz did not derive his views
about a substance's expression of the universe solely from the
premisses which he stated, but also had in mind some other,
suppressed premiss or premisses.[2] Perhaps he reasoned as follows. Let us consider Alexander from the standpoint of a creative deity. God decides to actualize the concept of an Alexander
who dies in Babylon;[3] that is, he creates an Alexander who *will*
die in Babylon. To speak of an Alexander who will die in
Babylon is to speak of an Alexander whose death in Babylon
follows with certainty (though, Leibniz would insist, not with
necessity)[4] from his preceding states; and since it follows from
them with certainty it could in theory be predicted from them,
i.e. they may be said to contain marks of the place of his future
death. Similarly, the Alexander who is created is an Alexander
who will have certain relations to the battle of Waterloo—for
example, the battle will occur at such and such a time after
his death; therefore the date of the battle must follow with

---

[1] § 1.1.

[2] That Leibniz made use of suppressed premisses in deriving from his
logic conclusions which relate to metaphysics has been suggested by C. D.
Broad, *Theoria*, 1949, p. 66. In Broad's view, Leibniz's argument was
probably this. Suppose, for example, that it is true that Queen Elizabeth I
sneezed at 5 p.m. on Christmas Day 1597. Since it was already true when she
was created that she would sneeze at this time, she must have been created
with a certain modification (i.e. a certain predicate) corresponding to this
part of her complete concept. 'Since it is true at every moment of her
history up to the date of reference … that she *will* then sneeze, this modification must have persisted until then. And, since it is true at every moment
after then that she *did* then sneeze, the same modification must persist in her
after then for as long as she continues to exist.' This persistent modification
in the substance is called by Broad the 'ontological correlate' of the timeless
fact of the Queen's sneeze. Broad's suggestion seems to be analogous to the
explanation to be offered above; he does not, however, say how this suggestion is to be used to explain Leibniz's views about a substance's expression
of the universe, including its own past and future states.

[3] Cf. *DM*, par. 14; G ii. 37, 54 (L 514); C 520 (L 414).

[4] See, e.g., *DM*, par. 13; C 520. Cf. § 4.6, p. 100.

certainty from his predicates; i.e. it can in theory be inferred
from them. If this is what Leibniz has in mind, then the expression of the whole universe by any substance does seem to follow; but, as will have been noticed, the premisses from which
it follows include Leibniz's theistic doctrines, and so are not
purely logical.

So far, the discussion has concerned the correctness of Leibniz's derivation of a conclusion. It is now time to consider, not
whether the conclusion follows, but whether it is true; indeed
whether it is, as Leibniz claims, necessarily true. No more need
be said at this stage about Leibniz's theism, but something must
be said about another of his premisses, the proposition that all
substances are connected. If this proposition is only a contingent
truth, then what follows from it will only be contingent; and
in fact the arguments which Leibniz brings do not seem to
establish its necessary truth. Sometimes Leibniz says merely
that 'there is no thing on which some true denomination, at
any rate of comparison and relation, cannot be imposed from
another'.[1] If this is true, it does not appear to be necessarily
true. We do say that certain things cannot be compared in
certain respects, in the sense that such a comparison would be
odd or inappropriate. In this sense, we say that a sonnet cannot
be compared with an epic, or that eating a peach cannot be
compared with hearing a symphony.[2] It seems possible, then,
that there might be certain substances which cannot be compared at all; if there are no such substances, this is only a contingent fact. Another argument which Leibniz uses to show
that all substances, or rather all material substances, are connected clearly has as its conclusion a contingent proposition.
The universe, Leibniz has argued, is a *plenum*; that is, there is
no vacuum in nature.[3] From this, he says, it follows that any
action of one body on another must be transmitted to all others,

[1] C 521 (L 414).
[2] We also say that there is no comparison between *A* and *B* when we
mean that the one is enormously superior to the other; this is not the sense
which is in mind here.   [3] § 4.8, p. 112.

somewhat as 'in a vessel full of liquid . . . a motion set up in the middle is propagated to the edges'.[1] If true, this is plainly a contingent truth, since the proposition from which it follows —that there is no vacuum—is itself contingent, being dependent upon the principle of the best.

It seems, however, that Leibniz could bring an argument for the necessary truth of the proposition that all substances are connected. Though he does not seem to say so explicitly, he may think that a substance can only be identified by its complete concept if it is considered in relation to all others. To take a crude example: suppose that someone says, 'Please give me that pen', and that somebody replies, 'What pen?' The answer may be, say, 'The pen on the desk', and if it is then asked 'The pen on what desk?' the answer may be extended to 'The pen on the desk in the corner', and so on. Leibniz would probably say that if the pen is to be identified by a description, then this must take in the entire universe. We, of course, do not identify objects in this way, but Leibniz would say that this can be done by an infinite intellect, and that it is the only absolutely precise way of identifying an object. If a substance, then, is to be identified by its description or concept, it must be related to all others, and since Leibniz regards the former as necessarily true, he would regard the latter as necessarily true also.

It seems, then, that Leibniz could have derived from his logic the necessary truth of the proposition that every substance is related to all others. However, there are other criticisms which can be brought against his view that each substance expresses the whole universe. One such criticism is that this view involves a logical contradiction. The being and activity of a Leibnizian substance, it is said,[2] lie exclusively in its representations. But then the whole world of substances is dissolved into a system of representations or expressions; each substance is nothing but a representation of others, which in turn are only representations. One is left with a system of relations without any terms,

---

[1] C 521 (L 415). Cf. PNG, par. 3; Mon., par. 61; C 15.
[2] Heimsoeth, op. cit., p. 280 n. 1. Cf. Mahnke, pp. 196–7.

which is a contradiction of the very notion of a relation. This would indeed be a self-contradictory view, but the supposition that Leibniz is committed to holding it seems to rest on a misunderstanding. It appears to be assumed that a representation—that is, a predicate of a substance—derives its character from what it represents, as a mirror-image may be said to do. But this is to take Leibniz's metaphor of the mirror literally, which he warns us not to do.[1] According to Leibniz, a substance derives its predicates from God, and from God alone; it behaves as if there were nothing but God and itself in the world.[2]

But even if this criticism can be met, another can be brought to which Leibniz seems to have no effective answer. It can be argued convincingly that his views about a substance's expression of the universe entail his theses about extrinsic denominations, and it has already been pointed out that these cannot be sustained.[3] There were, it may be remembered, a weaker and a stronger thesis, the weaker stating that relational propositions are reducible to subject-predicate propositions.[4] (The term 'predicate', here and in what follows, is taken in the narrow sense,[5] which excludes relations.) That this is a consequence of Leibniz's view that a substance expresses the universe can be shown as follows. Suppose, for example, that A is father of B, and that A (as Leibniz would say that he is) is a substance. The complete concept of A must contain the concept of being father of B; there must therefore be some mark or trace in A, such that an omniscient being could tell from it that A is father of B. But a mark or trace is a predicate, from which it follows that an omniscient being could tell that A is father of B by his knowledge of the predicates of A alone. In other words, from a knowledge of the predicates of A alone it can be inferred that he is father of B. For Leibniz, however, the statement that something is inferred from something else is the statement that it is contained in that something else.[6] The relational term 'father of', therefore, must be contained in the predicates of A;

[1] G vi. 626.   [2] Cf. § 5.5, p. 150.   [3] § 2.3.
[4] § 2.2, pp. 42 ff.   [5] Cf. § 2.2, p. 40.   [6] Cf. § 1.6.

and since it is not itself a predicate, it must be a way of referring to a certain predicate or predicates of *A*. In short, the relational term 'father of' is logically superfluous, being (in the terminology used in Chapter I) 'reducible to' a predicate or predicates.[1] The same can be said, not only of the proposition '*A* is the father of *B*', but of all propositions about the relations between substances.

This is a large part of Leibniz's weaker thesis about extrinsic denominations, but it is not the whole of it. What has been said so far concerns only the relations between substances, whereas Leibniz would also say that relational propositions about the states of one substance are also reducible to subject-predicate propositions; that, for example, a proposition such as '*A* is now more alert than he was yesterday' is reducible to subject-predicate propositions which describe *A*'s states at certain times. However, this too can be derived from what Leibniz says about expression. It will be remembered that he asserts each *state* of a substance to express all states of all substances at all times, including the past and future states of the substance itself; in the soul of Alexander, for example, there are at all times traces of all that has happened to him, and marks of all that will happen to him.[2] Leibniz could say, then, that from a present state of *A*, and from this state alone, it can ideally be inferred that *A* is more alert than he was yesterday. From this stage, the argument is the same as in the last paragraph. A state of a substance is a predicate of a substance; therefore the relational proposition '*A* is more alert than he was yesterday' is reducible to a subject-predicate proposition about *A*.

It may be replied that the whole of Leibniz's weaker thesis about extrinsic denominations has still not been derived. The propositions just established, it might be said, are about substances only, whereas Leibniz's original thesis made no mention of substances, and may therefore be about all relational propositions without exception. To this it may be answered that Leibniz would say that all propositions are ultimately reducible

------

[1] § 1.6, p. 33.   [2] *DM*, par. 8.

to propositions about substances,[1] so that if all propositions about substances either are or are reducible to propositions of the subject-predicate form, the same can be said of all propositions absolutely.

The same arguments which establish Leibniz's weaker thesis about extrinsic denominations also establish his stronger thesis. This was, that the relations between A and B can be inferred from a knowledge of A or of B alone,[2] which is clearly just the view that each substance expresses the whole universe. That Leibniz sometimes means this when he says that there are no purely extrinsic denominations can be shown in the following way, adapting an example used by Leibniz himself. Suppose that B, the only son of A, dies; on his death, A ceases to have a son.[3] From what Leibniz has said about a substance's expression of the whole universe, it follows that there must be some mark or trace of this in A; consequently, however distant from each other A and B may be, there must be some change in the predicates of A when B dies. Leibniz also accepts this conclusion as following from his view that there are no purely extrinsic denominations. 'Taking things as one perceives them', he says, it is indeed true that when a man's son dies the man ceases to have a son without there being any change in him. 'In metaphysical rigour', however, this cannot be said; there are no purely extrinsic denominations, and so there must be some change in the man.[4] This shows, then, that Leibniz

---

[1] Abstractions as logically superfluous: C 243, 389, 433, 435, 512–13; Grua, pp. 547, 548 (C 400). [2] § 2.3, p. 45.

[3] Slight alterations have been made to Leibniz's text. Leibniz, who took his example from Locke (*Essay concerning Human Understanding*, 2. 25. 5), writes of a man ceasing to be a father on the death of his son—presumably an only child. This, however, is not in accordance with modern usage: a man may still be called a father after his only child dies, perhaps because 'to be father of . . .' is taken to mean 'to have engendered . . .'.

[4] *NE*, 2. 25. 5; cf. G vii. 321–2 (L 606): 'No one becomes a widower in India on the death of his wife in Europe without a real change occurring in him.' This also seems to be what is meant when Leibniz says in C 520 (L 414) that 'As often as the denomination of a thing is changed, there must be some variation in the thing itself'.

sometimes takes the statement that there are no purely extrinsic denominations to mean that a knowledge of the relations of a substance *A* to others can ideally be derived from a knowledge of *A* alone.

The upshot of these arguments has been that Leibniz's view that each substance expresses the whole universe implies the truth of his two theses about extrinsic denominations. But as these have already been shown to be false, the proposition which implies them must be false also.

§ 5.5. Besides saying of each substance that it expresses the whole universe, Leibniz says that a substance itself is 'like a whole world'.[1] At first he might seem only to be putting in another way what he has already expressed by the metaphor of the mirror, and to be saying that a substance is like a whole world, much as the Lady of Shalott's mirror was a kind of world for her. However, he means more than this. He says not only that each substance is like a whole world, but that it 'is like a world apart, independent of everything but God';[2] that a substance behaves as if 'there were nothing but God and itself in the world'.[3] He also adapts his metaphor of the mirror to express this, saying that each substance mirrors the universe 'from its own point of view',[4] so that 'it is as if there were as many universes as substances'.[5] Stated without metaphor, Leibniz's view is that, strictly speaking, no created substance acts on any other,[6] though it is always dependent on God.

[1] *DM*, par. 9.

[2] Ibid., par. 14. Cf. G ii. 46–47, 57 (L 518).

[3] G ii. 57. Cf. *DM*, par. 14; G iv. 484 (L 747); G vii. 312.

[4] G iv. 557 (L 937); *DM*, par. 9; *PNG*, pars. 3, 12; *Mon.*, par. 57; *To Clarke*, § 5.87; C 15.

[5] *Mon.*, par. 57; cf. *DM*, par. 9. See also G iv. 557, which links the notion of a 'point of view' with the idea that a substance is a 'little world'. Leibniz also (*To Clarke*, § 5.87) links this notion with that of the pre-established harmony, which (as will be seen later in this section) is designed to answer some of the problems posed by a substance's independence.

[6] G ii. 57, 69; G iv. 483 (L 746); G vii. 312; *DM*, par. 14; *Mon.*, par. 7; C 521 (L 415).

This view is stated by Leibniz to be another consequence of the fact that the complete concept of a substance involves all the substance's predicates.[1] In arguing for this conclusion, he says that since all our thoughts, for example, are only the consequences of the nature or concept[2] of our soul, and arise in it by virtue of its concept, it is pointless to ask for the effect of some particular substance on it.[3] All that can happen to us is only a consequence of our own being, and our own being is what it is because God has actualized a certain complete concept.[4] This is clearly similar to the argument by which, as suggested in the last section, Leibniz tries to prove that a substance expresses the whole universe. The same conclusion could also have been reached from what was argued in the last section to be a consequence of the proposition that each substance expresses the whole universe—namely, Leibniz's view that there are no purely extrinsic denominations. Leibniz has claimed that a complete account of substances can be given in subject-predicate terms; but to say that one substance acts on another is to state a relational proposition, which must therefore be reducible to subject-predicate propositions about these substances.

All this raises problems for Leibniz. First, he has to take account of the fact that it is very often said that one contingent thing does act on another. It is not enough to say that such propositions are, strictly speaking, always false; it must also be explained how they come to be asserted so often. Second, some explanation is required of the fact that, although no created substance really acts on another, each is such that a knowledge of all states of all other substances can be derived from a consideration of its complete concept alone. A third difficulty concerns the relations between God and other substances. It has already been mentioned[5] that Leibniz argues that God

---

[1] G ii. 69; G vii. 312; *DM*, pars. 9, 14; C 521 (L 415).
[2] For this equivalence, see G ii. 69; *DM*, par. 14.
[3] G ii. 69; cf. *DM*, pars. 14, 32.
[4] *DM*, par. 14.   [5] § 4.5.

conserves all substances, and does so by creating them continually; he also says that when God creates substances continually he acts on them.[1] This is called by Leibniz God's 'ordinary concourse';[2] besides this, he speaks of God's 'extraordinary and miraculous concourse',[3] by which he means that action or 'influence' of God on a substance which enables it to perform a miracle, which is an act which exceeds its own powers.[4] Now the difficulty is this: from the complete concept of a substance there is said to follow everything which can truly be stated of it, and this (it may be argued) must include the propositions which describe God's actions upon it. But this must imply that the supposed actions of God on a created substance are no more real than the supposed actions of one substance on another.

Leibniz might answer the last objection by reminding the objector[5] that from the mere concept of a substance other than God it cannot be inferred that it exists; that is, it cannot be inferred that it has been created and is continually created. All that can be inferred is that if there is a God, and if the substance is such that only if it exists will the best possible world exist, then God will create and conserve that substance. This, then, would probably be Leibniz's answer to the problem about God's 'ordinary concourse'. With regard to God's 'extraordinary concourse' Leibniz's view seems to be that action of this type does not differ essentially from the action by which God conserves a substance. For example, he might say that God enables Lazarus to rise from the dead in the same sense that he enables the living Lazarus to rise from his bed; we only call Lazarus's rising from the dead 'supernatural' because our concept of the nature of Lazarus, which is the concept of what Lazarus expresses 'more perfectly', does not include such an act.[6] But if we include in a substance's 'nature' everything

---

[1] DM, pars. 28, 30.   [2] G ii. 91–92; DM, par. 30.
[3] DM, par. 16.
[4] Ibid., par. 16; cf. G ii. 93; G iv. 520 (L 803); G vi. 265; To Clarke, §§ 3.17, 5.107, 5.112.   [5] Cf. §§ 4.7, 5.1.   [6] Cf. DM, par. 16.

which it expresses, 'nothing is supernatural to it, since it extends to everything'.[1] This might seem to imply that Leibniz believes that human beings may ultimately have no use for the term 'miracle', as their understanding of the universe increases and everything which was regarded as miraculous comes to be regarded as natural. However, this is not his view. As already mentioned,[2] he believes that there are events which are inexplicable by (as opposed to not at present explained by) human beings, and these are what he calls 'miracles'. He seems to hint that some so-called miracles, such as the miracle at Cana, might be explicable in natural terms,[3] but he insists that there are miracles in his sense of the term, such as the creation and annihilation of a substance.[4]

There now remain the other two questions asked earlier, of which the first was why we should make such common use of the concept of the action of one thing on another. Leibniz would reply that he does not wish to deny that a sentence of the form 'A acts on B' has a use. All substances, it has just been remarked, express all others; but it often happens that, for human beings, substance A expresses substance B 'more distinctly' or 'more perfectly' than B expresses A. When this is so, and in so far as this is what the assertion that A acts on B is taken to mean, then what is said is true.[5] In other words, to say that A acts on B is to say something which can be true, so long as it is taken to mean that it is possible to infer from A to B, and that it is easier to infer from A to B than from B to A. But if it is taken to mean that A makes some change in B, that something is transferred from the one to the other,[6] then the assertion is always false.

Leibniz gives the same account[7] of statements to the effect that a substance A is the *cause* of a change in some other

[1] Ibid.   [2] § 4.6, p. 102.   [3] G vi. 265.   [4] Cf. § 5.6.
[5] G ii. 47, 69, 71; cf. G vii. 322 (L 607). The same view is stated less precisely in *Mon.*, par. 50 and G iv. 486 (L 749), in which it is asserted that A can be said to act on B in so far as one can find in A reasons for what happens in B.   [6] G iv. 486 (L 749); G vii. 313; C 521 (L 415).
[7] G ii. 57, 69, 71; G vii. 312.

substance, B, perhaps on the grounds that to say that A is the cause of some change in B is the same as saying that A acts on B in a certain way, and the statement must therefore be interpreted in the same fashion. He argues, then, that 'A is the cause of some change in B' must be taken as saying, 'A expresses B, and expresses B more distinctly than B expresses A'; that is, that it is easier to infer from A to B than conversely. 'That thing is thought to be the cause', he says, 'from whose state a reason for changes is most easily given'[1]—somewhat as we attribute motion to a ship rather than to the sea as a whole.[2] It may be added that this indicates another difference[3] between the concepts of divine causality and causality as exercised by created substances. Leibniz could not sensibly say that it is possible to regard the contingent universe as the cause of God, and that it is only because God expresses the universe more distinctly than the universe expresses God that we do not.

To some extent, what Leibniz says about causality in the created world is an interesting anticipation of Bertrand Russell's views about causation, as expressed in his essay 'On the Notion of Cause'.[4] Russell argued that the concept of cause is imprecise, and that it had been replaced in the exact sciences by the idea of a law which applies to a system, enabling inferences to be made from a state of the system at any given time to its state at any other time.[5] This is not exactly what Leibniz said, and is not advanced for the same reasons; yet it does not seem farfetched to take Leibniz's views about 'expression' as containing the germ of the views about scientific explanation which Russell put forward. This is not mentioned as a justification of what Leibniz says about causation, but only as indicating that it may be rather more than an *ad hoc* way of solving a problem.

The remaining question is how substances are so related

[1] G vii. 312.   [2] G ii. 57; cf. G ii. 69.
[3] Cf. § 4.5, pp. 97 ff.
[4] *Proceedings of the Aristotelian Society*, 1912–13. Reprinted in *Mysticism and Logic* (London, 1918), pp. 180 ff.
[5] Op. cit., p. 194. This seems in essence to have remained Russell's view: see, e.g., *Human Knowledge, its Scope and Limits* (London, 1948), pp. 326 ff.

that from a full knowledge of any one it is possible to know everything about all other substances, in spite of the fact that no substance acts on any other. Three explanations seem possible. First, it may just happen that each substance expresses all others: this is an ultimate, inexplicable fact. Leibniz would reject this, on the grounds that it contradicts the principle of sufficient reason. Second, it may be that the relations between substances are the result of God's constant intervention in the universe. When it is said, for example, that one body moves another, it would be more accurate to say that God has given motion to the one 'on occasion of' the motion of the other. The order which holds between substances, therefore, exists only by virtue of the constant activity of God on each substance. This is not the same as saying, as Leibniz does, that God conserves the universe; on the theory now being considered the universe is thought of as a going concern, the substances in it being, as Leibniz would say, conserved by God, who is also regarded as constantly intervening in this universe. Such was the theory of 'occasionalism', as Leibniz understood it.[1] Leibniz's solution of the difficulty is to say that the order or harmony which is to be found among substances is 'pre-established'.[2] This is to say that God created a universe such that, without further interference from him (beyond his 'ordinary concourse'), every substance would behave with perfect spontaneity, and yet 'with a perfect conformity to things outside it'.[3]

Leibniz rejects occasionalism because it regards every case of what we call the action of one thing on another as a miracle.[4] According to the occasionalist, the ball which is commonly

[1] G iv. 483–4 (L 746).
[2] G iii. 566; NE, 4. 10. 9–10; To Clarke, § 5.87; Mon., par. 80. Leibniz often calls this the 'hypothesis of concomitance' (G ii. 58 (L 519), 68–70, 74, 95; C 521 (L 415); G vii. 313), and he also calls it the 'hypothesis of agreements' (hypothèse des accords: G iv. 485 (L 748)). But, as he points out (G iv. 486 (L 749)), it is strictly speaking more than a hypothesis for him, since he regards it as being known to be true.
[3] G iv. 484. Leibniz also regards the existence of a harmony between substances as a proof of the existence of God: e.g. G iv. 485; G vi. 541 (L 955–6); NE, 4. 10. 9–10; C 13.   [4] G iv. 483; cf. G ii. 57–58, 92–93.

said to move because it was hit by another is really moved by God; that is, it performs an action which is beyond its nature, supernatural.[1] Leibniz says that this is to call in a *Deus ex machina*, which is really no solution.[2] It might be replied that he is himself open to the same charge; for what is his postulation of a God who pre-establishes a harmony between substances, if not the introduction of a *Deus ex machina*? Leibniz might answer that he takes the term *Deus ex machina* in its original sense of a God who interferes in human affairs, or in the affairs of the universe in general, and that his God does not interfere in this way. If the term is taken in a wider sense, to mean an arbitrary use of the concept of God to solve a difficulty, Leibniz would probably say that his explanation is forced upon us, as the only really satisfactory solution. He might agree that the theory of the pre-established harmony is similar to that of occasionalism in that it makes reference to the miraculous; but, he would say, it postulates only one miracle, and only 'in the beginning of things'.[3] This miracle is the act of creation itself,[4] at which the harmony between substances is established once and for all.

It might perhaps be asked why Leibniz should count it a virtue that he postulates only one miracle to account for the order between substances. If there is to be one miracle, why should there not be a multitude of miracles? Leibniz replies that we ought to try to explain naturally all that we can;[5] to refer everything to miracles is to make explanation too easy,[6] and is to open places of refuge (*asyles*) for ignorance and laziness.[7] The theory of the pre-established harmony, then, is claimed by Leibniz to have the virtue of explaining the supposed action of one substance on another by reference to their nature; that is, it makes possible the natural explanation of such action.

---

[1] Cf. p. 152.   [2] G iv. 483; G vii. 313.   [3] G iii. 143.
[4] Cf. § 4.6, p. 102.   [5] G iv. 483.   [6] *To Clarke*, § 2.12.
[7] *NE*, Pref. (A vi. 6, 66; G v. 59). This may be an echo of Spinoza's phrase, *asylum ignorantiae* (*Ethics*, Book I, Appendix: Gebhardt, ii, p. 81).

It is clear that the solutions which Leibniz gives to the problems posed in this section are not derived from his logic; not that he claims that they are, though he would have said that they are answers to problems generated by a consequence of his logic. It may also be objected that the consequence in question—the proposition that each substance is independent of all others—does not follow from Leibniz's logic alone, but requires other, non-logical premisses such as the view that God actualizes certain complete concepts, creating substances which will act in ideally predictable ways. As the truth of this view may be doubted, Leibniz may seem to have been spending time in finding solutions for what are not real problems. However, Leibniz's ingenuity has surely not been wasted; what he says, in the course of giving his solutions, about the nature of causation and about the misuse of the notion of the miraculous is valuable on its own account.

§ 5.6. The proposition that the concept of a substance must be complete has other consequences for Leibniz: it implies, he argues, that a substance can only begin by creation and perish by annihilation, that it cannot be divided, and that one substance cannot be made out of two.[1] In the *Discourse on Metaphysics* he writes as if these conclusions were derived independently of one another, but in fact they are related. The proposition that a substance can only begin by creation and perish by annihilation will be found to depend on the premiss that a substance is indivisible, whilst the proposition that one substance cannot be made out of two seems to depend on the indivisibility and indestructibility of substance.[2] The indivisibility of substance, then, is the primary consequence from which the others are derived. It must be added that Leibniz sometimes says that a substance's indivisibility can be derived from the proposition that a substance has no parts,[3] but it seems that he might with equal justice have argued in the reverse direction, so that the two propositions are equivalent, each

[1] *DM*, par. 9.   [2] Cf. § 5.7.   [3] G iv. 479; *Mon.*, par. 3.

being derivable from the other. In what follows, it will be assumed that this is what he meant, and the statement that a substance is indivisible will be taken as equivalent to the statement that it is without parts, that is, 'simple', genuinely one, a 'monad'.[1]

Leibniz does not make clear how he thinks the indivisibility of a substance to follow from the completeness of its concept. He might be arguing from the premiss that the concept of a substance is indivisible, in the sense that to remove from it one or more of its component concepts would make it incomplete and so the concept of an abstraction, not that of a substance. Given Leibniz's views about the concept of a substance, the premiss is sound; on the other hand, no inference can be made from the indivisibility of a concept to the indivisibility of the substance of which it is a concept. For example, it is part of the complete concept of Lord Nelson that he lost an arm in battle; now, the complete concept of Nelson may be indivisible in the sense just explained, but it does not follow from this that Nelson did not lose an arm. It is tempting to see in this another example of a metaphysical argument which rests on Leibniz's confusion between the subject of a proposition and the concept of the subject.[2] What is true of a subject, in the sense of that which a proposition is about, is not necessarily the same as what is true of the concept of the subject.

It may be, however, that Leibniz's argument is different, and that it rests not only upon the assumption that the concept of a substance is complete, but also upon the assumption that every substance is connected with all other substances, so that it expresses the whole universe. The argument would then be that if it were divided, a substance could not express the whole universe, which it must do. But even allowing that Leibniz has shown that each substance must express the whole universe,

---

[1] Substance as 'simple', PNG, pars. 1–2; Mon., par. 1; as genuinely one, G iv. 478–9 (L 741). For the connexion between 'monad' and 'unity' see PNG, par. 1; NE, 4. 10. 9–10; G. M. ii. 295.

[2] Cf. § 5.4, p. 143.

which he has not,[1] it may be pointed out that this argument
assumes that a substance is economically constructed; that is,
that there is no more in the substance than is necessary to
express the whole universe. This can only be justified by an
appeal to the principle of the best, which is a non-logical
principle.[2] Leibniz might reply that a substance could not contain more than it does; it has to express an infinite universe, and
so must be of infinite complexity. This, however, does not get
rid of the need for the principle of the best, since it is from this
principle that Leibniz derives the view that there must be an
infinity of substances.[3]

As the indivisibility of a substance does not follow solely
from Leibniz's logic, the same can be said of what Leibniz
claims to be the consequences of a substance's indivisibility.
However, these consequences are worth discussion because of
their importance. Leibniz argues that because substances have
no parts they cannot be made or unmade, that is, they do not
begin or cease to exist.[4] More exactly, a substance can only begin by creation and end by annihilation; that is, by a miracle.[5]
Given that a substance has no parts, this is to some extent true,
in so far as it illustrates a certain use of words such as 'creation'
and 'destruction'. Leibniz may be taken as saying that any
compound can be destroyed in two, and only two, ways. On
the one hand its constituents may continue to exist, but no
longer as constituents of that compound: for example, when
a child has dismantled a house which it has made of bricks the
bricks themselves remain, ready for other uses. On the other
hand, the constituents themselves may be destroyed, in the
sense that absolutely nothing remains. In the first case, what
ceases to exist is a certain way in which simple parts are
organized, whilst in the second, the simple parts themselves
cease to exist. What occurs in the first case may be called
a destruction of order, and what occurs in the second may be

[1] Cf. § 5.4.   [2] Cf. § 4.7, p. 105, and § 4.8, p. 113.
[3] § 5.3, p. 140.   [4] PNG, par. 2; Mon., pars. 4–5; C 15–16.
[5] G iv. 479 (L 742); DM, par. 9.

called annihilation.[1] It follows that no substance can suffer destruction of order, for this applies only to compounds, whereas substances are simple—indeed, they are the only genuinely simple things. The child's bricks, for example, which served as an example of simple parts, can in turn be destroyed; but they are not genuinely simple, and what they undergo is a destruction of order. If a substance is destroyed, then, it can only be by annihilation. In the same way it is possible to distinguish between what may be called the formation of order, which occurs when simple parts are put together to make a compound, and creation, which takes place when a simple part comes into existence. Here it is obvious that a simple part can only be created, since what is made in the case of formation of order is a compound.

So far, Leibniz's conclusions cannot be challenged. If 'destruction of order' and 'formation of order' are terms which apply only to compounds, and if no substance is a compound, then it follows that if a substance is produced or destroyed it must be in some other way; and if the only other kind of production or destruction is creation or annihilation, then if a substance is produced or destroyed it must be created or annihilated. This, however, does not of itself justify Leibniz's further assertion that creation and annihilation are not natural events.[2] Here he is saying something about the limits of human understanding,[3] and it may be asked with what justification he places these limits where he does. Leibniz might reply by asking how the appearance of a new substance in the universe could be explained. According to the principle of sufficient reason, it must be explicable; but, by hypothesis, it cannot be explained in terms of the combination of other substances. If we could grasp God's plan, we might understand how the creation of such a substance is a necessary condition of the existence of the best

---

[1] It is not implied that this is a full account of the ordinary use of the term 'annihilation'. For example, when an army is said to be annihilated, the soldiers do not vanish from the face of the earth; on the other hand, they can be said to cease to exist *as soldiers*.

[2] Cf. G ii. 76, and *Mon.*, pars. 4–6.   [3] Cf. § 4.6, p. 102.

possible world; but we cannot do this, as it would involve the consideration of a universe of infinite complexity, which is beyond the powers of finite minds. Similar arguments apply to the annihilation of any substance.

Leibniz has also said that not only cannot one substance become two, but two cannot become one.[1] He does not seem to argue explicitly for this conclusion, but it is easily deducible from what he believes himself to have established already. Suppose that one substance is made from two; then either these two substances will retain their identity, or they will not. If they do not, they must have perished, which contradicts the proposition that a substance is naturally indestructible. If they do, a substance must consist of substances, that is, it must have parts, which contradicts the proposition that a substance is indivisible. It follows, therefore, that one substance cannot be made out of two.[2]

§ 5.7. From the fact that a substance must be indivisible, uncreatable, and indestructible it follows that no aggregate can be a substance; for it is obvious that an aggregate can be divided, can be produced, and can be destroyed.[3] Leibniz would not deny that an aggregate has some kind of unity, but he insists that this unity is only in the mind.[4] Such unity he sometimes declares to be a product of the reason; for example, if

---

[1] Cf. p. 157. It is true that in par. 1 of the *Principles of Nature and of Grace* Leibniz speaks of 'compound substance' (*la substance composée*), but this must be an inaccurate way of saying 'compound of substances'. In the nearly contemporary *Monadology* Leibniz is careful to speak, not of compound substances, but of 'compounds' simply (*des composés*) (*Mon.*, pars. 1–2). Cf. C 13–14, where Leibniz begins by speaking of composite substances, but then says that, strictly speaking, only simple substances exist.

[2] Cf. a similar argument in Spinoza, *Ethics*, Book I, Prop. 13.

[3] Cf. G ii. 76. In G ii. 72 Leibniz argues from the unreality of aggregates to the indivisibility of substance; this passage, however, comes from a study for a letter to Arnauld, and in the letter itself (G ii. 76) Leibniz reverses the order of the argument.

[4] G ii. 97, 119 (L 529), 261; *NE*, 2. 12. 3, 7. Leibniz also makes this point by saying that an aggregate is not *unum per se*, but *unum per accidens* (G ii. 76, 96).

one speaks of a pair of diamonds, one of which belongs to the Grand Duke and the other to the Great Mogul, the pair is an 'entity of reason', which serves only to 'abridge our thoughts' and exists merely 'for the convenience of reasoning'.[1] Sometimes the unity of an aggregate is said to be the work of imagination or perception; for example, if the two diamonds just mentioned are mounted in the same ring, the pair will constitute what Leibniz calls 'an entity of the imagination or perception, i.e. a phenomenon'.[2] This seems to mean that the diamonds are seen as a unity,[3] though in fact they are still separate entities.

Not only is the unity of an aggregate contributed by the mind, but its very being is in the mind also.[4] 'What is not genuinely *one* being', Leibniz says, 'is no more genuinely one *being.*'[5] This explains how he can say of what he calls 'moral entities', such as a people, an army, a society, or a college, that they have about them 'something of the imaginary and of dependence on mental fiction'.[6] He does not mean by this that aggregates are mere illusions; they have, he says, 'a basis in reality',[7] and this is probably why he sometimes calls an aggregate semi-mental, or a semi-entity.[8] This basis, the 'ingredients' of the aggregate, consists of the genuine entities which make it up, together with what Leibniz calls their 'modes' (by which he seems to mean their predicates) and their relations.[9] It is because aggregates have this basis in reality that we can have more or less reason for regarding as one what is really a number of entities.[10] So, according to Leibniz, an ordered society has more unity than a confused mob, and a machine more unity than a society, 'since there are more relations between the ingredients'.[11] Nevertheless, Leibniz insists that an aggregate has no real existence of its own, outside that of its constituents.

---

[1] G ii. 96, 101. Cf. *NE*, 2. 12. 3, which states that the understanding (*l'entendement*) is responsible for aggregates.   [2] G ii. 96.
[3] Cf. G ii. 517.   [4] *NE*, 2. 12. 7.   [5] G ii. 97.
[6] G ii. 76.   [7] G ii. 97; *NE*, 2. 12. 3.   [8] G ii. 304, 504 (L 1001).
[9] G ii. 72, 97, 101.   [10] G ii. 96.   [11] G ii. 100.

The view that no aggregate is a substance is doubly important for Leibniz. On the one hand, it helps him to make the negative point that no substance can be material; on the other, it enables him to state positively that every substance is an ego or soul, or at any rate is like one. To begin with the second of these: Leibniz does not seem to produce explicit arguments for his assertion that the ego, the self, is a soul,[1] but it is possible that he has in mind his view that the proposition that there is an 'I' which thinks is a primitive truth of fact,[2] and that he regards it as obvious that thinking is the work of souls. Neither does he argue explicitly for his view that the ego is no aggregate, but genuinely one.[3] Here, however, it is not clear what his argument would be, and the lack of a clear indication is serious, in view of the argument (to be found later in Hume) that to speak of the self is to speak of an aggregate, a 'bundle' of impressions and ideas. However, Leibniz has other reasons for saying that substances are souls, and therefore for his view that the ego provides as it were a model on which we may conceive substances, that is, that every substance is an ego, or something like it.[4] These reasons will be discussed in the next section; the rest of this section will be devoted to a discussion of the way in which Leibniz tries to establish the negative proposition that no substance can really be material. It must be said at the outset that he does not attempt to establish this conclusion solely from the premiss that no aggregate is a substance, but uses that premiss in conjunction with a definition which states that anything material, anything 'extended', is an aggregate. He could not, therefore, justifiably claim that his conclusion follows solely from his views about the nature of truth, but he could claim that these views (through their consequences that the concept of a substance must be complete, and that no substance is divisible) help to establish this conclusion.

[1] G ii. 76; G iv. 473, 482 (L 745).   [2] Cf. § 4.4.
[3] To the references in n. 1 add *Mon.*, par. 30, and Dutens, ii, p. 223 (L 964).
[4] G ii. 45, 76, 251 (L 863); G vi. 488, 493, 502 (L 891); G iv. 473, 482; Dutens, loc. cit.

The definition mentioned above is that the concept of extension is 'analysable into plurality, continuity, and coexistence, that is, the existence of parts at one and the same time'.[1] These parts, Leibniz asserts, are 'things', or rather substances.[2] No single member of this trio of plurality, continuity, and coexistence is peculiar to extension; plurality it has in common with number, continuity with time and motion, and coexistence with non-extended things.[3] What distinguishes extension is the fact that it has all three. For example, time and motion are continuous, but they are not coexistent, being the *successive* 'diffusion or repetition of a certain nature'.[4] Now, since anything extended is an aggregate of coexisting parts, it follows that these parts cannot themselves be extended. If they were, 'they would again be multitudes, and by no means true and pure unities, such as are finally required to constitute a multitude'.[5] From this it follows that although it seems to us that there are extended things, their extension has to be regarded as only a phenomenon;[6] that is, it is merely a perception, an appearance which is in the mind.[7] Hence the metaphor of the rainbow, which Leibniz often uses in this connexion:[8] just as an aggregate of colourless particles of water is seen as coloured, so an aggregate of unextended substances is perceived as extended. There is a further point: since the components of an aggregate which appears to us as extended are themselves unextended, they are in a sense not *parts* of the phenomena which are present

[1] G ii. 169 (L 838). Cf. G ii. 183 (L 843), 227 (L 855), 234, 269 (L 874), 339; G iv. 364 (L 642), 394, 467; C 361, 408. Leibniz sometimes distinguishes between extension and what is extended, saying that 'extension' designates a *possible* 'continuous plurality of coexisting things' (G ii. 195 (L 850). Cf. G iv. 568 (L 949)). But the distinction is not important here.
[2] G ii. 183, 227, 234, 269; G iv. 364, 492.
[3] G ii. 183, 227.
[4] G ii. 269. Cf. G ii. 227; G iv. 394.   [5] G vii. 552.
[6] G i. 391-2; G ii. 73, 77, 97, 118-19, 268 (L 873), 275, 281 n., 435, 473, 504, 517; G iii. 567 n., 623, 636; G iv. 473; G vii. 314, 444, 468; C 523; Grua, p. 322.
[7] G ii. 70; G vii. 319 (L 603); C 14.
[8] G ii. 77, 97, 119, 268, 281 n., 504, 517; G vii. 314; C 523; Grua, p. 322.

to us; not, that is to say, in the way in which bricks are parts of
a wall. Rather they should be called the foundations or bases
of phenomena, which are not so much constituted by them as
the result of them.[1]

When Leibniz says that extension can be defined in terms of
plurality, continuity, and coexistence he must not be supposed
to mean that anything which appears to us as extended is not
only an aggregate of coexisting substances, but is also an aggregate which is in some way really continuous, all that is apparent
being that form of continuity which is called extension. In his
view it is not extension alone, but anything continuous, which
is an appearance. His chief argument for this is that it provides
the only solution to the problem which he calls 'the labyrinth
of the continuum'.[2] Briefly, the problem is this. We are aware
of what is continuous, such as extension and duration; further,
anything continuous is infinitely divisible, in the sense that,
however small a segment of time or space we take, we can
always conceive one smaller.[3] But we also know, Leibniz
claims, that any substance must be indivisible; if, then, any substance is really continuous it must be both indivisible and infinitely divisible. Leibniz's solution is that anything continuous
is an appearance whose basis consists of substances; each extended thing, for example, is the appearance of an infinity of
substances.[4] This shows that the terms 'continuity', 'plurality',
and 'coexistence', which occur in his definition of extension,
are not, so to speak, on the same logical level. Continuity is
something which can be predicated of appearances only, whereas plurality and coexistence can be predicated of what is real.
In sum, Leibniz would have stated his views less misleadingly
had he defined extension as an aggregate of coexisting substances,
which appear to be continuous.

[1] G ii. 268.
[2] G ii. 119, 282, 379. Cf. A ii. 1, p. 111; G iv. 491; G vi. 29; *DM*, par. 10;
NE, 2. 23. 31; C 609; FC, pp. 179–80 (L 406). The term was borrowed by
Leibniz from a book by Libert Froidmont (Fromondus), *Labyrinthus, sive
de compositione continui* (Antwerp, 1631).
[3] G i. 403.   [4] G iv. 492.

Now that Leibniz's definition has been clarified, some comments can be made about it. It is obvious that this is the kind of
definition of which it may be asked whether it is correct or not;
Leibniz is not simply proposing to use the word 'extension' in
a certain way, but is claiming to say something about the nature
of that extension with which we are all familiar. However, his
reasons for defining extension as he does are not clear; he tends
simply to assert the definition, without arguing for it. It may
be asked first why he regards extension as the appearance of
anything. He has said that we can escape from the labyrinth
of the continuum only if we regard extension as a phenomenon; why, then, should he not say, with Berkeley, that to
speak of something material is simply to speak of the perceptions which someone has? This would not affect his view[1] that
we have good reason to say that there are physical objects; it
merely provides an analysis of what we mean when we talk
about such objects.

There were indeed times when Leibniz toyed with phenomenalism, suggesting that to talk about physical things is only
to talk about perceptions.[2] The idea which he puts forward is
that physical things might be 'true phenomena'[3]—that is, that
each physical thing is simply a coherent set of the appearances
present to a soul or souls.[4] However, the idea is put forward
only to be rejected, Leibniz arguing that it can be proved that
there exist physical things as well as souls. 'I am asked', he
writes,[5]

why God does not content himself with producing all the thoughts
and 'modifications' of the soul, without these 'useless' bodies which

---

[1] Cf. § 4.4.

[2] A ii. 1, 248–9 (L 239); deleted passages from *DM*, pars. 11, 12, 34, 35
(Lestienne ed., pp. 40–41, 87, 89: see also the Lucas and Grint translation).
Cf. L. J. Russell, 'Leibniz's Account of Phenomena', *Proceedings of the
Aristotelian Society*, 1953–4, pp. 167 ff.

[3] *DM*, Lestienne ed., pp. 87, 89; G ii. 77; G iv. 473; G vii. 314. The term
phenomena bene fundata is sometimes used in the same sense: e.g. G ii. 435;
G iii. 623; G vii. 468.

[4] On coherence among phenomena, cf. § 4.4, p. 90.   [5] G iv. 495.

the soul, it is said, can neither 'move' nor 'know'. The answer is easy. It is that God willed that there should be more rather than fewer substances, and that he found it good that these 'modifications' should correspond to something external.

In short, the answer to Berkeley is provided by the principle of the best.

Such, then, are Leibniz's reasons for regarding extension as an appearance of something. It now has to be asked why he regards it as the appearance of a plurality of coexisting substances. He does not seem to have in mind the fact that it is always possible to conceive an extended thing as containing coexistent parts. Parts which can be assigned as one pleases, and which are not already in a thing, he calls 'indefinite',[1] and he is emphatic that the coexistent parts of which he speaks are not of this kind.[2] Further, any such 'indefinite' part of what is extended would itself be extended, whereas Leibniz is asserting that what we call 'extended' is really an aggregate of non-extended substances.

It might perhaps be suggested that Leibniz means that if anything is to be extended it must contain at least two points. This suggestion is better than the last, in that a point is not itself extended, and is also indivisible. However, Leibniz makes it clear that this is not what he means. A point, he says, cannot be called a component part of anything;[3] it is not something which is real, capable of existing by itself. A point is only a 'modification' or 'modality';[4] to be more exact, it is only a limit.[5] This seems to mean that a point may be defined as the limit of a process of infinite subdivision. For example, if one conceives a straight line to be divided into two equal parts, and one of these parts to be similarly divided, and so on without

---

[1] C 377. Cf. G ii. 268, 278, 282, 379; C 438–9.
[2] G ii. 268, 282.
[3] G i. 416; G ii. 300, 370 (L 971); C 615.
[4] G ii. 370; G iv. 483 (L 745).
[5] G ii. 370; G. M. iii. 536; C 522 (L 416), 622. Cf. G iv. 478 (L 741), 491; C 615.

end, the segments which are produced in this way will converge towards a limit. This limit is what Leibniz calls a 'point', and of which he says that it cannot be called real. All that is real in the construction just described is the line and such segments as have been cut off at any given time, and no segment, however small, can be called a point, since it is always possible to divide it further.[1]

Both these suggestions, then, are expressly rejected by Leibniz, and some other explanation must be sought. On the whole it seems most likely that he would attempt to justify his definition in the following way.[2] He might begin by pointing out that his definition corresponds to the ordinary use of the word 'extension', in that his contemporaries normally meant by something 'extended' something which has a number of coexisting parts.[3] But, he might continue, these parts were thought of as smaller extended parts; these, however, are themselves divisible, and so cannot constitute the reality of extension, as everything real must be simple. The usual definition of extension, then, must be corrected to read 'Everything extended is an aggregate of *simple*, coexistent parts'.

As a postscript to this discussion of extension, something must be said about the related topic of Leibniz's views concerning time. The topic is an important one. Clearly, if Leibniz is to be able to say consistently that each created substance expresses the future and the past, he must accept the reality of time, in some sense of the word 'time'. Yet, as Russell has pointed out,[4] he often says things which imply that time is not real. The unreality of time might, indeed, seem to follow from what has already been said about the labyrinth of the continuum;[5] for if time is continuous, then it can only be an appearance. The question is, whether this contradiction is real, or only apparent.

[1] G. M. iii. 536; cf. G iv. 492.

[2] I owe this suggestion to Mrs. Kneale.

[3] Cf. the definition of a body (*corpus*) as that which has parts outside parts (*partes extra partes*): e.g. Jungius, p. 20.

[4] Russell, pp. 50 ff., 127 ff.   [5] Cf. p. 165.

What Leibniz says about this subject is only fragmentary,[1] but is enough to allow of a probable answer. It must first be noted that Leibniz draws a distinction between time and duration. Duration is to time, he writes, as extension is to space; duration and extension are attributes of things, whereas time and space serve to measure things.[2] Often, time is called an order—an order among changes or successions,[3] just as space is called an order of coexistence.[4] This is why time and space are called 'entities of reason':[5] they involve concepts of measurement, whereas duration and extension do not. It must be added that in calling duration and extension 'attributes', Leibniz does not mean that they really belong to substances; it has already been made clear that he thinks that they are only appearances. What he probably means is that substances appear to be extended and to endure even when their extension and duration are not measured.

So far it has been seen that Leibniz regards duration as an appearance and time as an entity of reason; the question remains, How can it be said that a substance really expresses the future and the past, or that it really has a history? Leibniz replies that although time may be an entity of reason, 'coexistence, and existing before and after, are something real'.[6] Exactly how he would develop this statement is not certain, but he sometimes says that instants are real,[7] and he may mean that it is correct to speak of a real (though discontinuous) succession of instants, but that to speak of a continuous succession is to speak only of appearances. If it is asked what is meant by calling instants real, Leibniz would reply that instants consist only in the successive

---

[1] A useful collection of texts will be found in Jalabert, op. cit., Chap. 4.
[2] G vi. 584 (L 1011). Cf. G ii. 183 (L 843), where duration and time are compared to extension and place.
[3] G ii. 221, 269 (L 874), 450 (L 983); G iv. 394, 523 (L 806); G. M. iii. 964; G. M, vii. 18 (L 1083); To Clarke, §§ 3.4, 5.105. Cf. § 4.6, p. 102.
[4] G ii. 277, 450; G iv. 394, 568; G. M, vii. 18; To Clarke, §§ 3.4, 5.29, 5.47, 5.104.
[5] G ii. 183 (L 844). On entia rationis, cf. § 2.2, p. 41, n. 2.
[6] G ii. 183 (L 844).
[7] G ii. 279; To Clarke, § 5.49.

order of things, and are nothing without things.[1] Perhaps, then, his views may be most accurately expressed as follows: the instantaneous states of things are real,[2] i.e. are predicates which really belong to substances, and coexistence and existing before and after are real in so far as they can be defined in terms of these states. Duration, on the other hand, is only the appearance of these instantaneous states,[3] and time a means of measuring duration. If this is what Leibniz meant, then his views about time and duration do not seem to contradict his belief that created substances have a history.

§ 5.8. The last section considered the consequences of a substance's indivisibility, uncreatability, and indestructibility; we turn now to the consequences of what, for Leibniz, is another feature of substance—namely, that it must have a present which is 'big with the future and laden with the past'.[4] It is hardly necessary to give another reminder[5] of the fact that this feature of substance is not validly derived by Leibniz from his logic alone, so that any inquiry into its consequences can only be an inquiry into what Leibniz thought to be derivable.

   The fact that a substance expresses both past and future means, according to Leibniz, that it is necessary to rehabilitate what the Scholastics had called 'substantial forms'.[6] As has already been remarked, they had used the term 'substantial form' to refer to the goal of a thing's endeavour, which they regarded as explaining changes in the thing, whether they are now in the future or now in the past.[7] This is what Leibniz has

---

[1] *To Clarke*, § 3.6.

[2] This may be what he has in mind when he speaks of 'the duration of things, or the multitude of momentary states' (G vii. 564; cf. G ii. 279).

[3] By analogy with what Leibniz says about substances and extension, he might be expected to say that instants are not parts of duration, but are its foundation or basis (cf. p. 165). In fact he comes close to this, saying that instants are not parts of time (G iii. 591; *To Clarke*, § 5.49). It must be added that in the *New Essays* (*NE*, 2. 14. 10) Leibniz says that the instant, like the point, is not a part in that it is only an 'extremity'. This seems to be a different concept of instant from that discussed above.

[4] § 5.4, p. 143.   [5] Cf. § 5.4.   [6] *DM*, pars. 10–11.   [7] § 4.8, p. 111.

in mind when he says that a form is 'a principle of action, which is found in that which acts'.[1] It is, it will be noticed, an *internal* principle of change: it is not, for example, like a cash prize which a man is trying to win, but is more like something which he is trying to become—successful, say, or healthy. In this way, Leibniz does not contradict his thesis that no substance can act on another.

Leibniz does not make wholly clear what he believes to be the relations between substance and form. Sometimes he seems to mean that a substance *is* a substantial form,[2] sometimes only that a substantial form is *an aspect* of a substance. He says, for example, that a substantial form is a 'substantial principle',[3] and that together with 'matter' it constitutes a substance which is truly one, a 'monad';[4] again, he distinguishes within a substance between the internal principle of change and the series of changes itself.[5] All this suggests that a substantial form is only an aspect of a substance; on the other hand, Leibniz also says[6] that 'vital principles', which may be called substantial forms, are indivisible substances or unities, and he remarks that the substance of a body must be a form.[7] However, there need be no genuine inconsistency here. In implying that a substantial form is an aspect of a substance, Leibniz may be thinking of a substance as something which strives for a certain end, while to say that a substance is form alone might serve to make the point that a substance cannot be extended, and that any distinction between form and matter—i.e. that which has the form—must not be made in terms which imply that extension is real.

[1] G vi. 149. Cf. G vii. 317 and 326, and Aquinas, *Summa Theologica*, i, Qu. 77, Art. 1, ad 4.
[2] Cf. the identification of form with substance which Aristotle sometimes makes: e.g. *Metaphysics*, 1029^{a}29, 1041^{b}4.
[3] G iv. 511 (L 818). Cf. the definition of a form cited above, n. 1, and G vii. 317, which states that the principle of action is the form *of the substance*.
[4] G iv. 512 (L 818). Cf. G ii. 512 (L 864), G iv. 478–9 (L 741).
[5] *Mon.*, pars. 11–12.   [6] G vi. 539 (L 953–4).
[7] G ii. 72.

So far, only matters of terminology have been discussed,
and it is now time to try to make clear the exact nature of
Leibniz's rehabilitation of substantial forms. He might mean
that 'substantial form' or 'containing a substantial form' are
simply other ways of referring to that which is big with the
future and laden with the past. If so, he will be saying that it is
true by definition that a substance is, or contains, a substantial
form. However, it does not seem likely that this is what he
means. A substantial form, he has said, is a principle of action;
that is, it is a source of action, it explains action. He seems to
mean, then, something of this sort: that it has been shown that
a substance is such that it is ideally possible to infer from any
of its states to its past and future states, and that it can only be
explained how this is possible if the substance is regarded as
having an end for which it strives.

A rough analogy can be derived from the game of chess.
From a knowledge of the position of the chess-men during
the game, it is to a certain extent possible to infer accurately
the past and future moves, given that the rules which govern the
movement and capture of chess-men are known, and that it is
known what each player is trying to do—namely, to put his
opponent's king in such a position that its capture cannot be
avoided. Something must also be known about the skill of the
players, and it is assumed that their play will be law-abiding.
However, all this can be known, or can be assumed, and correct
inferences to future moves (which are what interest the chess-
player) are often made.[1] The analogy breaks down in that
chess-men do not contain their own end and are therefore not
Leibnizian substances, nor is knowledge of the purpose of chess
alone a sufficient basis for the prediction of moves. The useful-
ness of the analogy is simply that it helps to show the relation

[1] That they can be made is assumed by chess-players themselves. This is
shown, for example, by the fact that in championship chess it is seldom,
if ever, that a game is won by actual checkmate; instead, one player infers
that, whatever move he makes, his king will be checkmated, and
resigns.

between inferring the past and future, and the purpose of an activity.

As Leibniz seems to mean that to talk about substantial forms is to explain how a substance can be big with the future and laden with the past, it follows that his justification of this language is not purely deductive, in the sense that the proposition that a substance is, or contains, a substantial form is not true by definition. Leibniz is claiming that if, and only if, a substance is or contains a substantial form can it be big with the future, &c., and this, if true, is certainly not definitionally true. However, it is because (though not necessarily only because) something which strives for an end satisfies the criterion of being big with the future and laden with the past that Leibniz rehabilitates substantial forms, and to that extent this rehabilitation is relevant to our theme.

'Substantial form' is not an isolated term in Scholastic philosophy, but is one of a cluster of related terms, such as 'entelechy', 'soul', and 'appetite'. It is not therefore surprising that Leibniz should use these words to explain what makes a substance able to express both future and past. He says, for example, that substances can be called entelechies because they have in them 'a certain perfection'.[1] It has already been mentioned[2] that, in both Leibnizian and Scholastic usage, to call something 'perfect' means that it has attained its fully developed state, that is, its form, so that Leibniz is again saying that a substance contains a form. Usually, however, Leibniz uses the word 'entelechy' to mean the form itself[3] rather than that which contains a form; in this sense, to say that a substance contains a form is expressed by saying that it contains an entelechy,[4]

---

[1] *Mon.*, par. 18; G vi. 150.   [2] § 4.8, p. 111.

[3] G iii. 339; G iv. 478–9 (L 741), 511–12 (L 818–19); G vi. 150; G vii. 529; cf. G ii. 121 (L 530). The same is meant when Leibniz identifies entelechy and 'act' (G iv. 469 (L 709), 472; G vi. 150. Cf. Aristotle, *Metaphysics* 1050ᵃ23). By 'act' he understands a substantial form, viewed as the fulfilment or complement of potency or possibility (G iv. 478–9; G vi. 150)—that is, as the perfect state of a thing, towards which the thing strives.

[4] G ii. 224 n., 252 (L 864).

while to call a substance an entelechy[1] might mean that it is a form.

Leibniz is also following Scholastic usage when he speaks of substance in terms of 'soul' (*anima*, *ame*). He recognizes two senses of the word: a wide sense, in which soul is defined as 'the same as life, i.e. the vital principle, namely the principle of internal action which exists in the simple thing or monad',[2] and a narrow sense in which the word refers only to sensitive life (*vita sensitiva*), that is, to that species of life which is accompanied by attention and memory.[3] In the wide sense, soul and substantial form seem to be identical, and it must be this sense which Leibniz has in mind when he says that all substances are souls and that there is life everywhere in nature.[4] Sometimes he seems to have the narrow sense in mind, as when he says that the substantial form which is, or is a part of, one of the substances which appear to us as a body is 'something which is related to souls'.[5] In neither case does Leibniz add anything to what has already been said of substance in terms of substantial forms. Nor is it likely that he would claim that he does; he clearly thinks[6] that anyone who is prepared to think of substances in terms of substantial forms will have no objection to the suggestion that substances may also be called souls, or at any rate soul-like. However, Leibniz understands by the term 'soul' not only a vital principle, but something which is percipient. This is additional to what has already been said; but as it relates to a substance's expression of the universe outside it rather than to its being 'big with the future', &c., it must be deferred until the next section.

Meanwhile, there is more to be said about the language which Leibniz uses in explaining how a substance can express the

[1] G iv. 558 (L 937–8).
[2] G vii. 529; cf. G iv. 511 (L 818); G vi. 539 (L 953–4).
[3] G vii. 529; cf. *PNG*, par. 4; *Mon.*, par. 19.
[4] G vi. 539; *PNG*, par. 4; *Mon.*, pars. 66–70.
[5] *DM*, par. 12; cf. G ii. 121 (L 530); G iv. 479 (L 741); *NE*, 3. 6. 42; Grua, p. 29.
[6] e.g. *DM*, par. 12.

future and the past. Another Leibnizian term which belongs in
this context is 'appetition', together with its equivalent, 'appetite'. By 'appetition' Leibniz seems to understand a thing's
aiming at or striving towards its goal; his definition of it is
'the action of the internal principle' of a substance[1]—that is, of
the substantial form. Since appetition or appetite is defined as
a predicate of a substantial form, Leibniz does not say that an
appetite is a substance, but rather that a substance contains
appetite.[2] For the Scholastics this 'appetite' might be found in
what are commonly called inanimate, as well as in what are
commonly called animate, beings, and Leibniz sometimes
writes as if he agreed with this.[3] Sometimes, however, he uses
the word only of what are usually called animate beings, when
he says that there is in substances either appetite or something
analogous to it.[4]

Scholastic terms are not the only ones used by Leibniz to
explain how a substance can express the future. Consider, he
says,[5] 'something heavy which is suspended and strains at the
rope which supports it; or . . . a taut bow'. These are examples
of the exercise of what he calls 'force'; now, in his usage the
term 'force' refers to 'what there is in the present state which
carries with it a change for the future',[6] so that it may also be
said that it is by virtue of containing a force[7] that a substance
is big with the future. It must again be remarked that Leibniz
is using the notion of force to explain, rather than simply to describe, the fact that a substance expresses the future. He would
reject the view that to say that there is a certain force in a bent
bow is no more than to say that if the bowstring is released the
bow will quickly resume the shape which it had before it was
pulled. It must be possible, he would reply, to explain why the

---

[1] *Mon.*, par. 15; cf. G iii. 575 (L 1077); *PNG*, par. 2.
[2] G iv. 512 (L 820).
[3] See the references cited in the two preceding notes. For Scholastic usage
see, e.g., Aquinas, *Summa contra Gentiles*, 1. 72. 3; 3. 3. 6; 4. 36. 6.
[4] G iv. 479 (L 741).   [5] G iv. 469; cf. G vii. 326.
[6] G iv. 523.
[7] G iv. 511–12 (L 818–19); G vi. 582 (L 1008). Cf. G iv. 469.

bow resumes its shape, and the answer to this question is that
there is a certain force in the bow.

The use of the word 'force' adds nothing to what has already
been said in terms of substantial forms, but Leibniz seems to
have wanted to make his point in non-Scholastic language.
At the same time, he is careful to relate the notion of force to
Scholastic concepts, but the definitions which he gives are confused, and as they add nothing of importance to what has
already been said they may be relegated to a footnote.[1] It will
be useful, however, to refer here to a distinction which Leibniz
draws between kinds of force. When speaking of force in connexion with substance, the term which he generally uses is
'primitive force',[2] which he distinguishes from 'derivative
force'.[3] The reason for the distinction is this. It has already been
seen that Leibniz believes that no substance can act on any
other, from which it follows that if a force belongs to a substance as the principle of its actions, no such force can act on
or be acted on by any other. Leibniz recognizes, however, that
it is often useful in the sciences to speak of a force as affected by
others, and it is this force which he calls 'derivative', as opposed
to 'primitive'. It is hardly necessary to add that, in Leibniz's
view, derivative forces cannot strictly speaking be said to exist.
The notion of a derivative force, like the notion of the action
of one substance on another, is justifiable only as an abbreviated
way of referring to relations between forces which are really
independent of one another.

---

[1] Leibniz sometimes uses the word 'force' (more exactly, 'primitive
force') as equivalent to 'substantial form' (G iv. 479 (L 741); G vii. 317);
sometimes the word seems closer in meaning to 'appetition', as when he
says that by 'force' he understands something which is 'a mean between
the faculty of acting and the action itself, and involves *conatus*' (G iv. 469
(L 709); cf. G iv. 472, 479). When relating the term 'force' to 'entelechy' he
sometimes says that a force 'includes' an entelechy (G iv. 472), sometimes
that an entelechy 'carries with it . . . what one can call force, effort, *conatus*'
(G vi. 150), whilst he sometimes regards a primitive force as *being* an
entelechy (G iii. 457; *NE*, 2. 21. 1).

[2] G iii. 457; G iv. 479, 511–12; G vii. 317.

[3] G iii. 457; G iv. 396–7; G. *M*. vi. 237 (L 715).

The term 'force', which plays an important part in Leibniz's science as well as in his metaphysics,[1] was free from what many of his contemporaries regarded as the taint of Scholasticism, and for that reason he did not feel that he had to defend its use. With terms such as 'substantial form', the case was different; these were regarded with contempt by many seventeenth-century scientists and philosophers, as providing only pseudo-explanations.[2] They had been associated with the attempt to explain the physical world teleologically, as analogous to a living and purposive being, an attempt which had been succeeded by the mechanistic explanations characteristic of the new science. Leibniz, for his part, had no wish to go back to Aristotelian physics. It is, he argues, a mistake to suppose that substantial forms can be used to explain 'particular phenomena';[3] these are explicable only in mechanistic terms.[4] However,[5] 'The general principles of corporeal nature and of mechanics itself . . . belong to certain forms or indivisible natures, as causes of appearances, rather than to corporeal or extended mass.' Leibniz means that it must not be supposed that substantial forms are in corporeal objects, as a kind of 'ghost in the machine',[6] affecting their behaviour. In his own words,[7] 'Souls change nothing in the order of bodies, nor do bodies change anything in the order of souls.' But the 'order of bodies' is what it is because what we call physical objects are the appearances of substances which can properly be described by such terms as 'soul' or 'substantial form'.

[1] Leibniz believed, indeed, that an adequate physics is impossible without such a concept, so that substantial forms can be defended on scientific as well as on metaphysical grounds (DM, par. 18; cf. G ii. 195 (L 850)).

[2] Cf. Gilson, 'La Critique cartésienne des formes substantielles', in Études sur le rôle de la pensée médiévale dans la formation du système cartésien (Paris, 1930); Spinoza, Epp. 13 and 56 (Gebhardt, iv, pp. 64 and 261).

[3] G iv. 479 (L 741); cf. G ii. 58, 77–78, 99; G iv. 346; G vii. 317; DM, par. 10.

[4] A ii. 1, 400 (L 289); G ii. 58, 77–78; G iii. 55 (L 542); To Clarke, § 5.115–116; C 12.   [5] DM, par. 18; cf. G ii. 58, 77–78.

[6] G. Ryle, The Concept of Mind (London, 1949), pp. 15 ff.

[7] G ii. 71; cf. DM, par. 12.

§ 5.9. Just as Leibniz has explained how a substance contains the marks of future and the traces of past events by using the notion of a form or soul, so he uses the notion of perception to explain how a substance can express the whole universe. A substance, he says, expresses the universe by virtue of perceiving it.[1] Stated briefly, Leibniz's reason for saying this seems to be that what is usually called perception, or a perception, is the expression or representation of a multitude in what is simple,[2] namely in a simple substance.[3] From this he apparently goes on to say that the word 'perception' may usefully be widened in scope, so that every substance may be said to perceive, and to perceive everything. Leibniz's thesis, then, seems to be based on a view about the nature of perception, and as such might appear to be outside the scope of this study. However, what he says about a substance's perception is meant to explain how it can satisfy a certain criterion, that of expressing the whole universe, which he declares to follow from his logic, and to that extent is relevant to our inquiry. It will also be seen later that what Leibniz says about perception depends in part on his views about causation, which are also related to his logic.[4]

Leibniz does not give a clear statement of his reasons for regarding perception as a kind of expression, but he says enough to enable them to be conjectured. First, he makes it clear that he thinks of a perception as something which is never deceptive; it is our judgements which deceive us, not our perceptions.[5] He obviously has in mind here the perceptions of rational beings, who are capable of judgement; when he wishes to distinguish such perceptions from the way in which what are commonly called inanimate beings express the universe, he calls them *sentiments*, a term which may be translated as 'sensations'.[6]

---

[1] G ii. 112 (L 521), 121 (L 530); *DM*, par. 14.

[2] G ii. 112, 311; G iii. 574–5 (L 1077) and G vii. 317 define perception as a faculty; G ii. 121 and *Mon.*, par. 14 refer to a perception, or to perceptions; G vii. 529 is ambiguous.   [3] G ii. 112; *Mon.*, par. 14.

[4] Cf. § 5.5, pp. 153 ff.   [5] *DM*, par. 14.

[6] *PNG*, par. 4; *Mon.*, par. 19. *Sentiment*, as used in this context, is sometimes translated as 'feeling' (e.g. L 1047, and Latta, *Leibniz: The Monadology,*

Leibniz goes on to assert that any perception is a 'transitory state' of a substance; or, it is an 'affection' of a substance, a quality or modification, an 'interior state'.[1] This explains how a soul can have many perceptions and yet be one, for to say that a substance has many modifications is not to deny its unity.[2]

Suppose, now, that a man is looking at a tree. According to Leibniz, the man will have a certain perception, or rather a certain sensation. He will not, incidentally, be perceiving a sensation; rather, the sensation is a state of his soul.[3] It now has to be asked what is meant by saying that the man is looking at a tree, or that he has a sensation or perception of a tree. Expressed in terms which Leibniz would regard as strictly speaking inaccurate, his answer would seem to be that the sensation is of a tree in that it is the effect of the tree, which causes certain events to occur in the man's brain and nervous system, which in turn cause the sensation. This could be put in a way which Leibniz would regard as preferable by replacing the notion of causation by that of expression, and saying that the sensation is of the tree in that it expresses the tree.

Leibniz would add, however, that the sensation does more than express the tree. So far, it has been supposed that all that has affected the percipient has been a limited number of things; namely, the tree and whatever else is necessary to make a connexion between the tree and his sense-organs. But according to Leibniz there are connexions between all things;[4] what affects the percipient's sense-organs and produces the sensation, then, is the whole universe. Since what is perceived is what causes the sensation, or rather is what the sensation expresses, it follows that the whole universe is perceived. Finally, since

---

p. 410). In philosophical terminology, however, 'feeling' is not so wide in scope as 'sensation'. To see, for example, is to have a sensation, but to see is not to feel.

[1] PNG, pars. 2, 4; Mon., pars. 13–14.

[2] PNG, par. 2; cf. G vi. 628.

[3] This means that Leibniz does not fall into the infinite regress to which sense-datum theorists are alleged to be liable: Ryle, op. cit., pp. 213–14.

[4] Cf. § 5.4, p. 141.

every substance expresses all others, and every substance is or is like a soul, it can be said that all substances in a sense perceive all others.

There are obvious objections to all this. It may be said, for example, that if each substance always expresses all substances, it is not clear why we should say that a man is perceiving a tree, rather than the whole universe. Indeed, it seems to follow from what Leibniz has said that we are always perceiving the same—that is, the whole universe—which is surely false. Leibniz would reply to the first that although a substance expresses all substances, it expresses some 'more distinctly' than others; that is, it is easier to infer from it to some than to others.[1] When we say, then, that a man is looking at a tree we mean that he is having a sensation which expresses the tree more distinctly than it expresses other substances.[2] To the second objection he would give a similar reply, saying that although a substance always expresses the whole universe, it does not always express distinctly the same part of the universe, and so we say that now one thing is perceived and now another.

Leibniz's account of perception has obvious affinities with what is generally called the 'causal theory' of perception, and to that extent is open to the objections brought against this theory: that, for example, to perceive is not to infer. It differs from the causal theory in that Leibniz claims that each perception 'expresses' the whole universe; but this in turn may give rise to another objection. It may be asked how a perception can express the whole universe; how, for example, it is possible to infer true propositions about remote parts of the universe from the sensation which a man has when he looks at a tree. Leibniz would answer by making use of the notion of a 'little perception' (*petite perception*). He asserts that every sensation has as its ingredients, or contains, or is composed of, an infinite number of 'little perceptions',[3] that is, of perceptions which

[1] Cf. § 5.5, pp. 153–4.
[2] Cf. G ii. 114 (L 524); C 15.
[3] G iii. 657; G iv. 523 (L 806); G vii. 501; *NE*, 2. 2. 1.

the percipient does not know that he is having,[1] perceptions which, in Leibniz's terminology, are not 'apperceived'.[2] By means of these little perceptions we are at all times perceiving all substances, though our consciousness of the universe is only 'confused', by which Leibniz means that we are unable to analyse a sensation into its components.[3]

The concept of a 'little perception' is far from clear. The term itself suggests that perception is a genus of which little perceptions are a species, somewhat as little boys are a species of the genus boy. But if the term 'perception' is taken in its usual sense, this is not so; to perceive something is to notice something, whereas we are said by Leibniz to have little perceptions without noticing what we perceive. Indeed, Leibniz's own definition of perception indicates an important difference between perceptions and little perceptions. A perception, he has said, is the expression of a multitude in what is simple. On the other hand, he seems to think of each of the infinity of little perceptions which constitute a sensation as expressing only one unit of an infinite universe. A little perception, then, seems to be regarded as an expression of the simple in the simple. In view of these confusions it may be doubted whether the concept of a little perception is of much value.[4] To speak of such perceptions is only to say that a substance somehow expresses the whole universe, whilst giving a delusive appearance of explaining how it does so. In favour of the term it may be said that it serves as a reminder of Leibniz's view that a substance is or is like a soul; but it is not clear that any more can be said for it.

[1] G ii. 311 n.; G iv. 523; G vii. 501.
[2] PNG, par. 4; Mon., par. 14; NE, Pref. (A vi. 6, 53–54; G v. 47).
[3] G iv. 422–3 (L 449). Cf. § 1.2, p. 13.
[4] It is not necessary to consider here Leibniz's detailed arguments for the existence of such perceptions: that, for example, we must have little perceptions of an unnoticed mill-wheel (G ii. 311 n.; DM, par. 33; NE, Pref., A vi. 6, 53), or of each singly inaudible wave, the mass of which is heard as the roar of the sea (G ii. 91, 113; NE, Pref., A vi. 6, 54). It is not denied that there are genuine problems here, but it is doubtful whether such a confused concept as that of a little perception can help to solve them.

VI

Conclusion

§ 6.1. The last two chapters have covered most of Leibniz's metaphysical doctrines: the chief exceptions are perhaps his views about primary and secondary matter (*materia prima* and *materia secunda*), which involve his dynamics;[1] his belief that substances form a hierarchy, some monads being 'dominant' over others, which is connected with what he says about the relative clarity of the expression of the universe by different substances;[2] and the obscure doctrine, developed towards the end of his life and perhaps adopted only for controversial purposes, of a 'substantial bond' (*vinculum substantiale*) between the substances which constitute a body.[3] But although nearly all of Leibniz's metaphysics has been considered, the upshot of these last two chapters has been that only a few propositions relating to metaphysics are, or can be, validly derived from his logic.

It will be worth while to put the results of this inquiry in another form, and instead of showing that Leibniz's metaphysics does not follow from certain premises, to try to find premises from which it can be derived. Russell claimed that there are five principal premisses from which Leibniz's philosophy follows 'almost entirely'. He states these as follows:[4]

  I. Every proposition has a subject and a predicate.
 II. A subject may have predicates which are qualities existing at various times. (Such a subject is called a *substance*.)
III. True propositions not asserting existence at particular times are necessary and analytic, but such as assert existence at particular times are contingent and synthetic. The latter depend upon final causes.
IV. The Ego is a substance.

---

[1] Cf. Russell, chap. 7.
[3] Cf. L 968–1002; Russell, pp. 151–2.
[2] See, e.g., G ii. 451.
[4] Russell, p. 4.

V. Perception yields knowledge of an external world, i.e. of
existents other than myself and my states.

This list is defective in many respects. The second item appears
not to be a premiss of Leibniz's philosophy at all, whilst each
of the rest, with the exception of the fifth, is incomplete or
inaccurate in some way. It has already been argued[1] that the
first premiss should read 'Every proposition either is, or is
reducible to, a subject-predicate proposition'. As to the second,
it is clear that this cannot be Leibniz's definition of substance
in general, since he regards God as a substance, but not as
existing through time.[2] Nor is it adequate as a definition of
created substance, since it would permit us to regard as a substance a class which has predicates referring to different times.
For example, it can be predicated of Rome that it was once
an obscure city, which later became famous; but Rome would
not be counted by Leibniz as a substance. In stating the third
premiss, Russell should have mentioned that the final causes
involved are the purposes of God, whilst the fourth should have
explained why Leibniz regards the ego as a substance—namely,
because it satisfies the criteria of unity and of being 'big with
the future and laden with the past'.[3] A more important defect
is that the list is seriously incomplete; Russell's five premisses
make no mention of the existence of a God of the kind in whom
Leibniz believed, nor can this be derived from them. This is no
minor deficiency, to be repaired by the addition of a few premisses of secondary importance; our inquiry has shown how
fundamental the concept of God is in Leibniz's metaphysics.

It remains, then, to find a number of premisses from which
Leibniz's metaphysics, as described in these pages, can be
derived. The definitions, axioms, and theorems which follow
are an attempt at giving one solution of this problem. Since
they amount to a restatement, in a more systematic form, of
arguments which have already been given in detail in the last
two chapters, the proofs of theorems are only sketched.

[1] § 1.6, p. 33 .   [2] § 4.1, pp. 78 ff.   [3] § 5.7, p. 163; § 5.8.

DEFINITIONS

D 1. By 'perfection' is meant reality or essence.

D 2. By 'God' is meant a being containing all perfections.

D 3. By a 'miracle' is meant an event which is beyond human comprehension.

D 4. A is said to 'express' B if the predicates of B can be inferred from the predicates of A alone.

D 5. By 'perception' is meant the expression of a multitude in the simple.

D 6. By a 'little perception' is meant a perception of which the percipient is not aware.

D 7. By a 'substantial form' or 'soul' is meant an internal principle of action, or the end state towards which a thing strives.

D 8. A concept is called 'complete' if it contains the concepts of every predicate of the subject to which it is ascribed.

D 9. By a 'substance' is meant that which has a complete concept.

D 10. By an 'identical proposition' is meant a proposition of the form 'A is A', 'AB is A', 'ABC is A', &c.

D 11. By a 'proof' of a proposition is meant the reduction to an identical proposition of the proposition to be proved.

D 12. A truth is called 'contingent' if its reduction to an identical proposition can be completed only in an infinite number of operations.

D 13. By 'extension' is meant a plurality of coexisting substances, which appear continuous.

AXIOMS

A 1. There exists a God.

A 2. The perfections of God include perfect wisdom, power and goodness.

A 3. Goodness communicates itself.

A 4. Moral perfection is natural to minds.

A 5. There is no created soul without a body.

A 6. Every true proposition is, or is reducible to, an identical proposition, and conversely.

A 7. The most economical method, whether of production or of explanation, is the best.

THEOREMS

T 1. Every identical proposition is true (the 'principle of identity') (A 6).

T 2. Every true proposition can be proved (the 'principle of sufficient reason') (A 6, D 11).

T 3. God has created a world (A 2, A 3).

T 4. The world created is the most perfect or best possible (T 3, A 2).

T 5. The world created contains most reality (T 4, D 1).

T 6. In the world, the most reality is realized with the greatest economy (T 4, T 5, A 7).

T 7. The world not only contains most reality, but is also morally perfect (T 4, A 4).

T 8. There exists an infinity of created substances (T 3, T 5).

T 9. All created substances are connected (substances exist (by T 8), therefore there exist instances of complete concepts (by D 9): such concepts are possible if, and only if, T 9).

T 10. No two substances are exactly alike (T 8, D 9, D 8, A 5).

T 11. Each substance expresses all states of all substances at all times (T 9, D 9, D 8, D 4, T 3).

T 12. No created substance acts on any other (T 11).

T 13. God pre-establishes a harmony between substances (A 7, T 11, T 12 if, and only if, T 13).

T 14. Each substance is indivisible or 'simple' (T 11, T 6).

T 15. No substance can be created or annihilated except by a miracle (T 14, D 3, D 12).

T 16. No aggregate is a substance (T 14).

T 17. Nothing extended is a substance (T 16, D 13).

T 18. A substance is or contains a substantial form (D 7) or soul (T 11 if, and only if, T 18).

T 19. There are substances besides what are commonly called souls (T 8, T 10).

T 20. A substance perceives (D 5) all other substances (T 11 if, and only if, T 20).

T 21. A substance has 'little perceptions' (D 6) of all substances (T 20 if, and only if, T 21).

§ 6.2. Our inquiry into the relations between Leibniz's logic and his metaphysics has now been completed. At first sight, its results might appear to be largely negative, and it could reasonably be asked whether the undertaking was worth while. All that has been shown, it seems, is that an attempt at establishing a deductive metaphysics has failed; but in these days hardly anyone expects such an attempt to succeed, so that time spent in showing that Leibniz has failed could surely have been spent more profitably. Such an objection, however, would not be justified. First, although criticism of Leibniz has been one of our concerns, the inquiry had another and logically prior aim— that of trying to see what Leibniz meant; of finding some, at any rate, of the reasons for which he held his metaphysical views. It may be replied that this does not, of itself, establish the worthwhileness of the inquiry. Granted, it may be said, that there is a certain fascination in piecing together Leibniz's philosophy from a host of fragments; granted, too, that the system which has been put together is elaborate and ingenious; nevertheless Leibniz's logic is still inadequate, and the attempt at basing a metaphysics on it is a failure, which is precisely what Russell said sixty years ago.

To this it may be answered that the results of our inquiry are by no means precisely the same as those of Russell's. For example, Russell argued that Leibniz's logic is inconsistent with his pluralism, whereas it now appears that it is not.[1] Again, there are some respects in which Leibniz's logic is better than Russell at first supposed, or at any rate is closer to Russell's later than to his earlier views—one may instance Leibniz's insistence on the analytic nature of all necessary truths, including those of mathematics, and his rejection of the idea that classes are real.[2] It may, however, be replied that although these points

---

[1] Cf. § 2.1.
[2] On necessary truths in Russell and Leibniz, cf. § 2.1, p. 38 n. 2; on classes, cf. § 5.7 with Russell's later view that classes are 'logical fictions' and that it is false to say that 'there are such things as classes' (e.g. 'The Philosophy of Logical Atomism' (1918) in *Logic and Knowledge* (London, 1956), pp. 253,

are important, they do not alter the fact that Leibniz's logic suffers from fundamental defects which Russell pointed out, just as his theology suffers from fundamental defects which were pointed out by Kant. This may be so; but it does not follow that a philosophy which is erroneous is therefore worthless. One can learn from mistakes, and in any case Leibniz's philosophy is not composed wholly of errors.

To see what can be learnt from Leibniz, let us begin with his logic. Almost any present-day student of philosophy will point out that not all propositions are of, or are reducible to, the subject-predicate form. The student will, of course, be right, but it is important sometimes to consider why one is right, and an examination of Leibniz's logic is a good way of conducting the inquiry. The chief problem here concerns the reducibility of relational to subject-predicate propositions, and if, as has been said, 'few have hammered relations so hard as Leibniz',[1] then something may be learnt from his failure to hammer relational propositions into another shape. Another major feature of Leibniz's logic is its intensional character, which was seen to be related to his attempt at interpreting propositions in such a way that no existential commitments are involved; here, too, his failure is instructive. His theory of truth may be criticized on the grounds that it fails to distinguish adequately between what is necessarily and what is contingently true; yet his account of contingent truth is not merely ingenious, since his use of the concept of hypothetical necessity may contribute towards the solution of the problem, or problems, of free will and determinism.

In discussing Leibniz's metaphysics, a distinction was drawn between his account of created substances and his account of the uncreated substance, the latter being in effect his theology. This is clearly of the type known as 'natural theology', which is based

262, 266). This contrasts with Russell's earlier view that classes were entities with a special kind of being: e.g. *The Principles of Mathematics* (London, 1903), par. 427.

[1] J. L. Austin, *Philosophical Papers* (Oxford, 1961), p. 18 n.

wholly on reason. The difficulties which led to the very possibility of such a theology being called in question were not raised
until long after Leibniz's death, and he can hardly be expected
to provide a full set of answers to them; what he does provide
are hints at answers. For example, Kant argued that to speak
of God as a 'cause' is to use, or rather to misuse, a term which
has meaning only within the limits of possible experience to
describe something which cannot be experienced, and many
regard this argument as sound. Leibniz would agree[1] that God
is not a cause in the sense in which this term is used in the natural
sciences; to speak of God's creation of the universe is, according
to him, to speak of something which is not a natural event. In
effect, he is suggesting that the justification of theistic language
is of a different type from the justification of scientific language,
and the hint may be helpful, even if Leibniz does not succeed in
making clear in what precise sense God is a cause.

Leibniz's God is called not only a creator, but also a 'necessary being'. It is often said (and not only by critics of theism)[2]
that one of the lessons which philosophers have learnt since
the time of Leibniz is that no existence is necessary; that there
is nothing of which it can be said that its non-existence would
involve a contradiction. Against this it has been pointed out[3]
that mathematics contains a number of instances of propositions
which are both necessary and existential: for example, the
proposition that there is a prime number greater than a
thousand. It is unlikely, however, that Leibniz would wish to
say that God exists in the sense in which a prime number exists,
so that it may still be asked what is meant by talking about
a necessary being. Perhaps the term has a twofold use in
Leibniz's philosophy. First, it may be pointed out that the proposition 'There is a God, but there might not have been' has
something odd about it, in a way that the proposition 'There

---

[1] Cf. § 4.6, pp. 102–3.
[2] Cf., e.g., I. M. Crombie, 'Theology and Falsification', in *New Essays
in Philosophical Theology*, edited by A. G. N. Flew and A. MacIntyre
(London, 1955), pp. 113–14.   [3] Kneale, p. 707.

is a King of Sweden, but there might not have been' has not. In company with Descartes and Spinoza, Leibniz took the oddity of the first proposition to reside in the fact that to say this of God is to assert a self-contradiction. In this they were undoubtedly wrong; yet the oddity remains. Second, it was seen earlier[1] that Leibniz's account of the necessary being is bound up with the principle of sufficient reason; that Leibniz is saying that everything has an explanation, and that that which has no explanation outside itself must be self-explanatory, a 'necessary being'. It is possible, then, to regard the concept of a necessary being as the expression of an attitude, the attitude that explanations must always be sought. The notion that there exists only one necessary being may have a similar function, the attitude it expresses being that all explanations form part of one system. This is related to Leibniz's idea of an 'alphabet of human thoughts', and to his idea of a universal symbolism, a 'universal characteristic'.[2]

It might be objected that although Leibniz's theism may be a way of saying that explanations must always be sought, it also provides him with too ready a means of giving explanations, by referring everything to the purposes of God. But it would be a caricature to represent Leibniz as a Doctor Pangloss, for whom the nose exists in order that we may wear spectacles. It has already been pointed out that Leibniz regards his metaphysics as compatible with a mechanistic interpretation of nature;[3] the principle of the best is used either to refute rival metaphysical theories or to make discoveries which could only have been made with great difficulty if the mechanistic approach had been followed.[4]

One of the best-known features of Leibniz's theology is its optimism—the view that God created the best possible world. It has been seen[5] that this optimism is not simply the expression of a sanguine nature. Under the placid surface of works like the

---

[1] Cf. § 4.3.
[2] Besides § 1.3, p. 15, and § 4.2, p. 80, cf. C. L., Chap. 4.
[3] § 5.8.   [4] § 4.8.   [5] § 4-7.

Theodicy it is possible to detect signs of tension—of the belief that, *in spite of* appearances, this *must be* the best possible world. This 'must' is a logical 'must'; Leibniz is calling attention to the logical consequences of theism, and is pointing out that belief in a perfectly wise, good, and powerful deity is inconsistent with the belief that this deity's work could have been better in any respect. It might perhaps be thought that the belief that this is the best possible world is objectionable on pragmatic grounds, in that it may lead to a passive acceptance of things as they are. In some people it may, but in Leibniz's case it clearly did not. For him, the best possible world is also one in which human beings, and indeed all created substances, strive to fulfil their ends; substances are essentially active.[1] Leibniz's life, which was one of the most strenuous activity, shows that this was not a doctrine to which he paid only lip-service.

Mention of created substances leads to the second main division of Leibniz's metaphysics. In previous chapters an attempt has been made to explain what Leibniz says about such substances; it now has to be asked how much of this is of more than historical interest. First to be considered is what may be called Leibniz's 'idealism'; that is, his view that all substances, including those which we call material objects, are strictly speaking souls, or at any rate soul-like. Leibniz's idealism has two aspects, the first concerning questions about the relations between perceptions and physical objects, and the second, questions about the identity of individual substances. The former, which could be called Leibniz's account of our knowledge of the external world, has been seen to be[2] in essence a causal theory of perception, modified by the view that in place of 'cause' one should speak of 'expression'. Leibniz, however, had also felt the lure of phenomenalism, of the view that material objects are nothing but perceptions.[3] Indeed, he

---

[1] Cf. Leibniz's rejection of the religious views of the Quietists: e.g. G vi. 536 (L 907); *DM*, par. 4; Grua, pp. 92, 114.

[2] § 5.9.   [3] Cf. § 5.8.

might be prepared to say that a Berkeleian universe, in which there exists nothing but what are normally regarded as souls, is a *possible* world; he would also say, however, that this is not the *best* possible world. There are some similarities here to Kant's account of perception; each philosopher asserts the existence of unextended entities, called by Leibniz 'substances' and by Kant 'things in themselves', which are responsible for the fact that we have any perceptions.

The other aspect of Leibniz's idealism referred to earlier is its teleological aspect—that is, his view that substances are souls in the sense that they strive to achieve their nature or form. This is Leibniz's answer to the question of what constitutes a thing's identity; a thing is one in so far as it has one end. Here Leibniz is in the tradition of Aristotle, and the doctrine which he propounds, although not beyond criticism, is worth consideration. One criticism may be mentioned here. It might be objected that the most that Leibniz can be said to have shown is that the statement that something is purposive is not of the same type or category as the statement that (for example) it is of such and such a colour, or so big; to argue from this that a substance has no colour and no size would be a logical error. This would indeed be an error; but what is in question here is not Leibniz's denial of the reality of extension, but rather his views about the relations between the concepts of purpose and identity.

It remains to comment on a few other Leibnizian theses about the nature of created substances. The principle of the identity of indiscernibles is closely related to questions about what constitutes an individual, and Leibniz's discussion of the principle is still of interest. With regard to the theory of the pre-established harmony, it has already been argued that this is relevant to discussions about the nature of causation;[1] but our last word about Leibniz will be in connexion with the view which raised the difficulties which the theory of the pre-established harmony was meant to solve—the view that no

[1] § 5.5, pp. 154 ff.

created substance acts on any other. A metaphysics is seldom, if ever, a mere set of propositions, but carries with it implications for conduct. Mention has already been made of the stress which Leibniz lays on the notion of a substance's activity, and it must now be recalled that this activity is not action on any other substance, but is *self*-fulfilment. This means that when, for example, Leibniz wrote letters in order (as we should normally say) to influence other people, he could not hope that what he did would really affect them; nevertheless, he behaved as if it could, since this was done in the course of fulfilling his own nature, and was part of the great schemes of God. This notion has some similarity to Stoicism, the Stoic image of playing a part on the stage coming to mind; it may also be prophetic of Kant's insistence, in his moral philosophy, on the concept of duty. It is a notion which will not be attractive to everyone, but it has its own impressiveness and, like other doctrines discussed in this essay, bears the stamp of a great philosopher.

INDEX

Titles in This Series

1

Barber, W. H.
Leibniz in France from Arnauld to Voltaire
A Study in French Reactions to Leibnizianism, 1670–1760
(Oxford, 1955)

2

Grua, Gaston
Jurisprudence universelle et Théodicée selon Leibniz
(Paris, 1953)

3

Grua, Gaston
La Justice humaine selon Leibniz
(Paris, 1956)

4

Jalabert, Jacques
Le Dieu de Leibniz
(Paris, 1960)

5

Jalabert, Jacques
La Théorie leibnizienne de la substance
(Paris, 1947)

<u>6</u>

Kauppi, Raili
Über die Leibnizsche Logik
(Helsinki, *Acta Philosophica Fennica*, Fasc. XII, 1960)

<u>7</u>

Leibniz, G. W.
The Leibniz-Arnauld Correspondence
Edited and translated by H. T. Mason
(Manchester, England, and New York, 1967)

<u>8</u>

Leibniz, G. W.
Lettres de Leibniz à Arnauld d'après un manuscrit inédit
Edited by Geneviève Lewis
(Paris, 1952)

<u>9</u>

Leibniz, G. W.
The Monadology and Other Philosophical Writings
Edited and translated by Robert Latta
(Oxford, 1898)

<u>10</u>

Leibniz, G. W.
*Textes inédits d'après les manuscrits
de la Bibliothèque provinciale de Hanovre*
Edited by Gaston Grua
(Two volumes. Paris, 1948)

<u>11</u>

Martin, Gottfried
Leibniz: Logic and Metaphysics
(Manchester, England, 1964)

12

Meyer, R. W.
Leibnitz and the Seventeenth-Century Revolution
(Chicago, 1952)

13

Parkinson, G. H. R.
Logic and Reality in Leibniz's Metaphysics
(Oxford, 1965)

14

Yost, R. M., Jr.
Leibniz and Philosophical Analysis
(Berkeley, University of California
Publications in Philosophy 27, 1954)